Elections in Britain Today

A Guide for Voters and Students

Second Edition

Dick Leonard

Foreword by David Butler

St. Martin's Press   New York

This edition first published in the United States of America in 1992

Printed in Great Britain

ISBN 0–312–01186–5

Library of Congress Cataloging-in-Publication Data
Leonard, R. L. (Richard Lawrence)
Elections in Britain today : a guide for voters and students /
Dick Leonard : foreword by David Butler. —2nd ed.
p.   cm.
Includes bibliographical references and index.
ISBN 0–312–01186–5
1. Elections—Great Britain.   I. Title.
JN955.L45   1992
324.6'0941—dc20   91–19697
                                                    CIP

ELECTIONS IN BRITAIN TODAY

For Irène, Mark and Miriam

Contents

Appendices

Foreword

The importance of elections is taken for granted but the nature of elections is little understood. Nationwide voting every four or five years is an essential safeguard of democracy and liberty – that, at least, is an axiom of contemporary democratic faith. But there is remarkable ignorance on the vital questions: what do elections really accomplish? what factors decide elections? and even, how are elections conducted? Anyone who studies carefully the press reports on by-elections will be struck by the self-confident but quite unproven assertions about what matters in electioneering. Few reporters are bold enough to say that campaigning takes the form of a traditional and often empty ritual, which, like all rituals, has become surrounded by hallowed myths.

No one – not the politicians, nor the professional party workers, the pollsters or the psephologists – knows with any certainty what does decide elections. The experts are only really confident about some of the factors that have far less influence than is popularly supposed, or even no influence at all.

One of the reasons why I welcome Mr Leonard's lucid and reliable account of the electoral process in contemporary Britain is that, while it sets out so clearly what is beyond dispute, it does not pretend to answer the central questions to which there is, as yet, no definitive answer. Why do people stay loyal to their parties? why do they switch? what specific government or party policies or outside circumstances lead them to change or to change back their vote?

Politicians and journalists spend a great deal of effort planning or analysing how votes may be influenced. The speculation on the subject is fascinating: sometimes it may hit on the truth but often it is far wide of the mark. Mr Leonard's book, which has been thoroughly revised in this new and enlarged edition, will help people to judge better than before between the rival theories that are propounded. It also has the down-to-earth virtue of providing the simplest and best account of the technicalities of electoral law and practice that I have encountered.

DAVID BUTLER

Nuffield College
Oxford

Acknowledgments

The author and publisher wish to thank the following authors and publishers for permission to use copyright material in various figures and tables included in this book: Mr Alfred J. Junz and the Hansard Society; Mr David Butler, Mr Donald Stokes, Mr Dennis Kavanagh, Mr Byron Criddle and Macmillan; Mr Richard Rose, Mr Ivor Crewe and the American Enterprise Institute; Mr Anthony Heath, Mr Roger Jowell, Mr John Curtice and Pergamon Press; Mr Paul McKee and the Cambridge University Press; *The Economist*, Economist Publications Ltd and *The Observer*. Detailed acknowledgment is made in the text wherever such material has been used.

He is greatly indebted to Mr Roger Mortimore, of University College, Oxford, for assistance in the final revision of the text. The responsibility for any errors remains that of the author alone.

1 Introduction

'The disadvantage of free elections', V. M. Molotov (the Soviet Foreign Minister in 1946) remarked to Ernest Bevin, 'is that you can never be sure who is going to win them.'

Perhaps, unconsciously, he had put his finger squarely on the feature which makes democratic systems of government so *interesting*. For it is the uncertainty which attends nearly every general election, at least in the United Kingdom, which adds spice to what might otherwise be regarded as a rather tiresome civic duty.

It is this, possibly, which explains a persistent paradox in British politics: that whereas only a tiny minority – probably less than one per cent – take an active part in politics between elections, well over three-quarters turn out to vote, without any compulsion, whenever a general election is held. Yet the choice which is presented to the thirty million or so electors who record their votes at elections is largely determined by the few thousands who take a continuing part in the activities of the political parties. It is they alone who participate in the selection of Parliamentary candidates and it is they who have a *direct* influence on the policies adopted by the political parties.

At most general elections about two million young men and women are entitled to vote for the first time. It was in the hope that it would be of assistance to some of them, and also to those older voters who are perhaps puzzled or uncertain about particular aspects of the electoral system, that before the 1964 general election the present author wrote a paperback entitled *Guide to the General Election*. It was intended to fill a gap which at that time seemed to exist for a book which explained the complexities of the electoral system in a simple manner and which also contained an account of how the political parties are organised, both locally and at national level, how their Parliamentary candidates are chosen and how the policies which they put before the electorate come to be adopted.

The reception which this book received was most encouraging, greatly exceeding the author's expectations, and a very considerable number of copies was sold. Shortly after the 1964 election the book went out of print and the author was urged to prepare a revised edition which would be equally relevant to future general elections. Moreover it appeared that the book was being widely used as a textbook in universities and polytechnics, as well as for civics courses in schools and adult educational colleges.

In the event, the revision was more fundamental than at first appeared necessary – substantial alterations and additions were made to nearly every chapter, and new chapters were added on by-elections and local elections, on opinion polls and on the evolution of the system. As the scope of the book was changed and enlarged to such a considerable extent, it was felt that a new title, *Elections in Britain*, more accurately reflecting its revised structure, was justified for the book which was published by Van Nostrand in 1968.

The years passed and that edition, which is now thoroughly out of date, has long been out of print. Meanwhile major changes have occurred to the electoral system (votes for 18-year-olds, elections to the European Parliament, the coming of referenda, two fundamental reorganisations of local government and so forth), to electoral techniques (as television and opinion polls have become more and more important) and to the party structure, with the creation of the Social Democratic Party and the subsequent merger to form the Liberal Democrats. New proposals for changes in the system, such as the introduction of public subsidies to political parties, have entered the field of public discussion, while older ones, such as the demand for proportional representation (PR) have gained more support without, as yet, being adopted. In preparing this new edition, the author has taken account of all these factors, and every chapter in the book has been comprehensively revised and rewritten, with the addition of a great deal of new material.

This book, now entitled *Elections in Britain Today*, is addressed to voters who support all political parties and to those who remain uncommitted. The author is not lacking strong political opinions, and for many years played an active role, fighting several elections, parliamentary and local government, and serving in Parliament as a Labour Member. But in this work he has attempted throughout to describe *how* the system works rather than explain *why* he approves or disapproves of its different features.

It should be emphasised that this work is an account of the British electoral system at the present time. It is not an historical work[1] or a general primer on the British constitution,[2] nor is it a work of comparative government.[3] Again, for the benefit of younger readers, however, it may be helpful to summarise in a few preliminary paragraphs the general characteristics of the British constitutional system in so far as it is relevant to elections.

1. The United Kingdom has a parliamentary form of government. The executive is not directly elected, but is formed from the membership of the legislature. Ministers are members of the legislature, the great majority, including those holding the leading offices, are members of the House of Commons. A minority are members of the House of Lords. This necessarily restricts the field of recruitment for ministers to a far greater extent than, for instance, in the United States of America.

2. It has evolved basically as a two-party system, though a third party, the Liberals, has invariably polled a substantial vote and has had a small representation in the House of Commons, and several smaller parties, from Northern Ireland, Scotland and Wales, are also represented in the House. The rise in support for the Liberals, and the recent creation of the Liberal Democrats, now places the whole concept in question. But in the past an election campaign, like a debate in the Commons, was basically a confrontation between the Government and the Opposition. The party which won a majority of seats in the House of Commons formed a government, and its leader became Prime Minister. Most elections have produced a clear Parliamentary majority for one party or the other, though occasionally only a small one. When a single party has not gained a majority of the seats a minority government has been formed rather than a coalition, which is a form of government unknown in modern Britain except in wartime.

3. The electoral system requires a single ballot and the candidate with the largest number of votes wins, even if he has polled only a minority of the total votes cast. This is sometimes known as the 'first past the post' system. It is not a system of proportional representation, and it penalises minority parties and inhibits their growth.

4. General elections in Britain are not held at fixed intervals, unlike in a majority of democratic countries. Though the maximum length of life of a single Parliament is five years, it may be dissolved at virtually any time at the wish of the Government. This gives the incumbent party a considerable advantage.

5. The United Kingdom has no written constitution; all laws, including electoral laws, may be changed by the passage of an Act of Parliament. It is technically easy, therefore, to change the electoral system at any time. In practice, only minor amendments are adopted with any frequency, and much of the present system is rooted in great antiquity.

Notes and References

1. See C. Seymour, *Electoral Reform in England and Wales* (New Haven, 1915); H. L. Morris, *Parliamentary Franchise Reform in England from 1885 to 1918* (New York, 1921); D. E. Butler, *The Electoral System in Britain since 1918* (Oxford University Press, 1963).
2. See John P. Mackintosh, *The Government and Politics of Britain* (London: Hutchinson, 1977), R. M. Punnett, *British Government and Politics* (London: Heinemann, 1976), J. Harvey and L. Bather, *The British Constitution* (London: Macmillan, 1964).
3. See Vernon Bogdanor and David Butler (eds), *Democracy and Elections: Electoral Systems and their Political Consequences* (Cambridge University Press, 1983), David Butler, Howard R. Penniman and Austin Ranney (eds), *Democracy at the Polls: A Comparative Study of Competitive National Elections* (Washington DC: American Enterprise Institute, 1981), Dick Leonard and Richard Natkiel, *World Atlas of Elections* (London: Economist Publishing Company, 1986), Richard Rose (ed.), *Electoral Behavior: A Comparative Handbook* (New York: The Free Press, 1974).

2 When Elections are Held

Apart from the result, the principal uncertainty about a British general election is its timing. Unlike in the United States and the great majority of democratic states outside the Commonwealth, there is no fixed date for British Parliamentary elections.

There is however a limit on the length of life of the House of Commons. In 1694 it was set at three years, which was increased to seven years in 1715. Under the Parliament Act of 1911 it was reduced to five years, which is the present limit. During both World Wars annual Prolongation of Parliament Acts were passed at the expiry of this limit to avoid the inconvenience of a war-time election, but though such a measure would theoretically be possible in peace-time it is inconceivable that it would be attempted.

No peace-time Parliament has in fact run its full five years, though that of 1959 came very close to it. Table 2.1 shows the length of each Parliament which has sat since 1918, the first to be elected under the 1911 Act.

Except in the case of a minority government or one with a very small majority (as in 1950, 1964 and February 1974) it will be seen that most Parliaments have continued for a period of between three and four and a half years. Unless an election is precipitated by a Government defeat on a vote of confidence in the House of Commons (which has not occurred, otherwise than to a minority government, since 1886),[1] it is in effect the Prime Minister who decides the date of a general election.

In theory the Sovereign may refuse the advice of the Prime Minister to dissolve Parliament. In practice she could not refuse any but the most frivolous request. Especially after a Parliament has passed its half-way mark, the Prime Minister may safely recommend a dissolution at any time.

The decision is his alone. In earlier times the agreement of the Cabinet was always sought, but in 1918 Lloyd George successfully set the precedent, which has never since been challenged, of not consulting his Cabinet on this decision. The Prime Minister may seek the advice of his senior colleagues, but is by no means bound by it. It is known that both in 1950 and in 1951, several senior Cabinet Ministers disagreed with Clement Attlee's decision to go to the country. Conversely, in September 1978 a large majority of Cabinet

5

TABLE 2.1

General Election	Duration of Parliament		Original Government majority
	Years	Days	
1918	3	265	263
1922	—	361	79
1923	—	266	None
1924	4	159	225
1929	2	105	None
1931	3	356	425
1935	9	200*	247
1945	4	189	186
1950	1	213	6
1951	3	183	16
1955	4	104	60
1959	4	342	100
1964	1	127	4
1966	4	41	97
1970	3	251	30
1974: Feb.	0	195	None
Oct.	4	166	3
1979	4	4	43
1983	3	345	144
1987	?	?	102

* Duration extended by annual Acts of Parliament during 1939–45 war.

ministers were known to be in favour of an election in the following month, but James Callaghan abruptly informed the Cabinet that there would not be one until the following year. There was no discussion, despite the fact that Callaghan's decision had taken his colleagues, and virtually the whole country, by surprise. When there is a coalition government the Prime Minister has less freedom of choice in the matter, unless his own party actually possesses a majority in the House of Commons. Thus in 1945 the Labour and Liberal parties would have preferred an election to be deferred until October but the Prime Minister, Winston Churchill, insisted on a July election and his view prevailed.

Numerous factors influence prime ministers in their choice of general election dates. The economic situation, the state of the government's legislative programme in the House of Commons, the need for the country to be represented at important international negotiations by a government with a fresh mandate from the people or, if the government majority is precarious or non-existent, as in the

February 1974 Parliament, the desire to increase its Parliamentary support. This list could be extended indefinitely, but there is little doubt that the principal factor was neatly summed up by Lord Poole, then joint chairman of the Conservative Party, in a speech at Newcastle in June 1963. 'The Prime Minister is likely to have a general election', he said, 'at the time when he thinks he is most likely to win it.'

The Prime Minister's own prerogative of effectively choosing the date of general elections is a powerful weapon for the Government and a serious handicap to the Opposition. It has moreover assumed greater significance during the past three decades when public opinion polls have provided a far more accurate and sensitive barometer to the relative standing of the political parties than existed in earlier periods. Traditionally, by-elections had been the main measure of political support, but the results of these can often be misleading. Thus in 1880, on the strength of two Conservative victories in by-elections at Liverpool and Southwark, Lord Beaconsfield (Benjamin Disraeli) went to the country, and saw his party defeated.

Sir Anthony Eden was, in 1955, the first Prime Minister to capitalise on the new precision with which public opinion polls enable a prime minister to choose a favourable moment for a dissolution, and all subsequent prime ministers have sought to follow in his footsteps. To have much hope of winning an election, under present conditions, it seems to be necessary for the Opposition party to lead the Government in popularity for three consecutive years, short of an error of judgement by the Prime Minister.

The advantage which 'naming the day' gives to the Prime Minister has never been more apparent than during the 1964 to 1966 Parliament. Despite the Government's tiny majority, it remained clearly in command of the political situation, mainly because the opinion polls showed, almost continuously, that Labour was well ahead of the Conservatives in the country and could increase its Parliamentary majority almost at will. Partly because of his cautious nature, and partly because of non-electoral considerations, Harold Wilson waited until a highly encouraging by-election result confirmed the opinion poll evidence – but there was then very little doubt that the ensuing general election would greatly augment his majority.

In a not dissimilar situation following the inconclusive election of February 1974, Wilson was able to choose his moment to call another general election in the hope of gaining an overall majority. This he achieved in October 1974, but only just – his majority was three

seats, and this majority was wiped out by by-election losses over the
next two years. Much more painful setbacks were suffered by Wilson
in 1970, and by the Conservative prime minister Edward Heath in
February 1974. Both called elections which the opinion polls indicated they would win, and both lost.

The timing of general elections has become of crucial importance
in British politics, as it is also in Australia, Canada and New Zealand
where, too, the Government effectively chooses the date of general
elections. Though the Prime Minister's advantage appears immense
(he can also utilise local government election results, including by-
elections which are held periodically throughout the year, as a
supplementary indicator), his area of choice is more limited than is
immediately obvious. For in practice there are normally only a
limited number of dates between which to choose.

The winter months are usually excluded from consideration for
climatic reasons, April is reserved for Budget legislation, early May
for local elections, Easter and Whitsun must be avoided and the
period from mid-June to mid-September is the holiday season. This
leaves early and late spring and early autumn as the only occasions
normally seriously considered for electioneering. Apart from 1945,
when the election was held on the earliest practicable date after the
German surrender, all general elections have been concentrated in
three periods – late February–March, May–early June and October–
early November. It may safely be assumed that the great majority of
future general elections will take place during these three 'windows
of opportunity'.

Over the last fifty years, general elections and the great majority of
by-elections and local government elections have been held on a
Thursday, which is generally considered to be the least inconvenient
day of the week for the purpose (see Table 2.2). There is no reason to
believe that this practice will not continue, particularly because the
advanced planning and allocation of election broadcasts, on radio
and especially television, are now all geared to the assumption that
polling day will be a Thursday.

Before 1918, polling had been spread over a fortnight or more and
results in the first constituencies to poll were already known when
voters in other constituencies went to cast their votes. This was
sometimes alleged to cause a 'bandwagon' in favour of the party
which made early gains. The only occasion since when voting has
been 'staggered' was in 1945 when, because of local holiday arrangements, twenty-three seats in the north of England and Scotland

TABLE 2.2   *Dates of general elections*

Year	Day	Date
1924	Wednesday	29 October
1929	Thursday	30 May
1931	Tuesday	27 October
1935	Thursday	14 November
1945	Thursday	5 July
1950	Thursday	23 February
1951	Thursday	25 October
1955	Thursday	26 May
1959	Thursday	8 October
1964	Thursday	15 October
1966	Thursday	31 March
1970	Thursday	18 June
1974: Feb.	Thursday	28 February
Oct.	Thursday	10 October
1979	Thursday	3 May
1983	Thursday	9 June
1987	Thursday	11 June

polled one or two weeks later. But as none of the votes in this election were counted until three weeks after the original polling day, to allow for servicemen's votes to be sent from overseas, there was no risk of a 'bandwagon' being created on that occasion.

Dissolution of Parliament is effected by Royal Proclamation, but it is customary for the Prime Minister personally to break the news with a statement giving notice of the dissolution. In 1983, for example, Mrs Margaret Thatcher issued a statement on Monday, 9 May, announcing the dissolution of Parliament on 13 May, and polling day was set for 9 June. The last-minute moves preceding the announcement were cryptically reported the following day in *The Times*:

10 am: Close Cabinet colleagues and Conservative Party advisers gathered at 10 Downing Street for final meeting before the election date is announced.

11 am: Mr Cecil Parkinson, party chairman, leaves briefly to break the news to Conservative central Office.

11.15 am: Mr Parkinson returns to Downing Street for a Cabinet meeting where June 9 date is revealed.

12.20 pm: The Prime Minister leaves for Buckingham Palace and asks the Queen to dissolve Parliament. After an audience lasting little more than half an hour, Mrs Thatcher returns to Downing Street at 1.10 pm.

2.15 pm: The Press Association releases the text of an official statement headed 'General Election, June 1983', and personal letters from the Prime Minister are sent to Mr Michael Foot, the Labour leader, and Mr David Steel, the Liberal leader, informing them of the decision.

Polling day is 17 days after the date of dissolution. But in reckoning the 17 days, Saturdays and Sundays are excluded from the calculation, as are Bank Holidays and the weekdays immediately before and after them. The 1983 election was the first in which Saturdays were excluded (under the terms of the 1981 Representation of the People Act), and the period also happened to include the May Bank Holiday. This meant that there were actually 27 days between dissolution and polling day, whereas the average number in postwar elections has been 20. But in giving only four days notice of dissolution, whereas most of her predecessors had given ten, Mrs Thatcher's announcement came exactly one calendar month before polling day. This conformed almost exactly to recent practice, though there is no legal requirement to give any notice at all of dissolution. In 1987 Mrs Thatcher followed a virtually identical timetable, announcing on 11 May an election to be held on 11 June.

In so far as the Government has the advantage of fore-knowledge in making its preparations, it may be presumed to gain by giving as short notice as possible. On the other hand, there is nowadays usually so much advanced Press speculation that the Opposition is not likely to be caught napping.

As soon as Parliament is dissolved, the Lord Chancellor is ordered by Royal Proclamation to issue writs for the holding of fresh elections throughout the country. The writs are issued as soon as practicable following the Royal Proclamation and are sent to the Returning Officers in each Parliamentary constituency. The Returning Officer is the person appointed to organise the conduct of elections, and in England and Wales he is normally the sheriff of the county, the chairman of the district council or the mayor of the London borough in which the constituency is situated. In Scotland he is a local government officer appointed by the regional or island council concerned. In Northern Ireland he is the Chief Electoral Officer for Northern Ireland, an official appointed by the UK government. The Returning Officer appoints an Acting Returning Officer, normally the Clerk of the Council, who in fact carries out most of the duties of the office.

Not later than four o'clock in the afternoon of the second day after the writ has been received the Returning Officer must publish, normally by means of posters outside public buildings and on commercial advertising sites, notices of election stating the place and times at which nomination papers must be delivered and the date of the poll. The election will only then be officially in train, though most people concerned in it will already have been extremely busy with their preparations for several weeks.

Note

1. On 28 March 1979 the minority Labour government led by James Callaghan was defeated on a confidence motion by 311 votes to 310. A general election was immediately called for 3 May.

3 The Voters

The franchise is enjoyed by all British citizens, other Commonwealth citizens and citizens of the Republic of Ireland, with few exceptions, over the age of eighteen. The only other qualification required is that of residence (or, in the case of British citizens only, to have been resident at some time during the previous twenty years).

Thus British Parliamentary elections are based on the principle of universal franchise. It was not always so, indeed it was only the abolition of plural voting (by university graduates and occupiers of business premises) by the Representation of the People Act of 1948, which finally established the principle of one man, one vote.

Like most developments in the British constitution, progress towards universal suffrage had been slow and gradual. Prior to 1832, voting was a privilege reserved for a mere five per cent of the population and it required five Acts of Parliament spread out over a period of one hundred and sixteen years for the transition from oligarchy to democracy to be effected. The growth of the British electorate since 1832 is shown in Table 3.1 and Figure 3.1.

Apart from minors and aliens, the following categories of people are ineligible to vote:

Peers, or peeresses in their own right, who have not disclaimed their titles. Irish peers are entitled to vote, as are the wives of all peers.

Persons of unsound mind, who may, however, vote 'during lucid intervals.'

Convicts. A convicted person detained in any penal institution is disqualified while serving his sentence.

Persons convicted of corrupt or illegal practices in connection with elections (see p. 111 below and Appendix 5) are ineligible to vote for five years from the date of conviction.

Although adults not in any of the above categories are qualified to vote they may not do so unless their names appear on the Register of Electors. This is prepared annually and the Registration Officer for each Parliamentary constituency is required by law to make 'sufficient enquiry' to ensure that it is accurate. The Registration Officer is normally the town clerk or the clerk to the council of the principal

12

TABLE 3.1 *Growth of the franchise*

Representation of the People Acts	Provisions relating to voters' qualifications		Total Electorate	Percentage of population 21 years and over
Prior to 1832	Counties	40s. freeholders.	509,000	5
	Boroughs	various and unequal franchises		
1832	Counties	40s. freeholders, £10 copyholders, £10 leaseholders, £50 tenants at will.	720,000	7
	Boroughs	£10 householders.		
1867	Counties	40s. freeholders, £5 copyholders, £5 leaseholders, £12 tenants at will.	2,231,000	16
	Boroughs	All occupiers of rated dwelling houses, lodgers occupying £10 lodgings.		
1884	Counties and Boroughs	A uniform franchise for householders and lodgers, giving a vote to every man over 21 who had a home.	4,965,000	28
1918	Men	Abolition of property qualification in counties. Qualification by either six months' residence or the occupation of a £10 business premises.	19,984,000	74
	Women	Enfranchised at the age of 30. Plural voting by university graduates and the holders of the business premises qualification restricted to two votes including the one for residence.		
1928	Women enfranchised at 21. Male and female adult suffrage.		29,175,000	96.9

continued on page 14

TABLE 3.1   *continued*

Representation of the People Acts	Provisions relating to voters' qualifications	Total Electorate	Percentage of population 21 years and over
1948	University constituencies and all plural voting abolished. 'One man, one vote.'	34,915,000	*
1969	Voting age reduced to 18	39,153,000	
1985	Vote extended to certain overseas voters	43,181,321	

SOURCE   This table is adapted from *The Student Guide to Parliament* by Alfred J. Junz (London: Hansard Society, 1960).
* Since 1948 the adult Franchise has been almost 100 per cent, subject to the deficiencies of the registration process (see page 21).

local government area (county or district) in which the constituency is situated. The Registration Officer is the same person as the Deputy Returning Officer, who is responsible, in practice, for the organisation of elections in the different constituencies.

To be included in the register one must be resident in a constituency on a qualifying date, 10 October, in England, Wales and Scotland. In Northern Ireland the qualifying date is 15 September, and it is necessary to have been resident at the same address for three months before the qualifying date. This is to prevent residents of the Irish Republic crossing the border for a short period only and registering as voters. During the weeks preceding the qualifying date the Registration Officer supplies forms, usually by means of a house-to-house canvass, to heads of households, requiring them to fill in details of all members of the household (including lodgers) who are eligible to vote.[1] Any person who refuses to comply or who gives false information is liable on summary conviction to a fine not exceeding £400.

In addition to eligible voters over the age of eighteen on 10 October, persons whose 18th birthday occurs within the following 16 months should be included on the form. They will be registered as 'attainers', and the date of their birthday will appear on the printed register. They will accordingly be eligible to vote at any election occurring on or after that date.

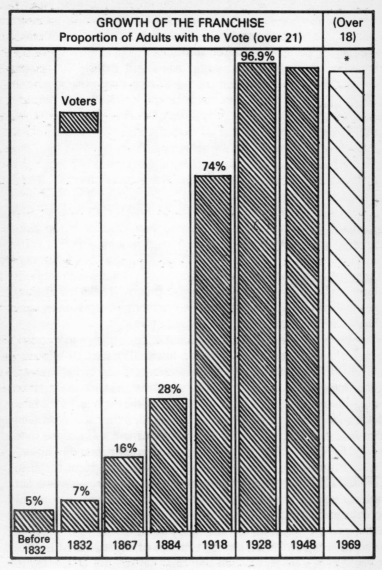

FIGURE 3.1 *Growth of the franchise*

A further special category are service voters, who were formerly marked on the register with an initial 'S', but are now no longer specially identified. In addition to members of the armed forces, these include persons employed in the service of the Crown outside the United Kingdom (such as diplomats and British Council employees and their wives), and the wives of service voters, who are residing with their husbands outside the United Kingdom. Wives of servicemen in the UK have the choice of claiming a service qualification or of being regarded as an ordinary voter. Service voters are eligible to vote either by proxy or by post.

On 28 November each year a provisional register is published by the Registration Officer and is displayed in post offices, public libraries and other public offices until 16 December. The provisional register is in three parts. List A is the register already in force, compiled at the end of the preceding year. List B is the list of proposed additions to the register, consisting of newly qualified voters, those who have changed their addresses or those whose voting status has changed (for example by ceasing to be attainers) from the previous year. List C is a list of proposed deletions from the register – consisting of those who have died or moved away or, again, those whose voting status has changed.

During the period that the provisional register is open to inspection claims and objections may be made to the Registration Officer, in respect of inaccurate entries or omissions. It is especially important that newly-qualified voters or those who have changed their address during the previous year should check that they are included in the provisional register; but there is no guarantee that voters who had been included in the previous years' register will be included in the next. If the head of the household has inadvertently failed to make an accurate return the voter might be included wrongly in the list of proposed deletions. There is also a possibility, on rare occasions, of a clerical error by the staff of the Registration Officer. The vast majority of voters who do not bother to check the provisional register each year nevertheless find, when they come to vote, that they have been properly registered. On the other hand, thousands of qualified voters at each general election find that they are not on the register and it is then too late to do anything about it.

Claims and objections may be made on or before 16 December (or 17th if the 16th is on a Sunday) on a form obtainable from the Registration Officer, who is entitled to make enquiries and to require proof of age or nationality from claimants. Since 1980 a new system has been introduced permitting late claims for inclusion on the register. These may now be considered up to the final date for the nomination of candidates. It is important to note, however, that the Registration Officer can only include the names of people who were duly qualified to be registered at a particular address on the canvass date (10 October), but whose names by some oversight were omitted.

The final register, which consists of the former list A, with the entries from list B incorporated and those from list C removed, together with amendments arising from successful claims and objections, is printed shortly before 15 February, on which day it comes into force and remains valid until 14 February of the succeeding year. Names added subsequently, under the late claims procedure, are published as a supplement. The Parliamentary register incorporates that used for local government elections and for elections to the European Parliament, the franchise for which is virtually the same. The only differences are as indicated on page 18 with regard to **L**, **E** and **F** voters. Copies of the register in each constituency are normally available for inspection in public libraries and certain other public offices, and free copies are provided for the agents of political parties and to Parliamentary candidates. They may also buy additional copies at the rate of 20p for each thousand names. Registers, or parts thereof, may also be purchased from the Registration Officer by members of the general public for £2 for each thousand names or part thereof.

The register is divided into polling districts (each of which is distinguished on the register by an initial letter or letters). Polling districts are devised by the Registration Officer to give each voter the minimum distance practicable to travel to cast his vote. They vary in number between a mere handful of voters (sometimes less than a dozen) in remote hamlets to over 5000 in densely populated areas in the centres of cities. The most usual number of electors in polling districts is, however, between 1000 and 2000. There are about 50 000 polling districts in the whole of the United Kingdom.

There are normally between one and a dozen polling districts in each Ward (the local government electoral area in towns), several of which normally comprise a borough constituency. In country areas each village would be a separate polling district and towns and larger villages would be subdivided. Within each polling district the electors are listed in street order, except in villages, where they are often listed alphabetically. Each entry consists of, reading from left to right, the voter's electoral number (counting from one in each polling district), his surname, first Christian name, the initials of any other Christian names and the number or name of the house. Within each household the names are given in alphabetical order. Certain special categories of voters are indicated by letters printed in bold type immediately preceding the voter's surname, as follows:

L voters are peers who, being members of the upper house of Parliament, are not entitled to participate in the choice of representatives to the lower house. They may vote in local government and European Parliament elections.

F voters are overseas voters who have the right to vote in Parliamentary and European Parliament elections, but not local government elections.

E voters (a very small category) are overseas peers who have the right to vote only in European Parliament elections.

Before February 1987 no overseas voters, other than service voters, were able to vote in any elections in Britain. Under the terms of the 1985 and 1989 Representation of the People Acts, a limited right has been granted to British citizens resident outside the United Kingdom. For 20 years following their departure they may qualify to be 'overseas electors' in respect of the address at which they were last registered (or at which they would have been registered if they were too young to vote when they last lived in Britain). In order to do so, they will need annually to register themselves through British consular posts. This will entitle them to vote, by proxy, at any Parliamentary or European Parliament election which occurs while the register is in force.

A portion of the 1986 register for polling district WW of the Knightsbridge Ward of the London and Westminster South constituency is reproduced in Figure 3.2.

Certain persons who would find it difficult or impossible to vote in person may claim the right to appoint a proxy or vote by post. There are two broad categories. Those who wish to be registered as absent voters for an indefinite period, and those who are seeking an absent vote for a particular election. In the first category are those for whom the special nature of their occupation (for example, long distance lorry drivers and merchant seamen) makes it unlikely that they would be able to vote in person. Registered blind persons and people in receipt of a mobility allowance also qualify, as do other disabled persons whose physical incapacity is attested by an appropriate

ENNISMORE GARDENS MEWS

SW7 1HK

402	Mappin, Mrs. Carol A.	1
403	Mappin, David J.	1
404	Mappin, Nicholas E.	1
405	St. Johnston, (Lady) Margaret	2
406	Baden, Mrs. Geraldine A.	3
407	Baden, Raymond R.	3
408	Guiver, Mrs. Molly M.	4
409	Shaftesbury, Countess of	7
410 L	Shaftesbury, Earl of	7
411	Rickett, Mrs. Alys P.	8
412	2/05 Rickett, Nicholas O	8
413	Norton, Miss Patricia	9
414	Sinclair, Mrs Mary J.	9

SW7 1HY

415	Grieve, Mrs. Nora	11
416	Skelsey, Mrs. Jenifer M	12
417	Romoff, Harvey M.	15
418	Romoff, Mrs. Suzanne	15
419	Laurenson, Mrs. Hilary J	16
420	Laurenson, James T	16
421	Schicht, Mrs. Ann	17
422	Schicht, Miss Caroline	17
423	Schicht, Ernest	17
424	Dixon, Mrs. Inga M.	21
425	Holliday, Mrs. Pamela	22
426	Holliday, Philip B	22
427	Holliday, Thomas B	22
428	Matthews, Guy C.	23
429	Matthews, Mrs. Sheila M.	23
430	Freedman, Adrian	25
431	Freedman, Jill A.	25

FIGURE 3.2 *The Electoral Register*

professional person – such as doctors, first level nurses trained in general nursing, Christian Science practitioners, those in charge of residential care homes and local authority residential accommodation and resident wardens. Electors who have moved house since the register was compiled are entitled to an absent vote 'if they cannot reasonably be expected to vote at the polling station for their old address'.

The second category was substantially enlarged by the 1985 Representation of the People Act, and from January 1987 onward any voter is entitled to apply whose 'circumstances on the date of the poll are likely to be such that he cannot reasonably be expected to vote in person at the polling station'. This means that not only people suffering from short-term illnesses, but holidaymakers (specifically excluded in the past) have now become eligible.

Absent voters are allowed the choice of voting by proxy or by post (providing they are able to supply an address within the United Kingdom where the ballot paper may be sent). Where they are qualified, absent voters may also vote by post or proxy in local government elections in Great Britain, including parish and community council elections in England and Wales. Full details of those who are eligible, and of how to apply for postal and proxy votes are given in Appendix 3.

Applications for postal votes must be made, on the appropriate form, to the Returning Officer of the constituency at the latest by the 13th day (excluding Saturdays, Sundays and public holidays) before the date of the poll. This is also the last day on which applications to cancel postal and proxy votes may be made. Applications may however be accepted by the Returning Officer until noon on the sixth day before polling in respect of sick voters who could not have foreseen on the 13th day that they would be unable to vote in person.

It is highly advisable however for people eligible to vote by post to make arrangements well in advance. Delay can be experienced in obtaining the appropriate form and, where necessary, getting it signed by a doctor, and at every election many voters who would be eligible find that they have left it too late to apply. The importance of the postal vote, especially in closely contested constituencies, is touched on in Chapter 13. In copies of the election register supplied to polling stations, postal voters are marked in ink on the register with the letter 'A' and proxy voters have the names of their proxies marked on the list.

An absent voters' list, including the addresses to which postal voting forms must be sent, is compiled by the Returning Officer and is available for inspection at his office, as is a separate list of overseas electors. Copies of the list are supplied free of charge, on request, to each candidate or his election agent.

Although considerable efforts are made by Registration Officers to ensure the accuracy of the election register, it is an imperfect instrument. It is already four months old when published and sixteen months old at the end of its life. Thus at all times large numbers of dead people are on the register while people who have moved are not registered in respect of their current address (probably only a minority of these apply for a postal vote or travel back to their previous neighbourhoods to register their votes on polling day).

Many years ago the Government Social Survey made a study of the accuracy of the election register. They found that when compiled it was 96 per cent accurate (that is, 96 per cent of electors were registered in respect of the address in which they were actually living on the qualifying date). By the time the register was published it was only 94 per cent accurate. There was thereafter a cumulative loss of one-half per cent per month, due to removals, until at the last month that the register was in force its degree of accuracy was only 87 per cent.[2]

A much more recent study, by the Office of Population and Census Surveys in 1982, suggested that the situation had deteriorated even further.[3] It showed that the October 1981 register was only 93 per cent accurate at the time that it was compiled. In some areas, and for some categories of voter, the position was a great deal worse than the national average. For example, over 50 per cent of unemployed black youths in the East End of London were not registered.[4] Since then there may have been some improvement, as changes in the law have permitted Registration Officers to correct individual errors and have extended the period during which late appeals for inclusion can be considered.

The 1948 Representation of the People Act provided for two registers to be compiled each year, but in 1949 as an economy measure the number was reduced to one. The apparent effect of this has been to disfranchise anything up to an additional three to four per cent of the population at any one time.

A proposal to produce a constantly up-to-date register, with the aid of computer techniques, was considered by the Speaker's Conference on Electoral Law in 1965–6. The conference recommended that a study of its feasibility should be made, but nothing emerged directly from this proposal. In the intervening period, however, Registration Officers have increasingly come to rely upon computers for storing data for the election register, and many of them are in a position to supply copies in the form of magnetic tapes or disks. Apart from political parties, the main purchasers of election registers are direct mail advertising agencies and many of these prefer to receive the information in machine-readable form. Registration Officers are permitted to sell printed labels showing electors' names and addresses, at the rate of £10 per thousand to those entitled to receive free copies of the register and £20 per thousand to others, which would include all commercial users.

Citizens of Commonwealth countries, resident in the United Kingdom are regarded as British citizens and are entitled to vote, as are Irish citizens. For many years relatively few Commonwealth immigrants availed themselves of this opportunity. There were a number of reasons for this. Many of the immigrants, particularly those from Asian countries, spoke little or no English and were ignorant of their rights. Some of them came from countries with authoritarian forms of government, and were strangers to the phenomenon of voting. Others regarded their stay in Britain as a purely temporary affair and took no interest in British politics.

However as the years passed, and as families established themselves here, more and more immigrants and their native-born offspring became more integrated in British life. It is clear that the proportion of Commonwealth citizens who are registered, and the proportion who actually vote, is still lower than for the electorate as a whole. But the margin is falling with each election. For example, in 1974 a poll carried out by Opinion Research Centre found that 30 per cent of eligible Asians and West Indians were not registered, compared to six per cent of whites.[5] By 1983 a more extensive poll by Harris Research[6] showed that 94 per cent of Asians and 82 per cent of Afro-Caribbeans were registered. A Gallup Poll taken during the 1983 election suggested turnouts of 68.3 per cent for Asian electors and 61.5 per cent for Afro-Caribbeans, against 74.6 per cent for white voters.[7]

The total number of registered voters is now over 43 million, including nearly 300 000 attainers and about the same number of service voters. There are some 36.4 million electors in England, 4 million in Scotland, 2.2 million in Wales and 1.1 million in Northern Ireland. Some 32 530 000 actually voted in the 1987 election, the largest number of electors ever to have gone to the polls in the UK. The percentage turnout however, at 75.3 per cent, was near to the postwar average, and far lower than the record 84.0 per cent who voted in 1950.

Notes and References

1. Merchant seamen who think that they may have been left off a householder's form may obtain from a Merchant Marine Office a special form (RPF 35) on which they can apply directly for registration.
2. See P. G. Gray, T. Corlett and Pamela Frankland, *The register of electors as a sampling frame* (London: Central Office of Information, 1950).
3. J. Todd and P. Dodd, *The Electoral Registration Process in the UK* (London: OPCS, 1982). See also J. Todd and B. Butcher, *Electoral Registration in 1981* (London: OPCS, 1982), and M. and S. Pinto-Duchinsky, *Voter Registration: Problems and Solutions* (London: Constitutional Reform Centre, 1987).
4. See David Butler and Dennis Kavanagh, *The British General Election of 1983* (London: Macmillan, 1984) p. 123. See also evidence given to the House of Commons Home Affairs Committee, Proceedings and Report (H.C. 32–1/1982–83).
5. See Monica Charlot, 'The Ethnic Minorities' Vote', in Austin Ranney (ed.), *Britain at the Polls 1983* (Durham, North Carolina: Duke University Press, 1985) p. 142.
6. *Ibid.*, p. 142.
7. *Ibid.*, p. 147.

4 Constituencies

The House of Commons has at present 650 members, each of whom is the representative of a single-member constituency. The origin of the different constituencies is diverse. Some constituency names, particularly those comprising medium-sized provincial towns, go back several hundred years, though the precise boundaries of the constituencies are unlikely not to have been altered at some time. The large majority of constituencies were in fact newly delineated prior to the 1983 general election.

The basis of representation in the House of Commons was, with few exceptions, two members for each county and two for each borough from 1264 to 1832. No attempt, however, was made to ensure that members represented equal numbers of voters, and enormous discrepancies in the size of constituencies had developed long before the 1832 Reform Act. Medieval boroughs which had declined almost to nothing retained their right to elect two members, while large cities such as Manchester, Leeds, Sheffield and Birmingham, which had grown up during the seventeenth and eighteenth centuries, had no separate representation. It has been estimated that by 1832 the largest Parliamentary constituency had more than one hundred times as many electors as the smallest. In 1832 and again in 1867 the worst anomalies were removed, but no systematic attempt was made to redraw the electoral map on the basis of approximately equal constituencies.

In 1885 a much more thorough redistribution was undertaken and the ratio between the largest and smallest constituency was reduced to 8:1. The Representation of the People Act of 1918 went one stage further and reduced the disparity to a maximum of 5:1. The 1885 Act also replaced the great majority of two-member constituencies with single-member seats, though the last of the two-member constituencies did not disappear until 1950.

Although the principle of approximately equal constituencies had been accepted in 1918, no provision was made to correct anomalies caused by future movements of population. Thus by 1939 the rapid growth of suburban fringes to London and other major cities had produced a large number of constituencies with an excessive number of electors, while depopulation of city centres and of remote rural areas had left many other constituencies with tiny electorates.

The Speaker's Conference on Electoral Reform in 1944 recommended the establishment of permanent machinery for the redistribution of seats, so that major anomalies should not again arise. An Act of the same year established four Boundary Commissions, one each for England, Wales, Scotland and Northern Ireland, which should make a general review of constituency boundaries at intervals of not less than three and not more than seven years. Each Commission consists of three members and each is chaired by the Speaker of the House of Commons, though his role is largely nominal.

The first reports of the commissions were, with one major amendment (mentioned below), approved by the House of Commons in 1948 and came into effect at the 1950 general election. They provided the first systematic delineation of constituencies which had ever been attempted, and of the 625 seats which made up the 1950 Parliament only 80 had retained their boundaries untouched. The Commission proposals were amended at the instigation of the then Labour Government, which argued that the English Boundary Commission had erred in recommending smaller electorates for county (average 55 360) than for borough constituencies (average 61 442). It proposed the addition of 17 extra borough seats, which reduced the average borough electorate to 57 883 – still more than 2000 greater than in the county seats. The Tory Opposition angrily accused the Labour Party of 'gerrymandering', but the results of the subsequent general election showed that Labour had gained virtually no net benefit from the amendment, and that the overall effect of the redistribution was a Conservative gain of between 20 and 30 seats.

In November 1954 the Commissions produced their second reports, which came into force in time for the 1955 general election. The recommendations which they made were much less far-reaching than in 1948. Altogether, major alterations were suggested to 172 constituencies and minor alterations to 43, and the creation of five additional seats was recommended.

The proposals of the Commissions, and particularly those of the English Commissions, were greeted with a storm of protest. There was general agreement, with which the Commissions themselves concurred, that if redistribution had previously been too infrequent it now erred very much on the other side.

Two groups of people were particularly incensed by the effects of this second redistribution within barely five years – Members of Parliament and active party workers in the constituencies. MPs of all parties were agreed that the normal hazards of political life were severe enough, without adding the further hurdle of a fresh bout of redistribution every five years or so. For a stiff hurdle it proved in a number of cases: safe seats were to become marginal or even hopeless, and marginal seats might become safe for the other side.

In 1950, of the 70 members who lost their seats at least half could blame redistribution, partly or wholly, for their defeat. In 1955 at least 11 members were in the same position. Sir Frank Soskice (Labour) and Sir Ralph Assheton (Conservative) were double casualties, losing their seats through redistribution on both occasions.

The inconvenience which redistribution brings to members of local political organisations was well described by Sir Kenneth Thompson, then Conservative MP for Liverpool, Walton, in a speech in the House of Commons on 15 December 1954. He said:

> We in the House are compelled to face the facts of political life. Political party organization consists of the little constituency club, a polling district committee, a ward organization, a constituency organization all pyramiding up from the modest humble, unobtrusive men and women who . . . do the slogging day-to-day work of a political party. . . . Every time a unit is taken from the electorate of a constituency, every time a boundary line is altered by however much or however little, some Mrs Jones is chivvied out of this organization and hived off to what is to her a foreign land, where there are a lot of people who do not speak her language. At the whim – if that is not an offensive word – of the Boundary Commission, she is expected to accept this as her lot and destiny and the pattern of her future political activity.[1]

The strong reaction to the 1955 redistribution led to amending legislation being passed by the House of Commons in 1958 which extended the period between general reviews of constituencies to a minimum of ten and a maximum of fifteen years. This meant that the next general review had to take place no earlier than the end of 1964 and no later than the end of 1969.

The Commissions duly reported in 1969, proposing the addition of five new seats, with changes to a further 429 constituencies, with only 201 unchanged. But the then Labour Home Secretary, James Callaghan, announced that the Government had decided not to implement the proposals in full because of the impending reorganisation of local government which would put local government boundaries completely out of line with those for the proposed constituencies. Instead he proposed that only the recommendations for the Greater London area, which was not affected by the local government reorganisation, should be implemented, while a handful of abnormally large constituencies should be divided. It seemed a reasonable proposal, but the Opposition Conservatives, who rightly believed that their party would gain from a redistribution, cried foul. The House of Lords duly voted down the bill promoted by Callaghan, who retorted by introducing orders to implement the Boundary Commissions' proposals, while inviting MPs to vote them down, which they proceeded to do. Accordingly the June 1970 general election was held on the old boundaries established in 1955, but the newly elected Conservative government lost no time in re-presenting the orders to the House of Commons, which approved them in October 1970. They took effect at the February 1974 general election.

The next redistribution proposals, which sought to align Parliamentary boundaries with those of the newly delineated local authorities, were presented in late 1982 and early 1983. Once again they led to political controversy, as the Labour Party, now in opposition and fearing that the net effect would again favour the Conservatives, tried to delay their implementation by legal action, based on the claim that the English Boundary Commissioners had misinterpreted the statutory rules which governed their work. Their appeal was rejected in January 1983, and the proposals were approved by Parliament in March, in time for the June 1983 general election. This was the most comprehensive redistribution so far, creating 15 new seats (five of them in Northern Ireland) and changing 569 more, leaving only 66 unchanged.

The statutory rules under which the commissions operate are few and simple. The total electorate in each of the four countries is divided by the number of constituencies to secure an electoral quota, and the number of electors in each constituency should 'be as near to the quota as is practicable'. Boundaries of local government areas should be respected but may be crossed if necessary to avoid 'excessive disparities' from the quota. However the commissions might depart from the rules 'if special geographical conditions, including in particular the size, shape and accessibility of a constituency, appear to them to render a departure desirable'. The number of constituencies in Scotland and Wales must not be less than 71 and 35 respectively and in Great Britain not substantially greater or less than 613, while Northern Ireland is to have between 16 and 18 seats.

This allocation gives more than their proportionate share of seats to Scotland and Wales, presumably as a sop to their national susceptibilities. Conversely Northern Ireland previously had less than its proportionate share, because its domestic affairs were dealt with by the Northern Ireland Parliament at Stormont. Of the 650 seats in the present Parliament 523 are in England, 38 in Wales, 72 in Scotland and 17 in Northern Ireland.

At the 1983 general election, as Table 4.1 shows, the largest constituency, the Isle of Wight, had an electorate of 94 226 – more than four times as large as the smallest, the Western Isles (in Scotland), with an electorate of 22 822. (By 1987 this disparity was even greater: the Isle of Wight had 98 694 electors, the Western Isles 23 507). This wide range had however been narrowed by the 1983 redistribution. On the previous year's register, the largest and smallest constituencies had been Buckingham, with 122 036 and Glasgow Central, with a mere 17 348 – only one-seventh the size. The overall effects of the redistribution were considerably more marked. Beforehand less than one-third of all seats had fallen within 10 per cent of the electoral quota, afterwards almost 70 per cent did so. Previously 39 per cent of all seats deviated by more than 20 per cent, afterwards only 5 per cent did so.[2]

TABLE 4.1   *Large and small constituencies (1983 electorates)*

England			
Isle of Wight	94 226	Surbiton	46 949
Crosby	83 274	Hammersmith	46 178
Devizes	83 211	Walthamstow	48 324
Eastleigh	82 447	Kensington	49 584
Berkshire East	81 512	Newham North-West	49 814
Scotland			
Gordon	65 537	Western Isles	22 822
Ayr	65 010	Orkney and Shetland	30 087
Inverness, Nairn		Caithness and	
and Lochaber	63 645	Sutherland	30 871
Aberdeen North	63 049	Tweeddale, Ettrick	
		and Lauderdale	37 075
Wales			
Pembroke	67 885	Meironnydd Nant	
		Conwy	30 459
Llanelli	63 826	Montgomery	37 474

Why is it that some constituencies are so much more populous than others, even when a redistribution has just taken place? The clearest explanation is given by Ivor Crewe.[3] 'The largest constituencies in the United Kingdom, which are all in England, are either in counties which just failed to qualify for an extra or second seat (Isle of Wight, Crosby, Devizes . . .) or in areas of population growth (Berkshire East) or both (Eastleigh). Eight of England's ten smallest constituencies are in Greater London, a consequence of the Boundary Commissioners' unwillingness to cut across London borough boundaries. . . . The smallest seats in Wales and Scotland are almost all in far-flung sparsely populated rural areas, usually of rugged terrain.'

With the passage of time, many of the larger seats tend to experience a disproportionate population growth, while the smaller seats tend to become progressively depopulated. The consequence is that the disparities grow year by year, providing ample demographic justification for the next redistribution some years before it is due.

The political impartiality of the Boundary Commissions is unquestioned, but their work certainly has a considerable effect on the fortunes of the political parties and some of their decisions, and particularly those of the English Commission, have been the cause of fierce controversy. It is obvious that individual decisions by the commissioners can greatly affect the political complexion of any particular constituency. Providing that there is no consistent bias in their approach, it would however be reasonable to expect that the overall effect of the cumulation of their decisions would be to cancel out the advantage which different parties enjoy. In fact the overall outcome of each periodic redistribution has been to benefit the Conservative Party. Table 4.2 shows the range of estimates by leading experts of the size of this benefit.

TABLE 4.2   *Conservative gains from redistributions*

Redistribution	General election	Net Con. gains in seats
1948	1950	20–30
1954	1955	2–10
1969	Feb. 1974	16–22
1983	1983	15

The reason for the consistent benefit which the Conservatives have gained is that redistributions cancel out the advantage that the Labour Party gains invisibly each year between one redistribution

and the next. For the seats which are becoming smaller are disproportionately Labour seats (mostly in declining inner city areas and in
the north), while those which are growing tend to be Conservative
constituencies in the suburbs and in the south and east of England. If
there were no redistributions the Labour Party would build up an
enormous cumulative advantage. As it is, the redistributions which
periodically eliminate the smallest seats and split up the largest tend
to overcompensate the Labour advantage, and for most of the
postwar period there has been a slight bias in the electoral system
towards the Conservatives. That is to say, that for any given distribution of votes they have tended to win more seats than the Labour
Party. In 1983 for example, it has been estimated that if the Conservative and Labour vote had been exactly equal the Conservatives
would have been ahead by 19 more seats.[4]

In the 1951 general election the Labour Party actually polled
231 067 votes more than the Conservatives, but a Conservative
government was elected with a majority of 26 seats over Labour, and
of 17 overall. Conversely, in the February 1974 election, the Labour
Party won five more seats than the Conservatives, even though it
polled 225 789 fewer votes. It was able to form a minority government, which managed to win a tiny overall majority of three seats at
the subsequent general election in October 1974.

While detailed criticisms can be made of the recommendations and
procedures of the Boundary Commissions, in general the difficult
problem of delineating constituencies appears to have been solved
more satisfactorily in Britain than in many other countries, and
serious accusations of gerrymandering are rare. If there are injustices
in the arrangements for British elections, they are due much more to
the electoral system than to the work of the Boundary Commissioners. Without a change in the system, it is doubtful whether the
method of revising constituency boundaries could be improved to any
significant extent.

All Parliamentary constituencies are now territorial ones, though
from 1603 to 1950 representatives of the universities (elected by post
by graduates) sat in the House of Commons. University representation was abolished, in accordance with the principle of 'one man, one
vote', by the Labour Government of 1945–51. This step was opposed
by the Conservative Party at the time and a pledge to restore the
university seats was given by Sir Winston Churchill. When a Conservative government was elected in 1951, however, no attempt was
made to redeem that pledge, and two years later Sir Winston announced that the question was to be dropped.

The method of election within each constituency is the simplest yet devised. Each voter has one vote which he records by marking an 'X' against the candidate of his choice on the ballot paper. The candidate who polls the largest number of votes in the constituency is elected, even if he is supported by only a minority of the voters. Where three or more candidates are in the field this is of course a common occurrence, and in the 1983 general election no fewer than 336 out of 650 Members were elected with a minority vote.

Where support for three candidates is very evenly balanced it is possible for a member to be elected with not much more than one-third of the votes, as happened in the Caithness and Sutherland constituency in 1945, when the result was as follows:

E. L. Gander Dower (Con.)	5,564	(33.47%)
R. McInnes (Lab.)	5,558	(33.43%)
Sir A. Sinclair (Lib.)	5,503	(33.10%)
Con. majority	6	

The lowest winning share of the vote in modern general elections came in a four-party contest for the Dunbartonshire East seat in October 1974:

Mrs. M. A. Bain (S.N.P.)	15 551	(31.2%)
J. S. B. Henderson (Con.)	15 529	(31.2%)
E. F. McCarry (Lab.)	15 122	(30.3%)
J. A. Thompson (Lib.)	3 636	(7.3%)
SNP majority	22	

A more recent example, also in a four-party contest, produced a winner with under one-third of the votes cast, at Renfrew West and Inverclyde in the 1983 general election. Here the result was:

Anna McCurley (Con.)	13 669	(32.7%)
J. Dickson Mabon (SDP/Alliance)	12 347	(29.5%)
George Doherty (Lab.)	12 139	(29.0%)
William Taylor (SNP)	3 653	(8.7%)
Con. majority	1 322	

It is of course theoretically possible in multi-sided contests for a candidate to be elected with considerably less than one-third of the votes. This has, however, never happened, at least in modern times, though in a by-election for the former Combined English Universities constituency in 1947, contested by five candidates, the winning Conservative polled just over 30 per cent of the votes.

The combination of single-member constituencies and a 'first past the post' (or 'plurality') method of voting leads to considerable discrepancies between the proportion of votes polled by parties and the number of seats which their candidates obtain in the House of Commons. Between the two larger parties this normally has the effect of exaggerating the majority obtained by the more successful and thus ensuring a larger majority for the Government in the House of Commons than could mathematically be justified.

Way back in 1909, the so-called 'cube law' was propounded by James Parker Smith, who stated that if the votes cast for the two leading parties are divided by the ratio $A:B$, the seats will be divided between them in the proportion $A^3:B^3$. This relationship was actually observed, with minor variations, in British election results over the next 65 years, as well as in some other countries, such as the United States and New Zealand, which have a similar electoral system. Yet there is nothing God-ordained about this relationship between seats and votes, and progressively since the February 1974 general election the advantage which the leading party has enjoyed over its main rival has shrunk. By the time of the 1983 general election the winning party's advantage was in fact even less than it would have been if a 'square law' had existed. In 1983 the Conservatives would have won 80 more seats and Labour 80 less if the cube law was still in operation.

The reasons why the cube law disappeared are complex, but they are due to population movements round the country and, in particular, to the fact that predominantly Conservative areas (in the south and in the country) have become steadily more Conservative, while Labour areas (Scotland, the north of England, inner cities) have become progressively more Labour. There are thus fewer marginal seats which are liable to change hands at general elections. Whereas in the mid-1950s some 17 seats changed hands, on average, for each one per cent swing between the two leading parties, by 1979–83 only 10 seats were changing hands for each one per cent swing.[5] (For definition of 'swing' see page 37 below).

The other wellknown consequence of the 'first past the post' system is that smaller parties tend to be seriously under-represented, especially those like the Liberal and Social Democratic parties, whose support is evenly spread across the whole country rather than being concentrated in geographical clusters (like the Scottish and Welsh Nationalists and the Northern Ireland parties). Table 4.3, which shows the proportion of votes and seats won by the three main parties since 1945, indicates the extent to which the Liberals (and in 1983 and 1987 the SDP–Liberal Alliance) have suffered.

TABLE 4.3 *Percentage of seats and votes won by the parties*

	1945		1950		1951		1955	
	votes	*seats*	*votes*	*seats*	*votes*	*seats*	*votes*	*seats*
Labour	48.1	62.2	46.1	50.4	48.8	47.2	46.4	44.0
Conservative	40.2	33.2	43.5	47.7	48.0	51.3	49.7	54.5
Liberal	9.0	1.9	9.1	1.4	2.5	1.0	2.7	1.0

	1959		1964		1966	
	votes	*seats*	*votes*	*seats*	*votes*	*seats*
Labour	43.8	40.9	44.1	50.3	47.9	57.6
Conservative	49.4	57.9	43.4	48.1	41.9	40.2
Liberal	5.9	1.0	11.2	1.4	8.5	1.9

	1970		Feb. 1974		Oct. 1974	
	votes	*seats*	*votes*	*seats*	*votes*	*seats*
Labour	43.1	45.7	37.2	47.4	39.2	50.2
Conservative	46.4	52.4	37.9	46.7	35.9	43.6
Liberal	7.5	1.0	19.3	2.2	18.3	2.0

	1979		1983		1987	
	votes	*seats*	*votes*	*seats*	*votes*	*seats*
Labour	36.9	42.4	27.6	32.2	30.8	35.2
Conservative	43.9	53.4	42.4	61.1	42.3	57.8
Liberal/Alliance	13.8	1.7	25.4	3.5	22.6	3.4

It is clear from a glance at the Liberal performance that third parties are very much under-represented under present conditions. The apparent injustice of the system led to demands in the period before the first World War for the introduction of a system of proportional representation (or PR) as practised in a number of other countries. The only system enjoying much support among British opinion was that of the Single Transferable Vote in multi-member constituencies (returning, say, three to seven members). Under this system, if in a six-member constituency the Conservative candidates polled half the votes, the Labour candidates a third and the Liberals a sixth, the Conservatives would get three seats, Labour two and the Liberals one. Over the country as a whole this system would still tend to benefit large parties and penalise small ones, but to a much lesser extent than does the present system.

STV (which is used for elections in the Irish Republic, and since 1970 for all elections in Northern Ireland except that for the House of Commons) is still the most likely proportional system to be adopted in Britain, though in recent years there has been some support for the Additional Members' System, based on the West German model. Party list systems, which are favoured in nearly all the other European democracies, have not attracted any significant support in Britain. Details of all these systems are given in Appendix 8.

Proportional representation was almost adopted in 1918, but support for it thereafter rapidly declined except, understandably, in the Liberal Party. A less drastic reform of the voting system, the alternative vote, was actually approved by the House of Commons both in 1918 and 1931. This provided for single-member constituencies, but if the leading candidate polled only a minority of the votes the lowest candidate would drop out and his second preference votes would be transferred until the winner emerged with more than 50 per cent of the votes. But defeat of the measure in the Lords in 1931, followed by a change of government, prevented it coming into force.

Both PR and the alternative vote were considered anew in 1965–7 by the Speaker's Conference on Electoral Law (see Chapter 15, below), which decided, however, by a margin of nineteen votes to one, to recommend no change in the present system.[6]

Since then however, interest in and support for PR has grown substantially, for two connected reasons. One has been the rise in the Liberal vote, and the formation of the Social Democratic Party, which fought the 1983 and 1987 general elections in alliance with the Liberals. The Liberal Party obtained almost one-fifth of the votes in February 1974, and the Alliance over one-quarter in 1983, yet obtained only 2.2 per cent and 3.5 per cent respectively of the seats. This was widely regarded as a scandal on a bigger scale than anything observed in the past. (In 1987 the Alliance obtained well over one-fifth of the votes, but only 3.4 per cent of the seats).

The second reason for misgivings was the relatively small proportion of the electorate who actually voted for governments recently taking power. The Labour Government elected in October 1974, with a majority of three seats, polled only 39.2 per cent of the votes cast (and 28.6 per cent of the total electorate). Mrs Margaret Thatcher's Tory Government was returned in 1987 with the far larger majority of 102 seats, but with only 42.3 per cent of the votes cast and 29.6 per cent of the electorate.

The Hansard Society set up a committee of enquiry which reported in 1976 in favour of introducing PR, using the Additional Members' System.[6] Without distinguishing between different methods of PR, opinion polls have since repeatedly shown large majorities in favour of changing the system. It is however extremely doubtful if any change will be made in the foreseeable future, unless the Liberal–Social Democratic Alliance is able to win sufficient support under the existing system to be able to force a change. Naturally a Liberal–SDP government would lose little time in introducing a bill to bring this about, but in the perhaps more likely event of them holding the balance of power in a 'hung' Parliament, the Alliance would try to bargain with either the Labour or Conservative Parties to trade its Parliamentary support for a change in the system. It might well require two successive parliaments to be 'hung' for them to be successful. If proportional representation does come to Britain, it may well do so for Euro elections or local government elections (see chapter 11, below) or even for an elected House of Lords before, or instead of, the House of Commons.

Historically it was quite common for there to be no contest in some constituencies at general elections in seats regarded as being very secure for the defending Member or his party. Since 1951 however, every single seat has been contested at every general election, the Labour and Conservative Parties fighting every constituency (except in Northern Ireland and, usually, the seat contested by the Speaker, who was always fought against by other candidates). But many constituencies had 'straight fights', between only two candidates, Labour and Conservative, as the Liberal Party was not able to field a full roster of candidates. In 1983 and 1987 however the Liberal–Social Democratic Alliance fought every constituency in Great Britain, which meant that there were at least three candidates in every constituency. In fact in both 1979 and 1983 there was an average of four per constituency. Table 4.4 shows the number of candidates in each postwar election (see also Appendix 1). There had been a steady rise since the mid-1950s, though there was a fall in 1987, probably due to the rise in the candidate's deposit from £150 to £500 (see page 101).

Although every seat is contested, relatively few change hands,

TABLE 4.4 *Seats and candidates 1945–1987*

General election	No. of seats	No. of candidates	Average per seat
1945	640	1682	2.6
1950	625	1868	3.0
1951	625	1376	2.2
1955	630	1409	2.2
1959	630	1536	2.4
1964	630	1757	2.8
1966	630	1707	2.7
1970	630	1837	2.9
1974: Feb.	635	2135	3.4
Oct.	635	2252	3.5
1979	635	2576	4.1
1983	650	2579	4.0
1987	650	2325	3.6

even in elections when one party achieves a sweeping victory. Some 47 did so in 1987, about seven per cent of the total. In 1979, when the Conservatives decisively defeated the defending Labour government, some 72 seats changed hands, just over 11 per cent of all seats.

Fewer than 100 seats have switched sides at each of the postwar elections since 1945 when, in a 'landslide' election, some 227 seats out of 640 changed hands, just over one-third of the total. The 1945 election was the first in ten years, and came after wartime conditions had changed the face of British politics. Such a dramatic turnaround seems hardly likely to recur.

In practice, constituencies are regarded as falling into three categories: safe, hopeless and marginal. A safe seat held by one party is of course a hopeless seat for the other. A marginal seat is one where the existing majority is small enough for there to be a realistic prospect for it to be captured by an opposing party. For most of the postwar period the great majority of marginal seats were at issue between Labour and the Conservatives. Only a small minority of seats (outside Northern Ireland) were regarded as being vulnerable to attack by another party, either the Liberals or the Scottish or Welsh Nationalists (Plaid Cymru). But the recent rise of the Liberal Party, and the creation of the Social Democratic Party and subsequently the Social and Liberal Democrats, has created a whole new category of marginal seats, most of which were previously regarded as being strongholds for one or other major party (usually the Conservatives).

It is impossible to give precise definitions of safe and marginal seats, but in practice those with a majority of more than 5000 (about 10 per cent of the votes cast) have been unlikely to change hands at a general election (much larger changes occur at by-elections, where many more seats should be regarded as marginal). On this rough-and-ready definition, some 151 out of the 650 seats in the House of Commons elected in 1987 can be regarded as marginal. Of these, 76 are defended by Conservatives, 56 by Labour members, 12 by the former Alliance parties, three by the SNP, one by Plaid Cymru and three by Northern Ireland parties. In fact rather more MPs, particularly Conservative, are likely to regard their seats as being marginal. The Labour Party would need a net gain of 97 seats to win an overall majority at the next general election, and the former Alliance parties are perceived as a potent threat by the Conservatives in a number of seats not included in the above figures. Probably up to half of the 375 Tory MPs in the 1987 Parliament, and certainly a third of them, would regard their seats as being to some degree marginal.

It has become common practice to convert the voting figures in constituency contests into percentages. This enables the 'swing' to be calculated. The term 'swing' was first applied to elections by David Butler. It is defined as the average of one party's gain and another's loss. Thus if at one election the Conservatives poll 50 per cent of the votes and Labour 45 per cent and at the next election the figures are reversed, there has been a swing to Labour of five per cent. (If both parties lose to a third it is calculated by taking half the difference between the two parties' losses, for example if at one election the Conservatives poll 60 per cent and Labour 40 per cent and at the next the Conservatives poll 50 per cent, Labour 38 per cent and the Liberals 12 per cent, the net swing from Conservative to Labour is four per cent. The utility of the swing concept is that it enables the overall change in a constituency between two elections to be expressed in a single figure, and thus allows easy comparison between the results in different constituencies. Table 4.5 shows an example from the 1983 general election.

The Labour percentage vote in Feltham and Heston fell by 8.9 per cent, and the Conservative percentage rose by 2.0 per cent, making a swing to the Conservatives of 5.5 per cent. With this figure one can tell at a glance that the Conservatives did better in Feltham and Heston than in the country as a whole, where the average swing to the Conservatives was 3.9 per cent.

Feltham and Heston was, in 1983, unusual in that its boundaries

TABLE 4.5   *Voting figures in Feltham and Heston, 1979 and 1983*

	1979	Per cent	1983	Per cent
Labour	28 675	(48.3)	21 576	(39.4)
Conservative	24 570	(41.4)	23 724	(43.4)
Liberal/Alliance	5 051	(8.5)	8 706	(15.9)
Others	1 066	(1.8)	696	(1.3)
Maj	(Lab.) 4 105	(6.9)	(Con.) 2 148	(3.9)

Swing to Conservative: 5.5%

remained unchanged from 1979, thus allowing a direct comparison to be made, but also because one of the main party's share of the vote increased, while that of the other decreased. In most constituencies in 1983 both the larger parties lost support to the Liberal–SDP Alliance. For some comparative purposes it may be more useful to exclude the votes obtained by third parties and only reckon the votes obtained by the two largest parties in calculating swing. This is known as 'two-party swing' or 'Steed swing', after Michael Steed who first developed this concept (by comparison, 'normal swing' is sometimes referred to as 'Butler swing' or 'all-party swing'). To take the earlier example for Feltham and Heston, the calculation of two-party swing would be as follows:

	1979	1983	
Labour	28 675 (53.9%)	21 576 (47.6%)	−6.3%
Conservative	24 570 (46.1%)	23 724 (52.4%)	+6.3%
Total two-party vote	53 245	45 300	

Two-party swing: 6.3

Note that in the case of two-party swing, one party's gain is always equal to the other party's loss, and that this is the net swing. Unless otherwise stated, all swing figures given subsequently in this book will be normal swing. The swing figure required for a seat to change hands is exactly half the percentage majority of the defending party, plus one vote. This is because one party's gain is another's loss. Thus in the above example of Feltham and Heston, where the Conservative candidate won by 3.9 per cent, a Labour swing of 1.95 per cent would have been needed for the Conservative majority to disappear.

Nothing is static in British politics and over the years safe seats have become marginal and marginal ones safe. This is due partly to the movement of population, partly to the effect of redistribution and partly to changes in political opinion. Each new Parliament elected alters the status of different constituencies.

Notes and References

1. Quoted by D. E. Butler in an article 'The Redistribution of Seats', *Public Administration*, Summer 1955. See also *The Electoral System in Britain since 1918* (Oxford University Press, 1963) by the same author.
2. See *The BBC/ITN Guide to the New Parliamentary Constituencies* (Chichester: Parliamentary Research Services, 1983), p. 4.
3. *Ibid.*, p. 5.
4. John Curtice and Michael Steed, 'An Analysis of the Voting', in David Butler and Dennis Kavanagh, *The British General Election of 1983* (London: Macmillan, 1984) p. 361.
5. See John Curtice and Michael Steed, 'Electoral Choice and the Production of Government: The Changing Operation of the Electoral System in the United Kingdom since 1955', *British Journal of Political Science*, July 1982, and Appendix 2, by the same authors, in Butler and Kavanagh, *op. cit.*, particularly pp. 360–3. In 1987 there was a slight reversal of recent trends, and an increase in the number of marginal seats. See Curtice and Steed, Appendix Two, and Butler and Kavanagh, *The British General Election of 1987* (London: Macmillan, 1988) pp. 353–7.
6. *Commission on Electoral Reform* (London: Hansard Society, 1976). For a description of the Additional Members System, see Appendix 8 below.

5 Political Parties – National

Although their existence is ignored in virtually all the laws and regulations governing the conduct of elections, it is the political parties which give them shape and purpose. The overwhelming majority of Parliamentary candidates are party adherents, and it is an exceptionally rare event for an independent candidate to secure election.

In this chapter and the next the organisation of each of the three major parties, together with that of minor parties who have put up candidates in recent general elections, is examined in some detail. Before discussing the individual parties it should be noted that there is a common pattern in the organisation of all three parties.

Each party is made up of three elements – the Parliamentary Party, comprising the MPs and peers who belong to the party concerned, the party bureaucracy and the mass membership throughout the country. The third element is discussed in Chapter 6, the first two are dealt with here.

Of these three elements, it is the Parliamentary Party which is dominant in each case. This is explicitly recognised in the Conservative Party, in which a strong Parliamentary group existed long before either a bureaucracy or a mass membership organisation was formed. The latter were set up in the mid-nineteenth century specifically to provide support for the Parliamentary Party and to ensure the continued election of Conservative MPs. In the Labour Party, the mass organisation was set up first. In the early days of this century when there were only a few Labour MPs they were clearly subordinate to the extra-Parliamentary organisation of the party. But, at least from 1924 onwards when the first minority Labour government was formed, the Parliamentary Labour Party secured for itself in practice, though not formally, a dominance comparable to that of the Parliamentary Conservative Party, though this has been diminished in recent years due to changes in Labour's constitution (see below). The Liberal Democrats were formed (originally as the Social and Liberal Democrats) in 1988 by a merger of the Liberal party, whose history was similar to that of the Conservatives, and the Social Democratic Party (SDP), which was founded in 1981, mainly by a group of defecting Labour MPs. Its constitution owes something to both traditions, protecting the autonomy of its MPs while reserving to the mass membership the final decision-making powers.

In all three parties, the leader of the party in the House of Commons and the leader of the whole party are one and the same, even in the Conservative Party where the other elements in the party play no direct part in the leader's election. The members of the Parliamentary Party – full-time professional politicians in daily contact with each other for eight months of the year – normally have little difficulty in monopolising the most important party decisions.

This is least true of the Labour Party, particularly in opposition. Labour Party leaders, and Labour MPs generally, have periodically had great difficulty in resisting dictation from the party's annual conference and from the National Executive Committee which it elects. In the early 1960s the conference successfully resisted an attempt by the then party leader, Hugh Gaitskell, to amend the party constitution, and against his wishes carried a resolution in favour of unilateral nuclear disarmament. Gaitskell was able to secure a reversal of this defeat the following year, 1961, and the supremacy of the Parliamentary Labour Party was reasserted. Twenty years later however, following Labour's severe defeat in the 1979 election, the conference once more insisted on voting for policies which the party leader and a majority of Labour MPs did not support, on EC membership, disarmament and the expulsion of American bases from Britain. The conference then proceeded to amend the party's constitution to take away from the Parliamentary Labour Party the exclusive right to elect the party leader and to submit Labour MPs to a mandatory process of reselection before each general election.

These decisions precipitated the breakaway of nearly thirty Labour MPs and the foundation of the Social Democratic Party. At one time it appeared that the Parliamentary Labour Party had suffered a permanent loss of power and influence to the conference, at least while the party was in opposition; in the late eighties, however, Neil Kinnock demonstrated a steadily tightening grip on the conference which has somewhat re-established the Parliamentary Party's position. When a party is in government, of course, much of the authority of the Parliamentary Party is assumed by the Cabinet, whose influence far outweighs that of any organ of the party.

The party bureaucracy in the Conservative Party is under the direct control of the leader. In the Labour and Liberal Parties it is responsible to the elected representatives or the mass membership. Because many of these elected representatives are also Members of Parliament the Parliamentary Party exercises a considerable indirect influence over the bureaucracy, and clashes of interest are rare. It is undoubtedly true that responsibility for the party machine is much more widely diffused in the Labour and Liberal Democrat Parties, in practice as well as in theory, than in the Conservative Party.

The party bureaucracy consists of a headquarters in London and a series of regional offices throughout the country. At one time the Conservative and Labour headquarters faced each other from different sides of Smith Square in Westminster, with the Liberal headquarters also in the same square. But in the early 1980s the Labour Party moved to premises at 150 Walworth Road, across the river in Southwark, and the Liberal Democrats' headquarters is now at 4 Cowley Street, very near to Smith Square. Though more scattered than they once were however, all three headquarters are still quite near to the House of Commons, emphasising their close relationship to their respective Parliamentary Parties.

The functions of the party bureaucracy are manifold. They are responsible for publishing a constant stream of pamphlets and leaflets for distribution through the constituency and local branches of the party. These range from the crudest propaganda handouts to sophisticated discussion pamphlets on policy, intended for the use of study groups within the party. Posters and other propaganda material are also produced in great quantities, and a steady supply of advice and information is supplied to constituency party secretaries who seldom experience a week without receiving at least one communication from head office.

Both the Conservative and Labour Parties' headquarters are now organised in three main departments, each under a director who is responsible to the head of the party organisation (the Chairman of the Conservative party, or the General Secretary in Labour's case). Conservative Central Office is divided into a research department, a communications department in charge of publicity, and a campaigning department which organises the political activities of the party; Walworth Road has an organisation department, a policy development department, and a communications and campaigns department. Although the names and divisions of responsibilities are somewhat different, both party headquarters carry out essentially the same wide range of functions. The department in charge of research has an essential job, briefing the party's speakers on the wide range of subjects on which they are called to speak, especially vital when the party is in opposition; much of the material contained in the party's publications will also originate here, although they will actually be prepared by the communications department.

The department in charge of communications and publicity, as well as looking after party publications, is responsible for the extensive advertising campaigns which mark the approach to a modern General Election, and for all aspects of the party's relations with the press and broadcasting media and for the image the party projects. Supervision of the party's own television and radio broadcasts is an important part of this function, but it is also essential to ensure that the party's spokesmen and prospective candidates are properly briefed and make a good impression when they appear on the TV companies' own programmes. The bureaucracy is also responsible for organising speaking tours by prominent MPs and supplying speakers on demand for speaking engagements throughout the country, both at election time and between elections.

The organising staff, who are responsible for maintaining an efficient vote-winning machine throughout the country, have the least glamorous but perhaps the most essential job at the party headquarters. Through their regional offices they keep a tight rein on the full-time constituency agents (although most of these are actually employed by the constituency parties), and are also responsible for ensuring that local parties are in a constant state of readiness to fight elections and that the selection of Parliamentary candidates proceeds according to the party rules. If there is any irregularity it is their function to bring the constituency party into line.

Head Office must also deal with such matters as local government, contacts with the European Parliamentary Party, international and Commonwealth affairs, relations with like-minded political parties in other countries, and fund-raising.

Although each party headquarters undertakes the same tasks, there has traditionally been considerable difference in the efficiency with which they have been performed. The Conservative Party has always had much the largest staff, although it was reduced considerably in the early 1980s to save money; it has also paid higher salaries, and has therefore often been able to attract better qualified people to its employ. Table 5.1 shows how the staff of the parties varies and is a rough guide to the thoroughness with which they were able to perform their tasks. It was compiled shortly before the last general election, in 1987, on the basis of information supplied by senior party officials. The numbers are not directly comparable in that the

TABLE 5.1　*Party staffs, 1987 general election*

Party	HQ	Regions	Constituencies
Conservative Party (England & Wales)	170	130	288
Labour Party (Great Britain)	150	25*	54
Liberal Party (England)	24	14	20*
Social Democratic Party (Great Britain)	44	4	20*

* Estimate

Conservatives have a separate organisation in Scotland, and the Liberals in both Wales and Scotland, so their total numbers are understated – particularly for the Conservatives. But the general picture is clear enough. Between general elections the number of party employees tends to decline, particularly constituency party agents, whose numbers are usually built up again in the year or so before the next election takes place.

The maintenance of a party bureaucracy is an expensive business, and the difference in size of staff is a direct reflection of the rival parties' financial resources. Historically the Conservative Party has been much the wealthiest party, but in recent years the gap between it and the Labour Party has narrowed considerably.[1] In the year ended 31 March 1986 the Conservative Party reported an income, at national level in England and Wales, of £5 015 000, compared to £4 574 000 for the Labour Party in 1985 for the whole of Great Britain. The comparable figures for the Liberal Party and the Social Democratic Party were, respectively, £405 192 and £818 604. Members' subscriptions figured as much the largest items in the incomes of the two smaller parties, but donations, mostly from business firms, provided four-fifths of the Conservative income, while trade union and other affiliations accounted for 78 per cent of Labour's. The Conservative Party's overall financial advantage is greater than these figures indicate. It is able to raise additional funds, through special election appeals to companies, which are substantially greater than the amount provided by the trade unions for Labour. Also local Conservative associations have larger and wealthier memberships than those of the other parties so that their expenditure in the constituencies is far greater. Despite the greater income of the Conservative party, however, in recent years they have had some difficulty in covering their costs; they were reported to be a million pounds in debt in 1986 (*Sunday Times*, 24 August 1986), and probably suffered a substantial shortfall in covering their expenditure on the 1987 election campaign.

The party bureaucracy is entrusted with the task of organising the annual party conference which provides the sole opportunity for the members of the mass organisation to give collective expression of their views. The three conferences are held in rapid succession – first Liberal Democrat, then Labour, then Conservative – in September and October each year at one of the small number of resorts which have the facilities to house such a gathering. Only Blackpool, Bournemouth and Brighton have a large enough conference centre and sufficient hotel accommodation to cater for the Labour and Conservative conferences, which alternate between these resorts each year. The other parties' conferences are somewhat smaller and a number of other towns, including Scarborough, Llandudno, Eastbourne, Harrogate and Cheltenham have been favoured by the Liberal Democrats and their predecessors in recent years.

Each conference receives a report on the work of the party bureaucracy during the year and a Parliamentary report, and then proceeds to debate a large number of policy resolutions which have been sent in by constituency parties or, at the Labour conference, by trade unions.

The Conservative conference is a cumbrous affair with some 4500 delegates and acts as little more than a party rally. It has no formal power to do more than proffer 'advice' to the leader, and for many years it appeared to have only a small influence on party policy. The two most recent leaders, Edward Heath and Margaret Thatcher, have taken its deliberations more seriously however, attending throughout the conference and taking care not to offend its sensibilities. The open contempt once shown by Tory leaders such as Arthur Balfour, who said he would no sooner take political advice from the conference than from his valet, is decidedly a matter of the past.

The Labour Party conference has about 1200 delegates of whom about half come from constituency parties, and the remainder mostly from trade unions. As the constituency delegates represent less than a third of a million members while the trade unionists represent over five million, the latter have a predominating influence on the voting, though spokesmen from the constituency parties enjoy the lion's share of the speech making and have had their voting weight magnified by recent constitutional changes. It is the Labour Party conference which decides the policy of the party and especially the election programme on which it is to fight. Theoretically therefore its influence is immense. In practice however the Parliamentary leadership consistently enjoys the support of several of the larger trade unions and this normally guarantees it a majority at the conference. It is only when one or more of the normally 'loyalist' trade unions disagrees with the Parliamentary leadership, as happened on the issue of defence policy in 1960, that the leadership runs a serious risk of defeat. This occurred with increasing frequency in the early 1980s, but things seemed to have settled back into their normal pattern by the end of the decade.

The majority of delegates to a Labour Party conference undoubtedly sincerely believe that they are there to frame the policy of the party, and the debates are vigorous and lively. And the great amount of time and trouble which both the Parliamentary leadership and many busy trade union leaders devote to the conference is strong evidence that its influence, though less than decisive, is far from negligible.

Unlike the conferences of the two larger parties, the federal conference of the Liberal Democrats meets twice yearly. In theory it has considerably less power than the Labour Party conference, although it is the final arbiter of party policy. In practice however its influence may prove fairly strong; the small number of Liberal Democrat MPs will probably leave the Parliamentary leadership in a weak position, as it did in the old Liberal assembly, and conference is likely to be very influential.

Since the early 1960s the party conferences have received extensive coverage on television, and this has to a great extent modified their function. Traditionally the Conservative conference was derided by its opponents as being 'stage managed' in order to provide a public image of unity and enthusiasm. Now all party managers exert themselves to achieve the same effect, and if they are successful they may well be rewarded by a spurt in their party's opinion poll ratings in the period immediately after the conference. Conversely a fractious or quarrelsome conference can lead to a sharp fall in a party's popularity.

The Conservative and Unionist Party is the oldest and most resilient of British parties. Its origins go back at least 300 years to Stuart times and the earlier name, Tory Party (still widely used by friends and foes alike), dates from 1679. 'Tory' was an Irish word meaning brigand and it was applied to the King's supporters, who were supposedly willing to use Irish troops against Englishmen to enforce the succession of James II. Tories were supporters of the Crown and drew their support principally from the squirearchy and the clergy.

The name Conservative was adopted following the Reform Act of 1832. Some thirty years later, finding themselves in a permanent minority in the then politically dominant urban middle class, the party, under the inspiration of Benjamin Disraeli (later Lord Beaconsfield) set out to form the basis of a mass party. Local Conservative associations were formed in many constituencies to secure the election of Conservative MPs. The 1867 Reform Act, which gave the vote to most of the urban working class, gave added impetus to this development and in the following three years the party took on substantially its present shape.

The Liberal Unionists, who broke away from the Liberal Party in 1886 because of their opposition to Irish Home Rule, finally amalgamated with the Conservative Party in 1912, hence its present unwieldy name.

Conservatives in Scotland and in Northern Ireland traditionally called themselves Unionists and Ulster Unionists respectively, but the term is infrequently used in England and Wales. The Official Unionist Party in Northern Ireland used to be the Conservative Party in the province. In 1972 however, the Conservative Government, under Edward Heath, imposed direct rule on Northern Ireland. The Unionists broke away, and their party is now completely independent of the Conservatives. After some years of refusing to countenance the possibility, the Conservative Party finally yielded to pressure in 1989, and has now permitted the foundation of constituency Conservative associations in the province.

Three distinct elements make up the modern Conservative Party. The Parliamentary Party, the National Union and the Central Office. They are linked at the apex by the leader, who enjoys very considerable formal power, much more than his Labour or Liberal Democrat counterparts. The most influential of the three elements is undoubtedly the Parliamentary Party, which is composed of all Members of Parliament who take the Conservative Whip. The management of the Parliamentary Party is the responsibility of the Chief Whip, who is appointed by the leader of the party.

From the Parliamentary Party and the Conservative peers, the leader chooses his Cabinet when a Conservative government is in power; when in opposition he appoints a 'shadow cabinet' and a deputy leader.

The Parliamentary Party has a number of specialist committees on defence, foreign affairs, trade and industry, agriculture and so on. When the party is in opposition the committees are attended by both front and back bench Members, when in government they are comprised entirely of back bench Members.

An unofficial body which wields considerable power is the '1922 Committee' (known as such because it was originally formed on the initiative of the back bench Members elected to the Parliament of 1922). This committee, known formally as the Conservative Members' Committee, meets every week while Parliament is sitting and consists, when a Conservative government is in power, of all the Conservative back bench Members. Its chairman, who is elected by the committee, is a prominent back bencher and his is a most influential voice in party affairs. When Conservatives are in opposition the 1922 Committee comprises the entire Parliamentary Party, and the back bench influence is diluted by the presence of the leading front bench Members.

The National Union of Conservative and Unionist Associations, which dates from 1867, is the body representing the mass following of the Conservative Party throughout the country. It is a federation of constituency associations, and its annual conference is, in effect, the annual conference of the Conservative Party. Despite its name, it includes only associations in constituencies in England and Wales; a parallel organisation, the Scottish Conservative and Unionist Association, being responsible for Scotland.

The governing body of the National Union is the Central Council, an unwieldy body of some 3000 members, on which every constituency has five representatives and which meets once a year in London. Its executive committee, with about 150 members, meets about every two months and is an important political body. Most of its more routine administrative work is normally delegated to its general purposes sub-committee, which meets monthly.

The executive of the National Union has a series of advisory committees on various aspects of organisation – local government, Parliamentary candidates, Young Conservatives, women, – and these committees are normally reproduced at area and constituency levels. The National Union has eleven provincial area councils on which the constituency associations are directly represented and which meet once a year. The National Union is not responsible for organisation – its function is to act as a two-way channel of communication between the leader, the Parliamentary Party and the rank and file members in the constituencies.

Organisation is the responsibility of the Central Office, which was established by Disraeli personally in 1870. Its direction has since remained firmly under the control of the leader who appoints its chairman (normally a Cabinet Minister or leading Parliamentary figure) and other officers. The general director of the Conservative Central Office, who is responsible to the chairman and is, in effect, his full-time deputy, is also traditionally the honorary secretary of the National Union and the Central Office agent in each of the provincial areas is also the honorary secretary of the area council of the National Union.

An unofficial body, the Bow Group (founded in 1957) which is modelled to a great extent on the Fabian Society, does a great deal of independent research on policy matters. Although its members are all Conservatives and it enjoys friendly relations with the party organisation, it has no formal link with it. Other unofficial groups, formed more recently, include the Tory Reform Group, on the left wing of the party, and the Monday Club, on the right.

The leader of the Conservative Party used to be nominally elected by the Party Meeting, a body which never otherwise met and which consisted of all the Conservative Members of the House of Commons and of the House of Lords, all prospective Parliamentary candidates and the executive committee of the National Union. In fact until 1965 there had never been a contested election, the leadership being decided by a process of informal consultation between the leading party figures in both Houses of Parliament and only one name was put before the meeting for formal endorsement.

When a Conservative Government was in power the Sovereign was normally advised to send for whoever was designated, even before the meeting to elect the new leader had been convened. On the resignation of Sir Anthony Eden in January 1957, the Queen was advised by Sir Winston Churchill and Lord Salisbury to send for Harold Macmillan, in preference to R. A. Butler, as the new Conservative Prime Minister. This process of involving the Sovereign in the selection of a political leader was widely criticised at the time, and some Conservatives felt that on future occasions their leader should be chosen by vote. But no change was effected and when in October 1963 Harold Macmillan announced his forthcoming resignation in the midst of the Conservative conference, ten days of the most intensive canvassing and speculation ever known in British politics ensued before the Queen, on the advice of the retiring Prime Minister, sent for the Earl of Home; the most fancied candidate, R. A. Butler, having again been passed over.

Although Lord Home was quickly accepted by the majority of the party, the degree of dissatisfaction at the manner of his selection was far greater than ever before. Following the Conservative defeat in the 1966 general election, Sir Alec Douglas-Home (as Lord Home was then known) instituted a one-man enquiry – carried out by the then party chairman, Lord Blakenham – into alternative methods of selecting the leader of the party. Upon receiving Blakenham's report, Sir Alec announced, on his own authority, that in future the leader would be chosen by a ballot of Conservative MPs.

The system he laid down had no exact parallel, and it was clearly devised to assist the evolution of a compromise choice should there be a sharp division between two controversial and mutually incompatible candidates. Under the new system a candidate needs to secure on the first ballot not only an absolute majority, but a lead of 15 per cent over his nearest rival. If the first ballot fails to produce a winner, a second ballot is held for which new nominations may be made. To be successful on the second ballot, a candidate needs only an absolute majority. If the second ballot is inconclusive a third and final ballot is held. The names on the ballot paper would be those of the three leading candidates in the second ballot. Voters are required to indicate their second as well as their first preference. The candidate with the smallest number of first preferences is eliminated and his second preferences are distributed between the other two. The winner of this ballot is then presented formally to the Party Meeting for election as party leader.

When Sir Alec resigned in July 1965 the new system was put into effect. Three candidates were nominated, and on the first ballot Edward Heath received 150 votes, Reginald Maudling 133 and Enoch Powell 15. Heath had received an absolute majority, but his lead over Maudling was less than 15 per cent and a second ballot was therefore necessary. However both Maudling and Powell declined re-nomination, and Edward Heath was elected unopposed.

The election system imposed by Lord Home contained no provision for periodic re-election, but in the autumn of 1974, following two successive Conservative election defeats, there was an overwhelming demand among Tory MPs for a fresh election, although Heath made it clear that he had no intention of resigning. Lord Home was asked to consider changes in the rules, and his three main proposals were:

1. There should be an annual election of the leader.
2. A candidate, to be elected on the first ballot, required not only an overall majority but also a lead over the runner-up equal to 15 per cent of those eligible to vote (it had previously been 15 per cent of those who actually voted).
3. Though only MPs had votes, the views of the Conservative peers and of the party in the country should be conveyed to them.

Heath submitted himself for re-election the following February, and was disconcerted to find himself led on the first ballot by Margaret Thatcher by 130 votes to 119, with 16 votes cast for a third candidate, Hugh Fraser, while 11 MPs did not vote. He immediately resigned and four more candidates were nominated for the second ballot, from which Fraser withdrew. This ballot, held on 11 February 1975, produced an absolute majority for Margaret Thatcher, as follows:

Margaret Thatcher	146
William Whitelaw	79
James Prior	19
Sir Geoffrey Howe	19
John Peyton	11
Did not vote	2

Although the new system provided for a theoretically annual election, even if the party was in power, the first opposed election after 1975 was in 1989, when Sir Anthony Meyer was persuaded to stand against Mrs Thatcher (who had by then been Prime Minister for ten years) to enable MPs to express discontent at the Government's progress and possibly to open the way for a challenge from a more senior figure should she fail to win outright on the first ballot. However Mrs Thatcher polled 314 votes while only 33 MPs voted for Meyer, with another 27 abstaining, although the public embarrassment for the party was considerable. Such contested elections seemed likely to remain very much the exception rather than the rule, but a year later Mrs Thatcher was challenged again, this time by Michael Heseltine, in the wake of the resignation of her Deputy Prime Minister, Sir Geoffrey Howe. Howe resigned in protest against her negative approach to the European Community, but Tory MPs were probably more influenced by the unpopularity of the poll tax which she had introduced, poor by-election results and the large Labour lead in the opinion polls in determining how to cast their votes.

In the event, although more than half of them voted for her in the first ballot, she failed by four votes to clear the hurdle of a 15 per cent lead over her rival. The result of this ballot, declared on 20 November 1990, was:

Margaret Thatcher	204
Michael Heseltine	152
Abstentions	16

Mrs Thatcher's immediate reaction was that she would fight on into the second round, but after having been warned by the majority of her Cabinet and by other senior party figures that her support was crumbling she withdrew, freeing both the Chancellor of the Exchequer, John Major, and Foreign Secretary, Douglas Hurd, to accept nominations. The result of the second ballot, declared on 27 November 1990, was:

John Major	185
Michael Heseltine	131
Douglas Hurd	56

Major was two votes short of the overall majority required on this ballot, but his two rivals immediately withdrew, making a third ballot unnecessary. The following morning Mrs Thatcher resigned as prime Minister and Major was appointed in her place. Many Tory MPs, as well as Conservative activists in the constituencies, were highly resentful that an electoral system designed when the party had been in opposition had been used to unseat a Prime Minister, and after the election the Chairman of the 1922 Committee, Cranley Onslow, was asked to carry out an enquiry as to whether different rules should apply when the Conservatives are in power. It seems probable that amendments will be introduced as a result of his enquiry.

The Conservative Party has always been one of the two principal parties of the State. In the period from 1832 to 1916 Conservative and Liberal governments alternated in power, though the Liberals had the lion's share of office. Since then the Conservatives became used to being the normal 'government party' and held power either separately or in coalition for all but nine of the forty-eight years between 1916 and 1964. Labour held power for 11 out of the next 15 years, but the Conservative victories of 1979, 1983 and 1987 may be the prelude to a further long spell in office.

The Conservative Party has not published membership figures for some years, but it is believed to have about 1½ million members. It is organised in each of the 633 constituencies in Great Britain,and it invariably contests every British seat at general elections except, on occasion, that of the Speaker. In 1987 it fielded a full roster of 633 candidates.

The Labour Party differs from all others in possessing a large affiliated membership (mostly trade unionists) in addition to its individual members. In fact for the first eighteen years of its existence it was impossible to become an individual member of the Labour Party.

The party was formed, under the title of the Labour Representation Committee, at a conference in London on 27 February 1900. The conference was convened by the Trades Union Congress, following a resolution passed at the TUC conference the previous year. It was attended by representatives of 67 trade unions and three small socialist organisations (the Independent Labour Party, the Social Democratic Federation and the Fabian Society). The purpose of the organisation established at this meeting was to secure the representation of 'working-class opinion' in the House of Commons 'by men sympathetic with the aims and demands of the Labour movement'. In the early years the Labour Representation Committee (which became the Labour Party in 1906) did no more than co-ordinate the political activities of its affiliated organisations and all Labour candidates at that time were financially sponsored by one or other of these affiliates.

Success at first came slowly to the new party. Only two Labour MPs were elected in the 1900 election (one being J. Keir Hardie who had been the driving force behind the creation of the party). But in the period from 1906 to 1923 the Labour Party progressively replaced the Liberals as one of the two principal parties, becoming the official Opposition in 1922 and forming its first (minority) government in 1924.

In 1918 the party adopted a new constitution. This at last made provision for individual membership of the party and the creation of constituency Labour parties throughout the country followed immediately after. The 1918 constitution also specifically committed the party for the first time to Socialist objectives. It has been amended a number of times, but it is still in force today. The most significant amendments, agreed at a special party conference in January 1981, altered the basis for electing the leader and deputy leader of the party. Previously there had been, in theory at least, an annual ballot of MPs, who elected a leader and deputy leader of the Parliamentary

Labour Party. Their choices were automatically accepted as being leader and deputy leader of the party as a whole. In practice such ballots virtually never occurred except on the death or resignation of the incumbent. Clement Attlee led the Labour Party from 1935 to 1955 and was never once challenged, nor was Harold Wilson between 1963 and 1976, when he resigned. Hugh Gaitskell, leader from 1955 to 1963, was challenged in 1960 (by Wilson) and in 1961, but these were exceptional occasions, due to the dispute in the party over unilateral nuclear disarmament. Neither James Callaghan (1976–80) nor Michael Foot (1980–3) had to face a further contest after their initial election, despite the fact that the electoral rules were changed immediately after Foot was chosen.

In January 1981, two months after Foot's election, Labour MPs lost the right to choose their own leader. Henceforth the Labour leader (and deputy leader) would be chosen by an 'electoral college' made up of MPs (with 30 per cent of the vote), constituency parties (30 per cent) and trade unions (40 per cent). Although nobody was nominated to run against Foot under the new procedure, his deputy, Denis Healey, who had been elected unopposed by the Parliamentary Labour Party, was challenged in 1981 by Tony Benn. Healey defeated Benn by a mere 0.8 per cent of the electoral college vote.

The first leadership contest under the new electoral system came in October 1983, following the resignation of Foot. The result was:

	Trade unions, etc.	Constituency parties	MPs	Total
		(*votes*)		
Neil Kinnock	4 389 000	571	100	–
Roy Hattersley	1 644 000	12	53	–
Eric Heffer	7 000	41	29	–
Peter Shore	5 000	0	21	–
Total	6 045 000	624	203	–
		(*per cent*)		
Neil Kinnock	29.042	27 452	14.778	71.272
Roy Hattersley	10.878	0.577	7.833	19.288
Eric Heffer	0.046	1.971	4.286	6.303
Peter Shore	0.033	0.000	3.103	3.137
Total	40	30	30	100

Neil Kinnock, with over 71 per cent of the electoral college vote, was easily elected on the first ballot. In a parallel election for the deputy leadership held later the same day, Roy Hattersley was also elected on the first ballot, with over 67 per cent of the electoral college vote:

	Trade unions, etc.	Constituency parties	MPs	Total
		(*votes*)		
Roy Hattersley	5 349 000	318	112	–
Michael Meacher	718 000	298	59	–
Denzil Davies	0	5	22	–
Gwyneth Dunwoody	5 000	2	8	–
Total	6 072 000	623	201	–
		(*per cent*)		
Roy Hattersley	35.237	15.313	16.716	67.266
Michael Meacher	4.730	14.350	8.806	27.886
Denzil Davies	0.000	0.241	3.284	3.525
Gwyneth Dunwoody	0.033	0.096	1.194	1.323
Total	40	30	30	100

In theory Labour holds elections for leader and deputy leader every year while in opposition (if Labour is in government they will occur only if a majority of conference votes for a contest, unless there is a vacancy), but Kinnock and Hattersley have been challenged only once up to and including 1990. In 1988 Tony Benn was nominated for the leadership and John Prescott and Eric Heffer for the deputy leadership; however Kinnock and Hattersley were both re-elected extremely comfortably:

	% Votes			
	Unions	CLPs	MPs	Total
Neil Kinnock	39.660	24.128	24.842	88.630
Tony Benn	0.340	5.872	5.158	11.370
	40.000	30.000	30.000	100.000
Roy Hattersley	31.339	18.109	17.376	66.823
John Prescott	8.654	7.845	7.195	23.694
Eric Heffer	0.007	4.406	5.430	9.483
	40.000	30.000	30.000	100.000

The Parliamentary Labour Party is made up of Labour MPs and peers, though the latter are relatively few in number and wield little influence. Each year when Labour is in opposition it now elects, by ballot, a Chief Whip and a Parliamentary committee (or Shadow Cabinet) of 15 members in the Commons and three in the Lords.

The leader of the party is also, when in opposition, chairman of the Parliamentary Party and presides at its weekly meetings. Policy and Parliamentary tactics are discussed at these meetings and are frequently put to the vote, which is binding on the leader and the Parliamentary committee. When Labour is in government the Parliamentary Labour Party elects a back bench Member as chairman and it comes to resemble more closely the Conservative 1922 Committee, though Ministers are entitled to attend and to vote, and frequently do so. A regular interchange of views between a Labour Government and its back bench supporters takes place through the 'Liaison Committee'. This consists of the chairman of the Parliamentary Labour Party, two elected vice-chairmen – also back benchers – and an elected representative of the Labour peers, with the Chief Whip and the Leader of the House of Commons representing the Government.

The party bureaucracy is not controlled, as in the case of the Conservative Party, by the leader, but by a National Executive Committee elected by the Labour Party conference. This committee, usually known as the NEC, consists of 29 members of whom 26 are elected by the conference. The remaining three are the leader and deputy leader of the party, and a representative of the Young Socialists' organisation, who is elected at their own conference. Except for its share of the electoral college vote for the leader and deputy leader therefore, the Parliamentary Labour Party has no direct link with the NEC, although some Labour MPs will normally be among those elected to it. Of the 26 elected members of the NEC, 12 are elected by the trade union delegates to the conference, seven by the constituency party delegates and one by the delegates of socialist and co-operative organisations. Five women members and the treasurer are elected by the whole conference, but as the trade unionists' votes predominate, the constituency party delegates have little influence on the election of these six members. In practice a majority both of the seven constituency party representatives and the five women members have invariably been Members of Parliament.

The NEC, which normally meets monthly, appoints the general secretary who is the chief official of the party and who is responsible to them for the running of the national headquarters at Walworth Road and of the party machine in the country. The NEC and its various sub-committees are also responsible for making appointments to other senior posts in the party bureaucracy.

In 1987 the Labour party had just under 290 000 individual members and over 5½ million affiliated members. The vast majority of these affiliated members belonged to one of the 38 Trade Unions which were affiliated nationally to the party, but also included were two co-operative societies (The Royal Arsenal Co-operative Wholesale Society and the London Region Co-operative Retail Society), the National Union of Labour and Socialist Clubs, and six small socialist organisations (the Fabian Society, Poale Zion (the Jewish Socialist Labour Party), the Socialist Educational Association, the Socialist Health Association, the Christian Socialist Movement and the Society of Labour Lawyers).

The largest of the affiliated Trade Unions at present are the Transport and General Workers' Union, the Amalgamated Engineering Union, the General, Municipal, Boilermakers and Allied Trades' Union, the National Union of Public Employees and the Union of Shop, Distributive and Allied Workers; these five alone commanded a majority of votes at the 1988 conference. Most of the other large unions representing manual workers are also affiliated, including the National Union of Mineworkers, once one of the 'big six' but now considerably reduced in size. The most important unions not affiliated to the Labour Party all represent white collar or professional workers, for example the Civil Service unions, the National Union of Teachers and the National and Local Government Officers (NALGO). Some white collar unions, such as the Association of Professional, Executive, Clerical and Computer Staff (APEX) are, however, affiliated to the party.

The Unions pay an affiliation fee for each member, set at £1 for 1989 (rising to £1.20 in 1990 and £1.45 in 1991 in preparation for the anticipated expense of an election campaign), which comes not from the general funds of the union but, by law, must come out of a special political fund established by a vote of all union members and from which any individual member may contract out if he does not wish to support the Labour Party financially. Individual members pay their subscriptions to their own Constituency Labour Party, and these are set at £10 per year (£3 for pensioners, students and the unemployed, who collectively make up not much under half of the individual membership) of which £5.30 (£1.80 at reduced rate) is passed on to the national party as an affiliation fee. Although this is substantially higher than the fee paid for each member affiliated through the trade unions, the total trade union membership is so much larger that it provides by far the larger part of the party's funds at national level.

The Fabian Society, which has been affiliated to the party from the beginning, is an independent socialist research organisation, whose principal function is the publication of books and pamphlets studying current political, economic, and social problems from a democratic socialist viewpoint. Although it is an affiliated body it expresses no collective viewpoint within the party and in practice its relationship to it is very similar to that of the Bow Group to the Conservative Party. The Fabian Society, founded in 1884, restricts its membership to those 'eligible for membership of the Labour Party'. This means, in effect, that non-members of the Labour Party may join, provided they are not members of other political parties.

Although it has been one of the two major parties since 1922, the Labour Party has until recently been markedly less successful than the Conservatives in securing office. In 1945 Labour was returned with a large majority in the House of Commons and formed a government which continued in office, introducing major legislative changes in a great many fields until the general election of October 1951. For thirteen years after 1951 Labour was in opposition, but in 1964 it snatched a narrow victory over the Conservatives which was consolidated in the 1966 general election. Defeat in the 1970 general election was followed by narrow victories over the Conservatives in the two 1974 elections. A further heavy defeat in 1979 was followed by widespread defections to the newly formed Social Democratic Party, and two more defeats in 1983 and 1987.

Minority Labour governments were in power in 1924 and in 1929–31, dependent on Liberal support in the House of Commons. Labour Ministers also took part in the wartime coalition governments of 1916–18 and 1940–45. For all the rest of its life the Labour Party has been in opposition, and this factor is undoubtedly reflected in its constitution which, unlike that of the Conservatives, is more fitted to a party in opposition than in government. The Labour Party normally contests every seat at general elections, except in Northern Ireland.

The Co-operative Party, founded in 1917, has been formally allied to the Labour Party since 1926. It has agreed not to put up candidates in opposition to Labour candidates and the only Co-operative nominees who are put forward are those selected by constituency Labour parties as Labour candidates. They are normally designated as Co-operative and Labour candidates, but otherwise are indistinguishable from other Labour candidates. The Co-operative Party has branches in more than half the Parliamentary constituencies. Co-operative Societies with eleven million members are affiliated to the party, but it is doubtful whether it has more than 3000 individual members. It sponsors its candidates financially in the same way as the trade unions (see Chapter 7). Its local branches are affiliated to constituency Labour parties, and it is financed more by contributions from the political funds of Co-operative Societies than by the subscriptions of its members.

In 1959 the Co-operative Party agreed with the Labour Party to limit the number of its sponsored candidates to a maximum of thirty. The table below shows the number who have been nominated at recent general elections.

TABLE 5.2   *Co-operative Party candidates*

Year	Candidates	Elected
1945	33	23
1950	33	18
1951	37	16
1955	38	18
1959	30	16
1964	27	19
1966	24	18
1970	27	17
1974: Feb.	25	16
Oct.	22	16
1979	25	17
1983	17	8
1987	20	10

The Social and Liberal Democratic Party (SLD, usually known by the shorter title of Liberal Democrats) was formed in 1988 by the merger of the Liberal Party and the Social Democratic Party (SDP). Of these, the Liberal Party was larger and far older. It grew out of the old Whig Party, which dated from the debates in 1679 over the attempted exclusion of the Duke of York, later James II, from the succession. The Whigs probably derived their name, which was at first meant contemptuously, from the Whiggamores, a body of Scottish Presbyterian insurgents who had marched on Edinburgh in 1648. The Whigs became identified as the party of those wishing to assert the authority of Parliament over that of the Sovereign, and later as the advocates of Parliamentary reform through extension of the franchise. In the years following the Reform Act of 1832 the new name of Liberal Party gradually replaced the old. Unlike 'Tory', the term 'Whig' passed completely out of common usage by the end of the century.

Under the leadership, successively, of Palmerston and Gladstone the Liberal Party dominated the Parliamentary scene during the greater part of the Victorian era. In 1886 however it suffered a major setback through the defection of the Liberal Unionists over the issue of Irish Home Rule.

In 1906 a Liberal government was elected with an immense majority, and remained in office until 1915, led successively by Campbell-Bannerman and Asquith, but by the 1920s the Liberals had been replaced by the Labour Party as one of the two main parties, a process which was aided by a bitter division between the supporters of the last two Liberals to be Prime Minister, Asquith and Lloyd George. The 1910–15 government was the last Liberal government; subsequently Liberals took part in the Asquith and Lloyd George coalition governments from 1915 to 1922, briefly in the Ramsay MacDonald National government from 1931 to 1932 and in the Churchill coalition government from 1940 to 1945. In 1977–8, under 'the Lib–Lab pact', the Liberal Party supported the Labour government of James Callaghan, which had lost its majority through by-election reverses, in the House of Commons, and there were regular consultations on policy matters. There was no suggestion however that the Liberal Party should join the government.

The electoral decline of the Liberal Party continued unabated until the early 1950s when it was reduced to a mere six seats in the House of Commons. After that it staged successive revivals, culminating in the 1983 general election when, in alliance with the newly-formed SDP, it polled over a quarter of the votes, almost as many as the Labour party.

The SDP, founded in 1981, had been established as a breakaway from the Labour Party, following the constitutional changes made at the special Labour Party conference in January 1981, which provided that an electoral college rather than Labour MPs should elect the Labour leader. The leading Social Democrats had already been dismayed by earlier Labour conference decisions, on defence policy and on projected British withdrawal from the EEC, as well as the general leftward trend of the party over the previous few years.

TABLE 5.3   *Liberal Party candidates since 1945*

Year	Candidates	Elected
1945	306	12
1950	475	9
1951	109	6
1955	110	6
1959	216	6
1964	365	9
1966	311	12
1970	332	6
1974: Feb.	517	14
Oct.	619	13
1979	576	11
1983	633*	23[†]
1987	633**	22[††]

Average vote per candidate in 1987: 23.7%
  * Including 311 SDP
 ** Including 306 SDP
  [†] Including 6 SDP
 [††] Including 5 SDP

The initiative in setting up the SDP was taken by the former Labour Chancellor of the Exchequer and Deputy Leader, Roy Jenkins, who had just completed four years in Brussels as President of the EEC Commission, and three younger ex-Cabinet Ministers, David Owen, Shirley Williams and William Rodgers. It was joined altogether by 26 sitting Labour MPs and one Conservative, and its parliamentary strength was subsequently increased to 29 by the election of Shirley Williams and Roy Jenkins in by-elections.

The formation of the new party had been actively encouraged by the Liberal leader, David Steel, and from the outset it was envisaged that the two parties would collaborate in fighting elections. Apart from policy issues, on which there were few serious differences between the two parties, both had a strong common interest in aiming to change the electoral system to one of proportional representation. They were forced however to fight under the existing system, which meant that they would only do themselves harm by putting up candidates against each other.

Within three months of the launch of the SDP, in March 1981, a joint programme, *Fresh Start for Britain*, was produced by the two parties, whose annual conferences formally approved an Alliance

between them the following autumn. The appeal of the new party
was immediate. It rapidly attracted some 70 000 members, two-thirds
of whom had not previously belonged to any political party. The
Alliance went on to achieve a string of by-election successes, and
easily led the other two parties in the opinion polls. By the spring of
1982 however the momentum began to slow down, though Roy
Jenkins did succeed in winning a hard-fought by-election in Glasgow
Hillhead in March 1982. But the following month saw the Argentine
invasion of the Falkland Islands, and the subsequent military campaign resulted in a patriotic rallying of support for Margaret Thatcher
and the Conservative government. This enabled it to sweep back into
the lead in the opinion polls, where it remained until the 1983 general
election a year later. The Alliance never recovered from the impact
of the Falklands War, and despite running a close third to Labour in
the 1983 election could take only 23 seats, 17 of them Liberal.
Although this total was slightly increased by by-election gains, their
total vote fell off in the 1987 general election and shortly afterwards
the parties announced that they were considering merger, which was
approved by ballots of both memberships and took effect early
in 1988.

A minority in both parties declared themselves implacably opposed to merger, and subsequently formed independent breakaway
parties under the old names. Of the two, the new SDP seemed the
more significant, having the allegiance of three MPs including former
leader Dr David Owen, but by the summer of 1990 it had become
increasingly obvious that they had no future as a national party, and
the Parliamentary Party was dissolved, all three MPs continuing to sit
as independents. The breakaway Liberal Party had no sitting MPs
and, although it has continued to fight by-elections has rarely looked
capable even of saving its deposit.

The Liberal Democrats' leader is elected by a postal ballot of all
members of the party. In the first (and so far only) contested election
shortly after the party's foundation in 1988, Paddy Ashdown won the
leadership, gaining 41 401 votes to Alan Beith's 16 202. Elections
take place in theory at least every two years, although in practice, as
with the two largest parties, contested elections are likely to be rare;
the role of the Parliamentary Party is provided for in that they have
the power to call for an election outside the normal two-year cycle by
passing a motion of no confidence in the leader.

The Liberal Democrats are organised in three separate party

structures, one each in England, Scotland and Wales (the party does not organise in Northern Ireland), with their own constitutions, bureaucracies and conferences, co-ordinated by a federal party head-quarters in London and represented on the main organs of the national party, the Federal Executive Committee and Federal Policy Committee. For most purposes the supreme body is the twice-yearly federal conference, which consists of representatives of the con-stituency parties in proportion to the party's strength in each constituency; however, the constitution also provides for decisions by a direct postal ballot of all party members.

The number of candidates put in the field by the Liberal Party in elections in the quarter-century after the end of the Second World War fluctuated wildly, but during the 1970s they began to attempt to contest as many seats as the Conservative and Labour Parties. In 1983 and 1987, in conjunction with the SDP, they contested all seats in Great Britain, and the Liberal Democrats are likely to do the same in the future.

The Scottish National Party (SNP), whose headquarters are in Edinburgh, was founded in 1928 with the aim of securing self-government for Scotland. Its first Parliamentary seat, Motherwell, which was won at a wartime by-election in April 1945, was lost three months later at the 1945 general election, and it had to wait until the Hamilton by-election in 1967 for its second success. This however heralded the start of an upsurge in strength which led to its capturing one seat in the 1970 general election, seven in February 1974 and eleven in October 1974, when it polled 30.4 per cent of the Scottish vote. This prompted the then Labour government to propose a separate elected assembly for Scotland (and also for Wales), but the proposal was stalled when a referendum in Scotland failed to produce 40 per cent of the electors in favour, as the House of Commons had stipulated, despite winning a narrow majority of those who voted. The SNP lost ground in both the 1979 and 1983 elections, but recovered somewhat in 1987.

The SNP contested all seats in Scotland in 1987 except Orkney and Shetland, where it stood aside for the candidate of the separate Orkney and Shetland Movement.

Plaid Cymru (the Welsh Nationalist Party), with headquarters in Cardiff, has contested all Welsh constituencies in all elections since 1970. It won its first Parliamentary contest ever in a by-election at Carmarthen in July 1966, but lost the seat in 1970. Since February

TABLE 5.4 *Scottish National Party candidates since 1945*

Year	Candidates	Elected
1945	8	0
1950	4	0
1951	1	0
1955	2	0
1959	5	0
1964	15	0
1966	23	0
1970	65	1
1974: Feb.	70	7
Oct.	71	11
1979	71	2
1983	72	2
1987	71	3

Average vote per candidate in 1987: 14.0%

TABLE 5.5 *Plaid Cymru candidates since 1945*

Year	Candidates	Elected
1945	8	0
1950	7	0
1951	4	0
1955	11	0
1959	20	0
1964	23	0
1966	19	0
1970	36	0
1974: Feb.	36	2
Oct.	36	3
1979	36	2
1983	38	2
1987	38	3

Average vote per candidate in 1987: 7.3%

1974 it has always been represented in Parliament, winning two or three seats at each general election. Founded in 1925, its programme is self-government for Wales. Its greatest strength lies in the Welsh-speaking areas of north and west Wales.

MINOR PARTIES

The Communist Party of Great Britain, founded in 1920, was formerly the most prominent of the minor parties with a national following. Communist MPs were elected to Parliament in 1922, 1924, 1935 and 1945, but the party has been without Parliamentary representation since 1950. Since then it has been in continuous decline, polling a smaller percentage vote than any other Communist party in the western world, amounting in 1983 to a mere 0.04 per cent of the total vote. It did even worse in 1987, when it contested a mere 19 constituencies, in which its average vote was only 0.8 per cent.

TABLE 5.6 *Communist Party candidates since 1945*

Year	Candidates	Elected
1945	21	2
1950	100	0
1951	10	0
1955	17	0
1959	18	0
1964	36	0
1966	57	0
1970	58	0
1974: Feb.	44	0
Oct.	29	0
1979	38	0
1983	35	0
1987	19	0

Average vote per candidate in 1987: 0.8%

Other far left Socialist groups of Trotskyist persuasion have tended to overshadow the Communist Party in recent years, but have done no better at the polls. The most active is the Workers' Revolutionary Party, which put up 20 candidates in 1983 who polled an average of 0.4 per cent of the votes each, despite the active participation of the actress Vanessa Redgrave in their campaign. Another Trotskyist group, the Militant Tendency has not fought independently but has sought with some success to infiltrate the Labour Party. Two of its supporters were elected as Labour MPs in 1983.

On the extreme right, various Fascist and–or racialist parties have contested recent general elections, the best known of which is the

National Front (NF), founded in 1966. Its candidates, who mostly contested working class seats in areas with many Commonwealth immigrants, polled an average vote of over 3 per cent in its first three general election campaigns, which encouraged it to fight on a much broader front in 1979, contesting nearly half the British seats. Its vote declined substantially, and it went down again in 1983, despite concentrating on its strongest areas; in 1987, blaming the increased deposit, it put up no candidates.

TABLE 5.7 *National Front candidates since 1970*

Year	Candidates	Elected
1970	10	0
1974: Feb.	54	0
Oct.	90	0
1979	303	0
1983	60	0

Average vote per candidate in 1983: 1.1%

Another right-wing racialist party, the British National Party (BNP), which split off from the National Front in 1983, did even worse, averaging 0.6 per cent of the votes against the NF average of 1.1 per cent.

The strongest minor party in Britain is now probably the Green Party, which changed its name from the Ecology Party in 1986. It was founded in 1975, and put up 53 candidates in the 1979 election, averaging 1.5 per cent of the votes. In 1983 it fielded 108 candidates, with an average vote of 1.0 per cent and in 1987 133 candidates with an average 1.4 per cent of the poll. It was the only party in 1983 and 1987 to run candidates both in Great Britain and in Northern Ireland. It has links with the Green Party in West Germany and with similar parties in the Benelux countries and Austria, but unlike them its growth is severely hampered by the first-past-the-post system, and it seems to have little prospect of winning parliamentary representation in the foreseeable future.[2]

NORTHERN IRELAND PARTIES

The party system in Northern Ireland is radically different from that in Great Britain, the major political divide being religious. The

Protestant majority mostly divides its support between two parties, both calling themselves Unionist.

The Official Unionist Party (OUP) is the successor to the Ulster Unionist Party, which until 1972 was affiliated to the Conservative Party. The Democratic Unionist Party (DUP), led by Ian Paisley, split off in 1971, and has adopted an even more stridently sectarian stance. Another Unionist splinter party, the Vanguard Movement, founded in 1974, was wound up three years later. In the 1987 general election the OUP won nine seats and the DUP three, with another seat being won by an Independent Unionist, running under the label of the Ulster Popular Unionist Party, which organises in only one constituency and is in effect a personal organisation of supporters of the sitting MP.

On the Roman Catholic side, the majority of votes in recent elections have gone to the moderately nationalist, Social Democratic and Labour Party (SDLP), which won a single seat in 1983, but gained a further one in a by-election in 1986 and a third at the 1987 general election. Provisional Sinn Fein, which is the political wing of the Provisional IRA, also won a seat in 1983 and 1987, which it refused to take up as a protest against British rule.

The non-sectarian Alliance Party, founded in 1970, tries to straddle the gap between Protestants and Catholics. It puts up candidates in most Northern Irish seats, and won 9.9 per cent of the votes in the province in 1987, without coming near to winning any seats.

A wide variety of Independent candidates, often wearing bizarre labels, offer themselves at each general election and at almost every by-election. Few independent candidates poll more than a few hundred votes, except when one of the major parties does not contest the constituency (a rare event). The only independents who have been elected in Britain since 1945 have been former MPs who have fallen out with their political parties and have stood again as Independents in their own constituencies. In Northern Ireland occasional independents have been elected, but this has normally been with the tacit or open support of one of the main Northern Irish parties.

The only other Members to be elected since 1945 without being official party nominees were the Speakers of the House of Commons who, in 1950, 1955, 1970 and 1979, were elected without opposition from the main political parties in the seats which they had formerly represented as Conservative or Labour MPs.

Notes and References

1. See Michael Pinto-Duschinsky, *British Political Finance 1830–1980* (Washington DC: American Enterprise Institute, 1981) especially pages 276–81.
2. For more information about minor parties see David Butler and Gareth Butler, *British Political Facts 1900–85* (London: Macmillan, 1986) pp. 162–73.

6 Political Parties – Local

The national organisations of the political parties monopolise publicity in the press and on radio and television, but it is the local branches with which the voter is likely to come into contact. Both the Conservative and Labour Parties have branches in each of the 633 constituencies in Great Britain, as have the Liberal Democrats in all but a few of them. None of the main British parties now has any significant presence in Northern Ireland.

A constituency party (or association as it is called by Conservatives) is not normally the nearest the parties get to the grass roots. Local branches are organised at ward level in towns and cities, and in villages and small towns in country areas. Here however the two main parties' coverage is less complete. In hopeless constituencies in industrial towns, and especially in mining areas, there are some constituencies where the Conservative ward organisation is rudimentary or non-existent. In the counties too there are many villages and small towns without any Labour organisation. Liberal Democrat organisation below constituency level is extremely patchy. In some constituencies they match or even better the coverage of the larger parties, particularly in the south and west of England. In probably a majority of constituencies, however, there is no Democrat organisation below constituency level.

It is the ward or local party, at least in the Conservative and Labour Parties, which is the basic level of party organisation. The ward party is the actual unit to which party members belong; it is responsible for recruiting new members and collecting subscriptions and for the great majority of party members it is the only organ of the party with which they have any contact. The typical ward or village party meets every month, usually in the house of one of its members, sometimes in a hired school room or village hall, occasionally on party premises. The number of members varies enormously, both according to the size of the electorate in the area covered (which will range from a tiny village to a large ward in a city with anything up to 15–20 thousand electors) and the strength of the party in that area. In practice the membership is unlikely to be less than half a dozen nor more than 1500. The great majority of members do no more than pay their subscriptions to the party when they are called on at their homes. The attendance at most ward or local party meetings is likely to range between 6 and 40, averaging between 5 and 20 per cent of the members in most towns, though in country areas the percentage attendance is likely to be considerably higher.

The minimum subscription to each of the parties is small – very small when compared to the subscriptions paid to political parties in most other countries. The Labour Party's minimum subscription is £10 (£3 for pensioners, students and unemployed). The Conservative Party, which has perhaps five times as many individual members, has no official minimum. Its current recruiting leaflet has four alternative boxes to tick, with suggested contributions of £25, £10, £6 and a blank amount to fill in. While emphasising that 'the amount is entirely up to you', the leaflet also states that 'we need to have an average annual donation of at least £6 per member'. The SLD has a minimum subscription of £2.50, and a 'recommended subscription', which in 1988 was set at £15.

Members of all parties are now encouraged to pay their subscriptions annually by post, banker's order or credit card, but they are otherwise collected by an annual visit to the member's home. In most areas the Labour Party made arrangements, in the past, for the monthly or even weekly collection of smaller amounts. With the fall in the value of money however such arrangements are now an exception. Most Labour members now subscribe quarterly or half-yearly, while an increasing proportion make a single annual payment. The collection of subscriptions is mainly carried out on a voluntary basis by keen party members, though all parties resort in some areas to paid collectors who may also receive a percentage of the amount that they collect. There is a great deal of inefficiency in the machinery for collecting subscriptions and it is apparent that each party loses a substantial amount each year because of this. Many branches with a potentially larger membership refrain from attempting to recruit new members because of a lack of volunteers to act as collectors.

The minority of party members who attend the monthly meeting of the party often find only a small part of its agenda is devoted to political matters. Many ward meetings have a speaker to address them on a subject of national importance, and there may be a resolution to discuss on the social services or a foreign policy issue. It is equally likely however that the agenda will consist almost exclusively of administrative matters, particularly those concerned with fund raising. It is not unusual for a local party to spend more time discussing who is to look after the sweet stall at the party's jumble sale than it devotes to considering possible resolutions for the annual conference of the party. It follows from this that local party branches are as much social as political affairs and the sense of comradeship at this, the lowest level of party politics, is strong.

In areas in which parties are weak, local and ward parties often have an ephemeral existence depending for their existence primarily on the enthusiasm of one or two members who provide the impetus for the others. A loss of interest on the part of one or two individuals, or their removal from the neighbourhood, may cause the branch to collapse altogether and go out of existence. Then, after an interval of perhaps several years, an enthusiastic newcomer will start things up again and with the aid of old and unreliable records will call on long dormant members and try to rekindle their interest. Even in areas in which a party is strong its local branches will not necessarily be flourishing. The absence of challenge from the other side may breed apathy and the party organisation, however strong on paper, may be sickly and lethargic. It is in marginal constituencies, where there is a constant electoral challenge, that the local parties on both sides are most likely to be large and active organisations.

There is a wide variation in the nature and circumstances of local branches. Differences within each of the three main parties are often greater than those between them. At this, the lowest level of organis-ation, the procedures and functions of branches of all political parties are very similar, so much so that there is no need here to distinguish between them. The only consistent difference is that there is less political discussion in Conservative than in Labour or Liberal Demo-crat branches, but even to this general rule there are manifold exceptions.

Depending on its strength and its circumstances, a local branch will have a number of officials. The minimum is normally a chairman, honorary secretary, and honorary treasurer, though in very small branches even these offices might be doubled up. There are normally also one or more vice-chairmen and a number of other functional offices, of which canvassing officer, social secretary, membership officer, literature secretary, and raffle officer or tote organiser are most common. There may also be an assistant secretary and, in the case of the larger and more active branches, an executive committee whose membership would include most or all of the officers listed above.

The most active members of the branch will also be delegates to the managing body of the constituency party, known as the Executive Council in the Conservative Party and the General Committee (GC) in the Labour Party. (In the Liberal Democrats all party members are entitled to attend the area party concerned). It is this body which contains the hard core of militants, usually of between 20 and 100 attending members (though the nominal membership may be higher), who keep the wheels of the party organisation turning throughout the country. At this level there is a notable difference between the parties. The managing body of a Conservative or Liberal Democrat constituency association will contain, in addition to representatives of ward and local branches, delegates from women's organisations and of the Young Conservatives and Young Liberal Democrats respectively. A Labour GC similarly contains representatives from wards, Young Socialists and women's sections but will also include delegates from affiliated organisations – trade unions, co-operative organisations and, perhaps, a local Fabian Society. For every individual member of the Labour Party there are perhaps 20 affiliated members and the nominal membership of a great many GCs is made up predominantly of the delegates from affiliated bodies. Many of these are inactive, and it is very rare for there to be a majority of delegates of affiliated organisations among those actually attending. On special occasions, such as the selection of a Parliamentary candidate, however, it sometimes happens that a meeting of a GC is crowded out by an influx of unfamiliar delegates who may never appear again.

The governing bodies of constituency parties are important and influential organisations. They are responsible for fighting elections, both Parliamentary and local government, and for all practical purposes are the voice of the national party within their own areas. Most of them meet monthly and, as in the case of local branches, much of their time is devoted to discussing financial and administrative matters. Constituency Labour parties, particularly those which are strongly left wing, frequently pass resolutions of a political nature, which are sent to Walworth Road for consideration by the National Executive Committee. Protests at the actions or omissions of the party leadership or of Walworth Road officials are also frequently registered, with little apparent effect. Conservative associations make their views known to their respective head offices with far less frequency. Liberal Democrat local parties behave more like those of the Labour Party.

Constituency parties elect delegates to the annual party conference, who may or may not be instructed on how to cast their votes on the most controversial issues to be debated at the conference. It is usual for each constituency party to send one resolution to the annual conference, though here again the right is more often asserted by Labour and Liberal Democrat parties than by Conservative associations. The most important *political* act of constituency parties is undoubtedly, however, the selection of Parliamentary candidates. This is discussed in detail in Chapter 7.

The ward and local parties are, in most respects, definitely subordinate to the constituency parties. Each constituency party has a full panoply of officers – chairman, vice-chairman, honorary treasurer, secretary, assistant secretary, and numerous other people designated to do specific tasks. In the Conservative and Labour Parties, subcommittees of the constituency party's governing body, known respectively as the finance and general purposes committee (Conservative) and the executive committee (Labour) are responsible for the day-to-day running of the constituency party. Conservative constituency organisations normally have several other standing subcommittees and make provision for both Young Conservatives and women members to be largely represented on all organs of the party.

The principal function of constituency parties is to maintain an electoral organisation in a constant state of readiness. Constituency parties able to maintain a full-time agent find this a much more manageable task. The Conservatives are much better placed in this respect. At the time of the 1987 general election they employed 280 full-time agents, including 70 in the 72 most marginal seats. At the same time the Labour Party had 68 agents in the field, a slight improvement over the 1983 figure, which was a mere 52. Nobody seems to have counted the number of agents employed by the Alliance parties, but it was certainly well below 50. In general the number of full-time agents has been declining fairly steadily over the past 20–25 years. In 1966 there had been 499 Tory agents, 202 Labour and about 60 Liberal.

Most agents earn between £7000 and £15 000 a year, the rate of pay in the Conservative Party being higher than in the Labour and Liberal Democrat Parties. It is the two latter, however, that experience the greatest difficulty in paying their agents' salaries, and many Labour and Liberal Democrat agents spend a great deal more of their time running money-raising schemes, the main purpose of which is to meet their own salaries. They then have little time left over for organising work. The headquarters of the Conservative and Labour parties have a limited amount of money at their disposal to help constituency parties to employ agents. Their money is channelled

into the marginal constituencies: other constituency parties wishing
to employ an agent are expected to pay their own way. Full-time
agents normally act as secretaries to the constituency parties which
employ them.

The activities of constituency parties between elections are varied.
Among the most important are to keep the name and activities of its
Member of Parliament or prospective Parliamentary candidate con-
tinually in the public eye. (Candidates are invariably known as
prospective candidates in the period until the general election campaign begins. Otherwise money spent on the candidate's activities
between elections might be legally chargeable to his election expenses, which are restricted by law. See Chapter 14 below.)

The traditional method of doing this is the public meeting. With
the spread of television and other mass media, interest in public
meetings has declined in the post-war period, though there is some
recent evidence that it is now increasing. Nevertheless few constituency parties in borough constituencies now organise more than four
public meetings a year and many do far less. The meetings, normally
addressed by the MP or prospective candidate and two or three other
speakers, are publicised through posters, local newspaper advertisements and by the delivery of leaflets. When one of the speakers is a
nationally known figure considerable extra effort may be put into
planning the meeting. In some areas a great deal of apathy is
encountered and the hard core of active party members will make up
by far the greater part of the audience. In other areas good attend-
ances are obtained, and lively meetings may be expected if 'the
opposition' turns up to have its say. It seems likely that many
constituency parties take an unduly defeatist view of the public
demand for meetings and that if they took the trouble to organise
them well, to obtain competent and varied speakers and to publicise
them widely and in good time, they would get better audiences than
they imagine.

Most Members of Parliament and some prospective candidates
hold regular 'surgeries' to which their constituents may come with
their personal problems. Pensions and housing are the subjects which
recur most frequently, but an extremely wide range of problems are
referred to MPs for their help and advice. Often it is a question of
referring the constituent to the proper authority – the Department of
Social Security, the housing department of the local council or the
public health authority. Sometimes however a Member can be of

direct assistance by taking up a case personally with a Minister or asking a question in Parliament. This 'welfare work' of MPs is one of their most important activities and it consumes an increasing proportion of their time and energies. In so far as MPs have a personal vote, it is more likely to be built up laboriously over the years through diligent application to the personal problems of constituents than by any more flamboyant action or gesture.

The agent or secretary will always be on the look out for other ways of pushing his MP or prospective candidate into the limelight. If a local organisation – a church or youth club, a dramatic society, a rotary club or any one of a hundred others – wants somebody to open a bazaar, distribute prizes or make a speech (quite often on a non-political subject) he has just the man for the job. The value of such assignments for prospective candidates lies at least as much in the report which will follow in the local newspaper as in the activity itself.

Most constituency parties organise membership drives from time to time in which their members call from house to house, usually in what are regarded as favourable areas, trying to persuade people to join. Little time is normally wasted on attempting to convert 'hostile' elements, but anyone who shows interest will be carefully fostered. In such cases a further visit by the Parliamentary candidate or party secretary may well be arranged.

A different sort of canvassing is designed to provide a reliable record of voting intentions of the electorate. The purpose is to obtain a 'marked register', so that the party has a good idea of where its support lies when the election is due. Copies of the election register are cut up and stuck on hard boards – and party members are asked to mark 'F', 'A' or 'D' against the name of each voter after calling at their houses. These abbreviations stand for 'for', 'against' and 'doubtful'. The proceedings at each house are crisp and seldom long prolonged. Most canvassers adopt an apologetic stance and mumble something along these lines: 'Good evening, Mrs Jones? I'm calling on behalf of the . . . Party. We wonder whether we can rely on your support at the next election'. The response to this enquiry is varied, but rudeness is extremely rare. 'Yes, you can depend on us' or 'We always vote on the day' are likely rejoinders from party supporters. 'I'm afraid we're on the other side' or 'You've called at the wrong house, old chap' are the limits to the hostility which the average canvasser can expect to encounter. There *are* voters who will say: 'If I had a hundred votes I wouldn't give one to your lot' or even 'If you come this way again I'll set my dog on you', but they are few and far between.

A subsidiary object of house-to-house canvassing is to discover invalids and other people who would be eligible for postal votes, so that they may be helped to claim them. Relatively few voters take this initiative themselves, without prompting from their party. The party which organises the largest number of postal votes in a marginal constituency may find that this has made all the difference between victory and defeat. There is no doubt that the Conservatives are more alive than the other parties to the need to build up a large postal vote and that they have hitherto enjoyed much greater success in this sphere.

Elections to local authorities absorb a great deal of the time and money of many constituency parties. Outside London they take place every year in May, with county council elections every four years in April. In London the local authority elections are also once every four years. Local elections help parties to keep their electoral organisation in a state of readiness for the general election and the canvassing results help the party to maintain an up-to-date 'marked register'.

It can happen, however, that excessive preoccupation with local government matters can hinder a constituency party's ability to fight an effective general election campaign. The more able members may have become councillors and may devote so much time to council affairs that they have little to spare for the party. If the party controls the town council, unpopular decisions by the council, such as raising council house rents, may adversely affect the party's electoral appeal at a Parliamentary election.

The ownership or tenancy of premises can have a similarly two-edged effect on a constituency party. Parties employing a full-time agent obviously need premises to provide an office in which he can work and to store the party records. It is a great advantage, too, to have a hall in which to hold meetings and to use as committee rooms at election time. And a permanent headquarters acts as a focus for a wide variety of party activities. There is danger however that if the premises are used extensively for social activities the political work of the party will suffer. In such circumstances the premises may be a heavy drain on the party's funds without producing any equivalent benefit to its electoral prospects.

Money raising is a perennial problem for constituency parties. Few of them derive sufficient income from subscriptions and donations to meet even their most essential commitments. The gap is met in nine cases out of ten by appeals to the gambling instinct. In all major parties it is normally the raffle or whist drive, the bingo session, the football pool or tote scheme which keeps the local branches solvent. The income which constituency parties derive from such sources varies from a few pounds to about £20 000 per annum. The latter amount is rarely reached but a large number of parties make between £1000 and £5000 out of their fund-raising schemes.

There is no regular published information about the funds of constituency parties, and the most recent and most comprehensive survey, carried out on behalf of the Houghton Committee on Financial Aid to Political Parties,[1] relates to 1973 and 1974. The second of these two years contained two general election campaigns, so the earlier year was probably more typical. This showed an average income for Conservative associations of £4713, for Labour parties of £1804 and for Liberal associations of £964. There is little reason to believe that either the real level of local party incomes or the relative wealth of the three parties has changed very much in the intervening period. One might therefore assume, taking account of inflation in the intervening period, that the average amounts in 1988 might have been around £18 000 for Conservative associations, £7000 for Labour parties and £4000 for Liberal Democrat parties. An indication of the main sources of income and expenditure in a moderately prosperous constituency party is given by the imaginary income and expenditure account shown in Table 6.1.

TABLE 6.1 *Sample accounts of a constituency party or association*

Expenditure	£	Income	£
Salaries/wages	8 500	Subscriptions	2 000
Rent/Rates	1 800	Company/trade union donations	1 500
Office expenses	850	Local branches	1 200
Postage, telephone	900	Lotteries etc.	7 500
Travel expenses	1 000	Social functions	1 500
Conference expenses	300	Bazaar	650
Hire of Halls	100	Financial appeal	2 400
Local government elections	1 500	Miscellaneous	250
Subscription to Head Office	1 300		
Miscellaneous	750		
Total	17 000	Total	17 000

Each of the parties has youth organisations which are made up of branches formed on a constituency basis or to cover a smaller area within a constituency. The branches are represented on the governing bodies of constituency parties.

The Young Conservatives, though there are no published membership figures, are undoubtedly much the largest and most powerful of the three organisations. Many of their branches are primarily social organisations, but Young Conservatives, particularly in suburban areas, provide much of the manpower for canvassing teams and other electoral activities. There is no doubt that they represent a valuable asset to the Conservative Party.

The Labour Party Young Socialists had around 17 000 members in 550 branches at the time of the 1987 general election. More political than their Conservative counterparts, they often embarrass the Labour Party by embracing policies well to the left of the leadership. Many branches play an important part in the party organisation, particularly at election times, but overall the Young Socialists have undoubtedly proved less of an asset to their party than the Young Conservatives to theirs.

The combined membership of the Young Liberals and the Young Social Democrats was probably somewhat larger than that of the Young Socialists. They have now combined into a single organisation, the Young Liberal Democrats.

All four parties have flourishing student organisations with membership in universities and colleges throughout the country. Except for the Conservatives, these bodies are probably somewhat stronger, despite their heavy turnover of membership, than the mainline youth organisations.

Note

1. *Report of the Committee on Financial Aid to Political Parties* (London: HMSO, Cmnd. 6601, 1976).

7 Candidates

WHO IS ELIGIBLE

No special qualifications whatever are legally required of Parliamentary candidates; the only positive requirements are virtually those which also apply to voters – that is, to be a British or Commonwealth subject or a citizen of the Republic of Ireland, and to have reached the age of 21. This has remained the minimum age for candidates, even though the voting age was reduced to 18 in 1969. It is not even necessary to be on the election register. There are, however, a number of disqualifications which together exclude a considerable number of people from being elected. People in the following categories are disqualified:

Peers. English and Scottish peers, unless they have renounced their peerage during their lifetime. Irish peers are not disqualified.

Clergy. Clergy of the Church of England or the Church of Ireland, ministers of the Church of Scotland and Roman Catholic priests. Clergy of the Church of Wales and non-conformist ministers are not disqualified.

Aliens, but those who have acquired British citizenship through naturalisation are eligible, as are citizens of Commonwealth countries.

Members of Legislatures outside the Commonwealth. These would normally be excluded as aliens, but the effect of this provision is to disqualify the exceptional case of people with dual nationality, and members of the Seanad and Dáil of the Republic of Ireland.

Certified Lunatics.

Bankrupts. Undischarged bankrupts are disqualified from six months after the date of adjudication and remain so until either the bankruptcy is annulled or a grant of discharge is awarded, accompanied by a certificate that the bankruptcy was not due to misconduct.

Convicted Criminals. Convicted persons serving a sentence of more than one year, or an indefinite sentence, while they are either detained or unlawfully at large. (This provision was enacted in 1981, following the Bobby Sands case. Sands, an IRA hunger striker in the Maze Prison in Belfast, was elected MP for Fermanagh and South Tyrone in April 1981. He died shortly afterwards as a consequence of his fast).

Corrupt and illegal practices at elections. Persons convicted of such practices may be disqualified for varying periods (see Appendix 5).

Much the largest number of people disqualified from membership of the House of Commons, however, are those who hold *offices of profit under the Crown*. This includes sheriffs, judges, policemen, civil servants and a very wide and varied list of office-holders, many of whom receive only nominal remuneration for their services. Before 1957 there was an immense degree of confusion as to what actually constituted an office of profit. Members elected to the House of Commons who performed public service, such as membership of Rent Tribunals, found to their dismay and astonishment that they were disqualified from membership of the House and liable to pay extremely high monetary penalties (£500 per day) for sitting and voting in the House. Ten members found themselves in this position between 1945 and 1955, and in nine cases the House passed emergency legislation to validate their position. In the other case Mr C. Beattie, the Member for Mid-Ulster in 1955, had to vacate his seat and a by-election was held to replace him.

The confusion which existed before 1957 was due to the fact that the different disqualifying offices had resulted from over one hundred Acts of Parliament enacted over a period of 250 years and there was no list of these offices to which would-be candidates could refer to see whether they were disqualified. The position was clarified however by the 1957 House of Commons Disqualification Act which contained two schedules, one listing specific offices which do disqualify, the other listing those which do not. It is highly advisable for all would-be candidates to study these lists before accepting nomination – as there is now little excuse for candidates who transgress through ignorance. It should perhaps be added that, though civil servants are disqualified from membership of the House of Commons, schoolteachers, employees of nationalised industries and local government employees are all eligible.

Armed forces. The final category of people disqualified from membership of Parliament are members of the armed forces. It had however been normal for a serviceman seeking nomination to be discharged. In 1962 an ingenious soldier, Malcolm Thompson, who had been refused a discharge in order to enrol as a university student, offered himself as an independent candidate at a by-election at Middlesbrough West and consequently secured his demobilisation. Later the same year twelve more servicemen followed his example, several of them discovering that they did not even have to be nominated (and thus have to pay a deposit of £150) to secure their discharge; it was sufficient just to apply for nomination papers.

By the end of the year, when further by-elections were expected at Colne Valley and Rotherham, it appeared that the trickle of servicemen using this means to obtain a cheap and easy discharge was threatening to become a flood. No less than 174 requests were received for nomination papers at Colne Valley and 493 at Rotherham. A Select Committee of the House of Commons reported that the problem was a most complex one and that it would take much care and thought to devise a permanent solution. As a temporary expedient, to meet the need to proceed with the by-elections already pending, it recommended the appointment of a small advisory committee which would vet applications by servicemen wishing to be candidates and would advise the appropriate service Ministers whether to grant a discharge.

This recommendation was approved by the House of Commons in February 1963 and a committee consisting of two Queen's Counsel and six former MPs was appointed by the Home Secretary. Its function was to examine the application of each would-be candidate (who would normally be personally interviewed by the committee) and decide whether he had genuine Parliamentary ambitions. The unsatisfactory nature of this expedient was soon apparent. Of the 26 servicemen who actually applied to the committee in connection with the Colne Valley and Rotherham by-elections only one was recommended for discharge. But as soon as he had secured his demobilisation he announced that he had changed his mind and did not offer himself as candidate.

In June 1963 the Select Committee reported that it was still unable to suggest a permanent solution to the problem, and it recommended that the advisory committee should continue to function. In the period up to October 1966 the committee interviewed 52 would-be candidates, of whom only four were recommended for release. The imposition of this stiff hurdle seems to have successfully staunched the flow of servicemen seeking discharge through this means.

Although all the above categories disqualify from membership of the House of Commons, there is in practice no means of preventing a disqualified person presenting himself as a candidate. The responsibility of a returning officer in vetting a nomination is confined to ascertaining that the nomination form has been properly filled in and signed by the requisite number of electors. He is not required to satisfy himself that the candidate is not a disqualified person.

In practice no political party, at least outside Northern Ireland where Sinn Fein has frequently done so, would normally agree to support a candidate known to be disqualified. Occasionally however such a candidate is nominated as a gesture. In 1961 Tony Benn (the former Lord Stansgate) successfully contested, as the Labour candidate, a by-election in his constituency of Bristol South-East, although disqualified at that time as a peer. This triggered a change in the law, under the 1963 Peerage Act, which enabled hereditary peers to disclaim their titles, and incidentally paved the way for Lord Home to become Prime Minister, as Sir Alec Douglas-Home.

In the event of a disqualified person being elected, it is open to his defeated opponent to apply to the High Court to have his election declared void. When this has occurred, the committee has held that if the facts leading to the disqualification had been generally known to the electors, those who have voted for the disqualified candidate should be deemed to have thrown their votes away, and the runner-up has been declared elected in his place. This indeed happened in the case of Tony Benn.

Where a disqualified person has been elected, without the facts leading to the disqualification being generally known to the electorate, the runner-up is not elected in his place, but a by-election is held to find a successor. This occurred in Belfast West in 1950, when the Rev J. G. MacManaway, a clergyman of the Church of Ireland, was elected, and it was not established until later that he was disqualified.

HOW CANDIDATES ARE CHOSEN

The procedures of the three main political parties for selecting candidates differ in a number of important details, but are basically similar. In each case the selection is the responsibility of the local constituency party and the influence of the party headquarters is relatively minor.

A pamphlet published by the Conservative Central Office for the guidance of local associations states: 'Subject to certain simple party rules each association has complete freedom to select the man or woman of its choice'. There are well-established procedures within the Conservative Party which limit, however, the degree of local variation in methods of selection.

The executive council of a Conservative association wishing to select a new candidate appoints a selection committee, usually of about six members, who would be amongst the most influential and senior members of the association. The chairman of the association is invariably included unless, which is not infrequently the case, he has ambitions to be selected himself. The purpose of the selection committee is to consider all the possible aspirants for the candidature and reduce them to a small number from which the executive council may make its choice.

The constituency chairman is expected to obtain from the Central Office a list of names of suitable people, together with biographical details. One of the vice-chairmen of the National Union, assisted by the standing advisory committee on candidates, is responsible for maintaining an official list of approved potential candidates from among whom a number of names would be sent. Any member of the Conservative Party may apply to be included on the official list, and he is then interviewed by the vice-chairman or by members of the standing advisory committee, and, if approved, his name is added to the list. In 1980 the procedure was tightened up and weekend residential selection boards (based on army, civil service and business executive recruitment practice) were arranged for batches of candidates before they were interviewed by the vice-chairman. In recent years only about 40 per cent of the applicants have been approved.

Together with the names obtained from Central Office, the selection committee considers any members of the constituency association who have expressed an interest in the candidature and also the names of Conservatives who may have written asking to be considered. If it is a safe Conservative seat there may be a large number of these and it is not uncommon for a selection committee to have over a hundred names from which to choose. The selection committee quickly whittle this number down to about seven or eight, and in the case of a safe seat few of the applicants would have much chance of surviving to this stage unless they were nationally known figures, were obviously extremely well qualified or were personally known to a member of the selection committee.

The seven or eight people chosen are invited to attend to be interviewed by the selection committee which then chooses normally two or three names from whom the executive council may make its final choice. Occasionally however, when the selection committee decide, in the words of the Central Office pamphlet, that 'a candidate is available whose record is so distinguished and whose qualifications are so outstanding that his adoption is practically a foregone conclusion' only one name is put forward to the executive council.

Before this stage is reached the names of any of the surviving nominees who are not included on the approved Central Office list are submitted to the standing advisory committee for endorsement. If endorsement is refused and the constituency proceeds to select a nominee in spite of this, he is not regarded as an official party candidate at the ensuing election. Cases of an association selecting a candidate who has not been previously approved are however extremely rare.

The nominees put forward by the selection committee attend a selection conference of the executive council. Each makes a short speech (normally limited to a period varying between 10 and 30 minutes) and answers questions put to him from the floor. A secret ballot is then held to choose who will be the candidate. There is no provision in the party rules as to the conduct of this ballot. It is possible for the nominee leading on the first ballot to be chosen forthwith, even though only a minority may have voted for him. It is far more usual, however, for an exhaustive ballot to be held, with the bottom candidate falling out if no overall majority is obtained on the first ballot.

The executive council's choice is submitted for approval to a general meeting of the whole association. This is normally a formality, but there have been occasions in which the executive council's choice has been challenged at this stage and another name substituted.

Money nowadays plays no significant part in the selection of Conservative candidates. This has not always been so. Up till 1948 it was very common for Conservative candidates to defray the whole of their election expenses and in addition to pay a large annual subscription to the constituency association. Consequently wealth was a prerequisite for potential Conservative Members, with very few exceptions.

The shock of defeat in 1945, however, led to a comprehensive reappraisal of the organisation of the Conservative Party following the report of a committee presided over by Sir David Maxwell Fyfe (who later became Lord Kilmuir). Its recommendations, which were accepted by the party, have fundamentally altered the financial relationship between Conservative MPs and candidates and their constituency associations. Under the new rules a Conservative candidate is precluded from making any contribution whatever towards the election expenses, other than his personal expenses. The maximum contribution which he may make to his association is £250. In no circumstances, state the party rules, may the payment of a subscription be made a condition of adoption.

There can be no doubt that the new rules are substantially adhered to, and the result has been that a large number of Conservative candidates without private means have been selected in the period since 1948. Whilst wealth is no handicap in the Conservative Party and rich men are often selected as candidates, money no longer plays a direct part in their selection.

The Labour Party's selection procedure is laid down in more detail in the party rules, and it is complicated by the existence of two classes of membership, individual and affiliated (principally trade unions). When a constituency party decides to select a candidate, its executive committee first consults with the regional organiser of the party to agree a timetable for the selection. The regional organiser is the representative of Walworth Road and it is his responsibility to ensure that the selection takes place according to the party rules. When the timetable has been approved by the general committee of the constituency party, the secretary writes to each local or ward party or affiliated organisation inviting them to make a nomination before a certain date, normally a minimum period of one month being allowed for this.

No person may be considered for selection unless he or she has been nominated by a local party or affiliated organisation. There is no provision in the Labour Party for members to nominate themselves, though if a member has good personal contact with organisations with the right to nominate it is often not difficult for him to obtain a nomination.

Like the Conservative Central Office, Walworth Road maintains a list of possible Parliamentary candidates. It is in two parts: List A contains the names of individuals nominated by trade unions and in respect of whom the appropriate trade union is prepared to assume financial responsibility for the candidature. List B consists of persons nominated by constituency Labour parties and for whom no financial responsibility has been assumed.

The executive committee of a constituency party may ask for copies of either list for its own reference or to circulate to affiliated organisations, but there is no compulsion on them to do so, and frequently, particularly in the case of safe Labour seats, they make no effort to obtain the lists. There is little point in local parties in safe Conservative areas consulting list A, as trade unions are rarely willing to sponsor candidates who have no prospect of being elected. The more hopeless the seat however, the more likely is a party to make use of list B and to write to perhaps a large number of the people included, asking them to accept nomination.

The number of nominations made varies enormously. In a 'hopeless' rural constituency many miles from a large centre of population there may be as few as two or three. In a safe Labour-held seat in a borough, with many affiliated organisations, there is likely to be anything from 10 to 25 nominations, and even the latter figure is often exceeded. Trade Union branches in safe Labour seats, particularly those of the larger unions, are likely to be approached by their union headquarters and asked to nominate a member of the union's parliamentary panel. These nominations must be accompanied by a letter from the general secretary of the union confirming that it will assume financial responsibility for the candidature. Trade union branches are also able to nominate unsponsored members of their unions whose standing is the same as that of nominees of ward or local Labour parties.

When the period of nomination has passed it is the responsibility of the executive committee (which itself has the right to make one nomination) to consider all the nominations received and to draw up a short list. If there are fewer than half a dozen nominations this is normally unnecessary, but this is a rare event, except in strong Tory areas. The executive committee may decide to interview all the nominees before drawing up a short-list, or it may send them questionnaires to fill in. Often however it does neither.

The executive committee usually recommends a short-list with from four to six names and this is reported to the general committee for its approval. (Under a rule change, approved in October 1988, at least one woman must be included in the short-list if there are any women nominees). It is open to any member of the GC to move the addition, substitution, or deletion of names and this occurs with considerable frequency, though more often than not amendments are voted down.

People on the approved short list are then invited to a selection conference of the GC whose procedure is not unlike that of the executive council of a Conservative association, though an exhaustive ballot is prescribed in the party rules. The choice of the GC does not have to be confirmed by a general meeting of members, as in the case of the Conservative Party, but his candidature must be endorsed by the national executive committee of the party. On very rare occasions this endorsement is withheld. This can be either because of alleged personal shortcomings by the candidate or because of the unorthodoxy of his political views. Even more rarely the NEC may impose a candidate of its own on the constituency party, and it was specifically given the power, in a rule change approved by the Labour Party conference in 1988, 'to require a CLP to select its nominee in the interests of the party'.

It is paradoxical that financial considerations now play a greater part in the selection of Labour candidates than of Conservatives. The restrictions on individuals are similar – no Labour candidate may subscribe more than £200 a year to his constituency party, and this rule is seldom transgressed.

The monetary element in the Labour Party is represented by the system of trade union sponsorship of candidates, which goes back to the early days of the party when there was no individual membership and every candidature had to be sponsored by an official organisation. Under the so-called Hastings Agreement, dating from the Labour Party conference at Hastings in 1933, a trade union is permitted to contribute up to 80 per cent of the election expenses incurred on behalf of its nominee and a maximum of £750 a year, or 70 per cent of the agent's salary, to the constituency party.

There is thus a strong temptation for hard-up constituency parties to choose a sponsored candidate, and this applies especially in safe Labour seats in industrial areas. Many constituency parties take a pride in choosing the best nominee available irrespective of financial considerations and many sponsored nominees are able and public-spirited men. There have, however, certainly been cases where more competent nominees have been passed over in favour of a mediocrity whose principal recommendation has been the income which his selection would ensure.

Under the party rules no mention of financial matters may be made at a selection conference and the regional organiser, who attends on behalf of Walworth Road, strictly enforces this rule. The significance of the distinction between trade union and local party nominees is likely however to be appreciated by at least the most alert of GC members. But it is at the short-listing stage that sponsorship carries the greatest weight. For the executive committee of a constituency party is acutely aware of the difference that a sponsored candidate can make and, composed as it is of the dozen or so people with the greatest responsibility for the party's affairs, financial worries are likely to be very much on its mind. If an executive committee is determined to have a sponsored candidate it will recommend a short-list made up entirely of those with financial backing, and there are fairly frequent examples of this occurring in safe Labour seats.

The Liberal Democrats' procedures differ in several respects from those of the two larger parties. The party maintains a national panel of approved candidates, and whenever a local party proceeds to select a candidate it must advertise the vacancy to people on the panel who are invited to apply to be considered. Biographical details and a statement in support of candidacy are demanded from all would-be candidates, and the local party is required to follow a precise procedure set out in the party's constitution.

The executive committee of the local party draws up a short-list, perhaps after interviewing the applicants, and it is required to include at least three and no more than seven names. The short-list must include both men and women nominees and 'shall be drawn up with regard to the desirability of securing proper representation for members of ethnic minorities'. Details of the short-listed applicants are then circulated to the entire membership of the area party, and a meeting or series of meetings are held to which all the short-listed applicants are invited to speak and answer questions. This somewhat resembles the selection conference procedure of the other parties, but there is no voting at the conclusion of the meeting(s). Instead, a postal ballot is held, in which all members of the local party may take part, irrespective of whether they have attended any meetings.

The methods of selection of minor parties differ considerably from those of the major parties, principally because they have so few members. Decisions normally taken in the larger parties by constituency associations, are more likely to be taken by the national committees of the smaller parties. Selection conferences of the type described above are the exception rather than the rule.

A few general points may be made about selection procedures of all parties. One is the small number of people involved in making the choice. The drawing up of the short-list – a vital stage – is the responsibility in the Conservative Party of less than a dozen people and in the Labour Party of less than 20. The final selection is seldom made by more than 200 people in the two largest parties and most often by between 50 and 150. In the SLD even smaller numbers are normally involved, though they sometimes achieve a substantially higher figure through the use of their postal ballots.

THE SELECTION CONFERENCE

The actual selection conference is the most dramatic stage in the selection process, and it is one that imposes considerable strain on the would-be candidates, as the author knows only too well from personal experience. It has been described by a former Tory MP, Nigel Nicolson, as 'a gala occasion for the selectors; slow torture for the candidate'.[1]

The nominees are asked to attend a conference lasting anything up to three or four hours, though most of the time they are cooped up in an ante-room with the other contenders while procedural matters are being discussed or one of their number is making his speech. There is a certain tactical advantage in being the last to speak (the order is normally decided by lot), but this is often offset by the tension of waiting until all your rivals have spoken. All one can hear of the proceedings are occasional muffled sounds of applause from which one imagines that one's rivals are making an extremely good impression. In fact the audience normally goes out of its way to encourage the nominees, whose ordeal they can imagine, and they are very free with their applause.

At last it is your turn. You are ushered into the conference, which as often as not is housed in a bleak Nonconformist church hall or school, but may occasionally be in the more regal surroundings of the council chamber of the town hall. Before you are perhaps 80 people, predominantly middle-aged, and you search eagerly for the encouragement of a familiar face, probably in vain.

You reach your seat on the platform, shake hands with the chairman, who announces that you are Mr X, whose biographical details have been circulated to all the delegates. You have fifteen minutes to speak and another fifteen minutes for questions. After fourteen minutes the chairman will sound a warning bell and after fifteen you will be stopped – if necessary in mid-sentence.

You stand up, try to show a confidence which you do not feel and launch into a well-prepared speech, which has been carefully timed in front of your bedroom mirror to last fourteen and a half minutes. In the event, you have either sat down after nine and a half minutes or are rudely cut short after fifteen minutes – less than a third of the way through your oration. You then deal rather better than you had expected with three or four questions and are surprised to hear that another fifteen minutes have gone by.

Back to the ante-room and the interminable wait while a succession of ballots is taken. At last after two or three false alarms the regional organiser of the party will come into the room, look at you straight in the eye and announce that Mr Y has been selected. You shake hands with Mr Y and utter a few modest words of congratulation. Meanwhile that blithering idiot Mr Z is slapping Mr Y on the back and saying he had always known that Y would be chosen.

Back to the conference chamber with the other nominees. Deafening applause. The chairman says that all the nominees were absolutely first class (even if this was patently not the case). They would have liked to have chosen all of them, nevertheless they had to make a choice, however difficult, and the mantle had fallen on Mr Y. He was quite sure that such excellent people as Messrs W, X and Z would have no difficulty in being chosen soon by another constituency, and the members of his constituency would follow their future careers with interest. Then votes of thanks all round, a few words from the selected candidate and a final rousing call from the chairman to rally round and ensure that Mr Y becomes the next member for the constituency.

It is not easy for nominees to decide what to talk about in their set speeches. Should they talk about party policy or their personal records of work for the party? There is no set formula for success. The speech which would be an utter failure in constituency A may turn out an unqualified success in constituency B. All the nominee has to go on is his experience and the degree of his knowledge of local feeling. His main consolation is that all his rivals are confronted by the same dilemma.

WHO IS CHOSEN?

Looking at it from the other side, what are the members of the selection conference looking for in their candidate? This varies with the nature of the constituency, and especially according to the prospect of electoral success. If it is a marginal constituency the delegates are most likely to be impressed by the vote-winning prospects of their candidate and a pleasing personality would be the number one qualification. In a safe seat delegates are conscious of choosing the future Member rather than a candidate and are more concerned to choose a man with the requisite knowledge and experience to perform what they conceive to be the functions of an MP. In a hopeless constituency energy and enthusiasm count a great deal, and younger candidates are much more likely to be chosen.

Policy differences are not all-important. It is commonly anticipated that left-wing constituency Labour parties are certain to select left-wing candidates and that right-wing Conservative associations, similarly, will pick extremist candidates. In fact this happens much less frequently than is imagined. Selection conferences of all parties will often pick the man or woman who 'looks the part' rather than to insist on the nominee whose political views most exactly coincide with their own.

Local interests undoubtedly often play a part. If one is nominated for a farming constituency it is prudent to show some knowledge of and interest in agriculture, similarly with industrial areas where one industry is predominant. But in mixed industrial areas and especially in suburban constituencies there is likely to be more interest in national than in purely local issues.

Age may play an important part in deciding between nominees, though this again will vary very much. There are a few parties which would regard a man of fifty as a 'young stripling', while others would regard a 40-year-old as a has-been. In general the optimum age range is from 35 to 45, with a certain preference for younger candidates in hopeless and marginal seats and for older ones in safe constituencies.

Unlike in the United States and certain other countries, it is not customary for a candidate to be resident in the area which he seeks to represent. In fact a large number of candidates in British Parliamentary elections are 'carpet baggers' with no personal stake in the community they seek to represent. At some selection conferences it is a major advantage to be a local man, but equally often it can be a handicap. To come in from outside with no previous connections with local factions, can in many cases be a strong recommendation.

One consequence of the substantial fall in party membership over recent decades, particularly in the Labour Party, has been that the number of selectors has been reduced. This has placed a premium on local wheeling and dealing, and a substantial number of recently elected Labour MPs have previously held office, usually as party secretary, in their own constituencies.

Regional prejudices seldom come into the picture in England, though in Scotland and Wales it is rare for a non-Scotsman or non-Welshman respectively to be chosen. Religion is not an important factor outside Northern Ireland, though Jews have been known to encounter strong prejudices in some local Conservative associations. In a few constituencies on Merseyside and in Glasgow Labour nominees who are Roman Catholics start with a distinct advantage.

TABLE 7.1   *Women candidates and members*[†]

General election	Con.		Lab.		Lib./SDP		Others		Totals	
	Cands.	MPs	Cands.	MPs	Cands.	MPs	Cands.	MPs	Cands.	MPs
1945	14	1	41	21	20	1	12	1	87	24
1950	28	6	42	14	45	1	11	0	126	21
1951	25	6	41	11	11	0	0	0	77	17
1955	33	10	43	14	14	0	2	0	92	24
1959	28	12	36	13	16	0	1	0	81	25
1964	24	11	33	18	24	0	9	0	90	29
1966	21	7	30	19	20	0	10	0	81	26
1970	26	15	29	10	23	0	21	1	99	26
1974: Feb.	33	9	40	13	40	0	30	1	143	23
Oct.	30	7	50	18	49	0	32	2	161	27
1979	31	8	52	11	51	0	76	0	210	19
1983	40	13	79	10	75	0	73	0	267	23
1987	46	17	92	21	105	2	84	1	327	41

[†] This table is based on information contained in *Women in Politics* (Conservative Central Office, 1986).

A certain prejudice undoubtedly exists against women candidates, which is stronger in the Conservative Party than in the Labour Party and in rural areas than in towns. Many fewer women than men are selected and they tend to be chosen for the less hopeful seats. The prejudice, however, seems to be diminishing, and the number of candidates has been rising steeply with each election since 1966, see Table 7.1. Despite the growth in the number of women candidates, there are still proportionately fewer women MPs than in most other European democracies. In 1987 some 41 were elected (21 Labour, 17 Conservative, two SDP–Lib. Alliance and one Scottish National party). This represented 6.3 per cent of the House of Commons, a record proportion and a steep increase from the 3.5 per cent of 1983. It seems scarcely conceivable that more women than this will not be successful in future elections. With all parties now putting up more candidates, with the SLD and the Labour Party both exercising a measure of positive discrimination, and the Conservative party having been led by a woman for over a decade, the circumstances should be more propitious than ever before. If the number of women MPs remains so small it is now clearly due, at least in part, to a lack of political ambition among women rather than to the obstacles raised against them by the political parties, which obstacles are progressively falling. One major obstacle remains the unsocial hours worked by the House of Commons (which sits from 2.30 till 10 p.m., and often late into the night). This militates against family life and is undoubtedly more of a barrier to women MPs than to men. Unless and until Parliament decides to reorientate its working day, many women who might otherwise be attracted by a political career are likely to be put off.

It is not only women candidates who have encountered difficulties in the Conservative Party. Despite frequent appeals from Central Office, it has proved almost impossible to persuade Conservative constituency associations to select working class candidates. A rare exception occurred in 1986, when Patrick McLoughlin, a former miner, was chosen to fight a by-election in the previously safe Tory seat of West Derbyshire. He just held the seat – by exactly 100 votes over the Liberal–Alliance candidate, but at the subsequent general election his majority rose to over 10 000.

One other category which has been seriously under-represented among candidates and MPs are blacks and other ethnic minorities. Although three Asians had been Members of Parliament at an earlier time, no blacks or Asians sat in Parliament between 1931 and 1987. Only a sprinkling of non-white candidates had been nominated before 1983, when between them the four major parties put up 18 – six Labour and four each by the Conservative, Liberal and Social Democratic Parties. None was elected, but in 1987, when the number of black and Asian candidates increased to 28 (14 Labour, eight Alliance and six Conservative), four were at last elected – all for Labour seats. In December 1990 the Conservative Party in Cheltenham, a Tory-held seat, selected a black barrister as its prospective candidate, a decision which was later challenged by a section of its members. The occupational backgrounds of candidates and elected members in the 1987 election are shown in Table 7.2.

TABLE 7.2   *Occupational backgrounds of candidates*[2]

	Conservative		Labour		Liberal		Social Democrats	
	Elected	Defeated	Elected	Defeated	Elected	Defeated	Elected	Defeated
	%	%	%	%	%	%	%	%
Professions	42	50	40	52	59	50	60	51
Business	37	34	10	9	12	27	0	25
Miscellaneous	20	14	21	24	30	22	40	19
Workers	1	3	29	14	0	1	0	5

In the professions category the law, particularly the bar, is dominant in the Conservative Party and in the two former Alliance parties, and is very well represented in the Labour Party. There are a number of reasons for this. Traditionally the bar and politics have been associated professions. By virtue of their training and professional practice barristers are skilled at arguing a case and it may be expected that they would face a selection conference with more confidence than most. Barristers and solicitors also undoubtedly find it easier than most to organise their time in such a way that they can combine their profession with their Parliamentary work.

There is a fair sprinkling from the other professions among the candidates of all parties, but it is only teaching – at both school and university level – which comes near to challenging the predominance of the law. In fact teachers form by far the largest occupational group among Labour candidates, nearly a third of whom in the 1987 election were teachers, either at university, polytechnic, adult education or school level. In the former Alliance parties, too, large numbers of candidates came from the teaching profession. Far fewer Conservative candidates have been teachers, though the number is growing.

It will come as a surprise to nobody to discover that business is largely represented in the Conservative Party. It made a good showing too, among defeated candidates at least, in the Alliance parties. The smaller number of Labour candidates with a business background are not really comparable, as a majority of these are small businessmen or employees of larger companies, whereas a majority of the Conservatives in this category are company directors or senior executives.

The largest groups in the miscellaneous category are journalists (in all parties) and farmers (nearly all on the Conservative side). Public relations and advertising men are well represented too, particularly in the Conservative Party. Amongst the workers, the largest single category is still the miners, though there are only half as many of these as a generation ago. Out of 17 miners who stood for Labour in 1987, no fewer than 16 were successful. In the 1966 general election there had been 35 miners standing as Labour candidates, 32 of whom had been elected. A good proportion of the 'workers' who stood in 1987 were full-time trade union officials, but many were working at their trades when first elected, and each general election brings to the Labour benches of the House of Commons reinforcements of

Members straight from the workbench. Most of these are sponsored candidates.

Only a derisory number of workers have at any time been selected as Conservative or Liberal candidates, and fewer still have been elected. In the Labour Party a majority of candidates would have been classified as workers in the period up to 1945 and a third of Labour MPs still fall in this category. But since that date the proportion of professional men (especially teachers) has greatly increased, and this has been largely at the expense of 'workers'. In very many cases the new aspirants have come from working class families; but unlike their parents have enjoyed the benefits of a grammar school and–or university education. Ironically, workers stand a much better chance of being chosen to fight safe Labour seats rather than hopeless or marginal ones. This is because of the system of trade union sponsorship described on page 85 above. In 1988, 29 per cent of successful Labour candidates were workers, but workers represented only 14 per cent of unsuccessful ones. A more comprehensive analysis of the occupational background of candidates in 1987 is contained in the table in Appendix 6.

In all parties there is a recognised route which the majority of would-be MPs are expected to follow. They must first fight a hopeless seat and, fortified by this salutary experience, they may then proceed to a marginal constituency, and later perhaps to a safe one. A fair number of aspirants in both major parties however succeed in by-passing this route and secure election to the House of Commons at their first attempt.

How much influence have the party headquarters on the choice of candidates? It is clear that no HQ can force an individual on an unwilling constituency party. The most they can do is to try to persuade the constituency, through the regional organiser or agent, to include someone whom Walworth Road or the Central Office would like accommodated on the short list. Very often a constituency party is quite willing to accede to this, but it frequently happens that the constituency party executive committee will have other ideas about whom to include on the short-list, and it is their view which prevails. Even when someone recommended from headquarters is included it is by no means always an advantage for this fact to be known. Once an officially recommended nominee is on the short-list he takes his chance with everyone else.

The negative powers which the party headquarters possess to

refuse endorsement to selected candidates are sparingly used. In the Labour Party it is in practice only used to exclude those with strong Communist or Trotskyist connections. Even then such intervention rarely occurs. For example, eight supporters of the Trotskyist Militant Tendency were selected before the 1983 general election and none was refused endorsement. Two were elected as Labour MPs. Even in 1986, after Neil Kinnock had spent two years fighting the Militant Tendency, and had succeeded in getting a number of its adherents expelled from the party, a leading Militant supporter, Pat Wall, was endorsed as prospective candidate for Bradford North. He was subsequently elected in the 1987 general election. In October 1986 however, Labour's National Executive Committee utilised its little-used power to nominate by-election candidates to impose its choice on the Knowsley North Labour Party, which was preparing to select a supposedly hard left candidate. In the Conservative and former Alliance parties, it is even rarer for selected candidates to be black-balled for political heterodoxy.

How much security do prospective candidates enjoy? Not very much. Their relationship to their constituency parties is a delicate one. Disenchantment easily sets in on either side. This is not perhaps surprising, as candidate and constituency party have usually had only the most fleeting view of each other prior to selection.

Opportunities for disagreement abound. Parties and candidates often differ on how much work the candidate is expected to put in. It frequently happens that a prospective candidate visits the constituency less often than his party would like; less commonly parties may decide that they see altogether too much of their candidate. Changes in the personal position of the candidate may also occur. He may be offered a better job, or his employers may prove unexpectedly difficult about allowing time off. His health may suffer, or that of his family. He may take on other commitments which leave him less time for his candidature. Or he may wish to be considered for another, more promising constituency; so, for one reason or another, a sizeable number of prospective candidates withdraw 'for personal reasons' long before polling day, and the procedure for selecting a new candidate has to be gone through all over again.

In the past, once a candidate had been elected as a Member of Parliament he usually had no difficulty in retaining the support of his own party, and unless his seat was a marginal one, he normally continued to represent it, if he wished, until the end of his working life. It was extremely difficult for a constituency party to rid itself of an unwanted Member, the required procedure for doing this in both the Conservative and Labour parties being heavily weighted on the side of the Member.

This situation was dramatically changed, so far as the Labour Party was concerned, by the adoption in 1981 of new rules requiring all Labour MPs to undergo a process of re-selection during the course of each Parliament. This 'meant that the sacking of a Labour MP by his local party could become a relatively routine matter instead of the messy and bitter experience it had traditionally been'.[3] Altogether eight Labour MPs were 'de-selected' by this process during the 1979–83 Parliament, and the list would undoubtedly have been much longer if 28 other Members had not defected to the SDP. It has been estimated that at least nine of these would have been casualties.[4] Moreover some at least of the 23 Labour MPs who retired voluntarily (mostly for age or infirmity) would probably have wished to stand again if they had been spared the re-selection process.

In the 1983–7 Parliament the procedure continued. A further six MPs were deselected, and a similar number were probably precipitated into retirement through fear of submitting themselves to the process.[5] In earlier parliaments only one or two Labour MPs had been refused re-adoption on average. The casualty rate has thus notably increased, though perhaps not as sharply as had been expected. Equally significantly, constituency parties had acquired a powerful weapon to force their Members to conform to their own views and prejudices. In the vast majority of cases such pressure has been applied to induce Labour MPs to adopt a more left-wing position than they otherwise would.

Partly in reaction to this, a determined effort was made after the 1987 general election to take away from the small number of activist members of constituency parties the right to select or de-select Members and Parliamentary candidates, and to give it instead to the entire party membership, which would normally mean several hundred people in a constituency rather than a few dozen. Proposals were put to the 1987 party conference, with the backing of the party leader, Neil Kinnock, that selections should in future be determined on a 'one person, one vote' basis rather than through representatives on the General Committee. The proposal was not in the event carried, due to the opposition of several of the larger trade unions which did not want to lose their share in the selection of candidates.

Instead it was decided to give the power to local 'electoral colleges', comparable to those responsible for electing the leader and the deputy leader of the national party. The formula adopted was that the colleges should be made up on the basis of 40 per cent of the votes for affiliated trade union branches, 30 per cent for individual party members on a one person, one vote basis, and 30 per cent for other party organisations such as Women's Sections and the Young Socialists. The new system only came into force in January 1989, and in October 1990 the party conference decided to scrap it in favour of the 'one person, one vote' system it had rejected three years earlier.

Many members of constituency parties would undoubtedly like their MPs to behave as delegates of the Labour Party rather than as representatives of the constituency as a whole. The national party has normally set its face against this concept, though it came close to accepting it during the late 1970s and early 1980s.

Similar pressures undoubtedly exist in local branches of the Conservative Party, though the party leadership has opposed them more explicitly. The Central Office pamphlet *Notes on Procedure for the Adoption of Conservative Candidates in England and Wales* quotes Burke, with approval: 'Your representative owes you not his industry only, but his judgment; and he betrays instead of serving you if he sacrifices it to your opinion . . . authoritative instructions, which the Member is bound blindly and implicitly to obey, though contrary to the dearest convictions of his judgment and conscience, are utterly unknown to the laws of the land, and against the tenor of our constitution'.

Although the Conservative Party has not adopted anything approaching Labour's re-selection proposals, Tory MPs also have felt more pressure to conform to the views of their party activists. This pressure is, of course, generally exercised from a right-wing standpoint, though it is perhaps strongest over such topics as capital punishment which are not party issues as such, but on which local Tories tend to have passionately-held views. Tory MPs are particularly sensitive when a parliamentary redistribution is in train, and they may well have to face competition from displaced rivals.

It used to be the received wisdom that MPs needed to keep well in with the party whips, but could be reasonably relaxed with their constituency parties if they wanted to have a long parliamentary career. Now the boot is very much on the other foot. It has become a rare event indeed for a Member to be dropped because of not voting with his party in the House (though preferment prospects may be damaged thereby). But MPs of all parties now know that their future as Members is very dependent upon the goodwill of their constituency parties or associations.

Notes and References

1. Nigel Nicolson, *People and Parliament* (London: Weidenfeld and Nicolson, 1958) p. 40.
2. The information in this table has been drawn from a more comprehensive table in David Butler and Dennis Kavanagh, *The British General Election of 1987* (London: Macmillan, 1988), pp. 204–5. The full table is reproduced below, as Appendix 6.
3. Byron Criddle, 'Candidates', in Butler and Kavanagh, *The British General Election of 1983*, pp. 219–20.
4. *Ibid.*, p. 241 (note 5).
5. See Butler and Kavanagh, *The British General Election of 1987*, p. 192.

8 The Campaign in the Constituencies

The announcement by the Prime Minister of an impending general election precipitates a flurry of activity in constituency and local party branches throughout the country. Emergency meetings are hastily convened to put the local party machines on a 'wartime footing' and to make arrangements for the formal adoption of Parliamentary candidates.

If the dissolution is announced unexpectedly a fair number of constituency parties may find themselves without a prospective candidate, but even when the election is anticipated a handful of parties find themselves in the same position because of the recent resignation of their previously selected candidates. A few other prospective candidates are likely to find, when the dissolution is announced, that an election campaign at that particular time would be inconvenient and they therefore withdraw from the field. All in all it is unlikely that fewer than half a dozen candidates have to be found at short notice at any general election by each of the Labour and Conservative Parties, and in such circumstances the selection procedures outlined in Chapter 7 are telescoped considerably.

In the past, the Liberal Party and each of the minor parties have usually had to find a higher proportion of their candidates at this stage. In many constituencies a decision to fight has been left in abeyance and the first question to be resolved at their emergency meetings is whether a candidate is to be put in the field at all. The Conservative and Labour Parties normally fight every single seat in great Britain, though on occasions both parties have allowed the Speaker a free run (this has not prevented other parties or independents putting up against him). In both the 1983 and 1987 elections, the SDP–Liberal Alliance also fought every British seat, and it is probable that the Liberal Democrats will do so in future, with the possible exception of the three seats currently held by SDP MPs.

In deciding whether to put up a candidate, a constituency party will seriously consider not only its potential voting strength in the area and the availability of a suitable man or woman to stand, but also its financial position. A deposit of £500 is required to be paid to the

Returning Officer at the time of the nomination, and this is return-able only if the candidate polls more than one-twentieth of the total votes cast. Until 1986 the threshold was much higher – one-eighth of the votes cast, though the deposit was lower, at £150, a sum un-changed since deposits were first introduced in 1918.

As soon as the question of a candidate is resolved the election agent, who is the key figure in every campaign, is appointed. The position is a statutory one and every candidate is required to notify the name and address of the person appointed, in writing, to the Returning Officer. The election agent is legally responsible for auth-orising all expenditure on behalf of a candidature and his name must appear as the publisher on all printed material, including posters and window bills, issued in support of the candidate. His official duties do not end until he has sent in a return of election expenses to the Returning Officer after the result of the election has been declared.

A candidate may act as his own election agent, though this rarely happens except in the case of independents and minor party candi-dates. When a constituency party employs a full-time agent, he automatically takes on the job. Otherwise it is assumed by an experi-enced member of the local party. Most 'amateur' agents arrange to take at least three weeks off from their regular work to devote themselves to their electoral duties. The work of an election agent is extremely arduous, beginning early in the morning and continuing far into the night, at least during the three weeks prior to polling day. His wife and family can expect to see almost nothing of him during this time.

Once the questions of a candidate and an agent have been settled, there is little more for a governing body of a constituency party to do. It is usual for a 'campaign committee', consisting of a handful of key workers prepared to devote virtually all their spare time to the election, to be appointed to supervise the details of the campaign, in conjunction with the agent and candidate. A financial appeal will be issued to members and known sympathisers and the agent will be authorised to spend up to a specified sum during the campaign. The party will then pass a resolution either formally dissolving itself or suspending all public propaganda activities for the duration of the election. The purpose of this is to emphasise that all activities on behalf of the candidature during the election period are the personal responsibility of the agent.

The first task of the agent is to obtain premises suitable for use as a campaign headquarters or central committee rooms, as they are called. When the party itself owns permanent premises which are suitable for this purpose there is no problem. Otherwise a frantic search is mounted for vacant shop or office premises, preferably in a prominent position in the main street of the principal town in the constituency. Labour candidates often experience great difficulties in obtaining premises of this kind because of the hostility of private commercial interests, but this is partly offset by the willingness of co-operative societies to make accommodation available. A high proportion of Labour committee rooms are housed above co-operative stores.

If commercial premises cannot be found or the party cannot afford to pay for them the committee rooms are likely to be established in the front room of a private house of a keen party member. The keenness of such a member will certainly be put to a severe test in such circumstances, for neither he nor his family is likely to be afforded much privacy in the succeeding weeks. Sub-committee rooms in each ward or polling district will also be set up; these will nearly always be in private houses.

Once established in his committee rooms, the agent is confronted with a bewildering multiplicity of duties. These come easily to the old hand, but to the inexperienced they can pose formidable problems. Fortunately the party headquarters run excellent correspondence and residential courses for those likely to be appointed as temporary agents and also publish handbooks setting out clearly the legal responsibilities of election agents and giving detailed guidance as to how their duties should be carried out. In case of difficulty a call to the party's regional organiser should elicit sound advice. The agent of an independent or minor party candidate is denied such help, and in practice it is he who is most likely to come unstuck. A prudent man in such a position would swallow his pride and equip himself with one of the agent's handbooks published by the major parties and freely on sale from their headquarters.

An election agent is unlikely to find himself short of willing helpers. The hard core of active party workers will devote the greater part of their spare time during evenings and weekends to the campaign, and they are likely to be supplemented by a larger number of normally inactive members who feel that they ought to rally round at election time. Many sympathetic members of the public, too, who are unwilling to become party members, will turn up at the committee rooms and offer to lend a hand. To keep this motley array of helpers happy and purposefully occupied requires high qualities of tact and diplomacy.

All the varied tasks undertaken by the election agent and his team of helpers are directed towards three objects: to familiarise the name of the candidate and underline his party affiliation, to identify the party's supporters within the constituency and to build up a machine capable of ensuring the maximum turn-out of these supporters on election day.

The first object has become less necessary since the passage of the 1969 Representation of the People Act. Before that time no mention of a candidate's party affiliation was made on the ballot paper, so it was up to parties to familiarise the electors with the names of their candidates. Hence all election literature and posters and window bills gave great prominence to linking the candidate's name with his party. 'Jones for Labour' or 'Vote Smith,' 'Conservative X' were slogans which became increasingly familiar to voters as polling day approached. Under the 1969 Act however, candidates are allowed to add up to six descriptive words to accompany their names and addresses on the ballot paper. Nearly all of them utilise this facility to indicate their party affiliation.

The activities of the candidate during the election campaign are a continuation and intensification of the work which he has been doing in the constituency in the months and years leading up to the election. The main difference is that the word 'prospective' is at last dropped from his title and that the public can now be asked to 'Vote for Jones' instead of merely for the party. The transition is usually marked by an adoption meeting, held as soon as possible after the election is announced, at which the candidature is formally proclaimed. This is usually a public meeting, which every party member is strongly urged to attend as a demonstration of enthusiasm and confidence. Speeches are made by the candidate and several other speakers, an appeal for financial support is made and a resolution formally adopting the candidate may be put to the meeting. It need hardly be added that such a resolution is invariably carried with acclamation. If the candidate is the retiring Member of Parliament for the constituency he will by this time have dropped the MP from his name, as he has ceased to be a Member since the dissolution of Parliament. During the election campaign he is merely a candidate and his status is no different from that of the other candidates in the constituency.

The adoption has no legal standing and each candidate must be formally nominated in writing. Nominations may be made on any day after the publication by the Returning Officer of the date of the election but not later than the sixth day after the date of the Proclamation summoning the new Parliament. This gives, in practice, a period of five days in which nominations may be made, and the final day for nominations is also the final day on which a nomination may be withdrawn.

The nomination form must be signed by a proposer and seconder and by eight other people, all of whom must be electors for the constituency in which the candidate is to stand. The nomination form contains the candidate's full name, address and 'description', and his proposers must sign their names in the same form in which they are listed in the election register and must also add their electoral numbers. Only one nomination form is required but it is usual for an agent to arrange for several to be filled in by different electors, partly as an insurance against one form being invalid and partly as a demonstration of support for his candidate.

The nomination form or forms must be delivered in person to the Returning Officer by the candidate or his proposer or seconder between the hours of 10 a.m. and 4 p.m. on one of the days when nominations may be made. The nomination must be accompanied by the £500 deposit, and by the candidate's consent in writing to nomination, which must be attested by one witness.

Provided a nomination paper has been filled in and delivered exactly as described above it will be deemed valid by the Returning Officer. Representatives of candidates may inspect the nomination papers of their rivals and may lodge objections if they suspect them to be invalid. The Returning Officer must then give his decision as soon as possible and if he decides that a nomination paper is invalid he must endorse the paper as invalid and state on it the reasons for his decision. This does not happen at all frequently, and when it does there is normally time for the candidate to send in another nomination paper which is correctly filled in, as few candidates are so imprudent as to leave their nomination to the very last moment.

If by the time that nominations are closed only one valid nomination has been received, the Returning Officer declares that person elected and publishes notices to that effect throughout the constituency.[1] Where there are at least two candidates, as happens in the vast majority of cases, the Returning Officer publishes a statement of persons nominated, together with the names of their proposers, seconders and assentors. This statement includes a notice of the poll, stating the date and time that the election is to be held, and gives particulars as to where people should go to vote. By this time things are hotting up; it is a mere nine days (excluding Sundays and Bank holidays) to polling day.

At least a fortnight before polling day, and probably a week or two earlier, the candidate will have moved into the constituency for the duration of the campaign. Unless he normally lives there, he will take a room at a hotel or lodge with one of his supporters. If he is married his wife will accompany him, family circumstances permitting, and she will be expected to take an active part in his campaign. Some idea of their daily life during the three weeks before polling day is given by the following imaginary timetable of a candidate in a county constituency.

7.30 a.m. Get up. Breakfast. Read all the papers – especially reports of the speeches of the party leaders and other election news.

8.30–9.30. Work in hotel bedroom on speeches to be delivered in the evening.

9.30. Meet reporter from local newspaper at hotel. Comment on speech given by rival candidate on previous day.

9.50. Arrive main committee rooms, in car driven by wife. Dictate replies to correspondence received from electors. Quick consultation with the agent on the day's programme.

10.30. Set off with woman councillor for door-to-door canvass of housewives on new housing estate.

12 noon. Visit hospital with wife to meet patients. Talk with matron to check that arrangements for postal votes for the patients have been made.

1 p.m. Quick lunch in café.

1.30 Drive to town at other end of constituency.

2.15. Set off on loudspeaker tour – making short speeches and answering questions at street corners.

3.15. Wife leaves to have tea with the Townswomen's Guild.

4.15. Meet a deputation of Roman Catholics to hear their case for more public money to maintain Catholic schools.

5.0 Interview with local radio station reporter.

5.30. Speak to factory gate meeting.

6.30. Return to main committee rooms, immediately set off with agent for quick tour of sub-committee rooms.

7.30. Supper at home of party chairman.

8.15. Leave for first of three village meetings.

9.45. Return to town hall for main evening meeting, which has already been addressed by a prominent visiting speaker.

10.15. Adjourn to pub with party supporters. Watch election news or party broadcasts on TV.

11.30. Return to hotel and to bed.

This kind of pace is sustained without much difficulty by nearly all candidates,[2] though elderly men who are defending safe seats tend to take it a lot easier. The constant excitement and the enthusiastic encouragement of supporters go a long way to create fresh reserves of energy which the candidate would not previously have suspected himself of possessing. A major problem is to restrain the ardour of one's supporters who will quite happily keep one up talking all night. Here a firm intervention by the candidate's wife is indicated.

It is notable how little the campaigns of rival candidates impinge on each other. The candidates may meet once or twice on neutral ground – at a meeting for all candidates organised by the United Nations Association, perhaps, or at an inter-denominational service held for election workers. One candidate may take up some remarks of another, as reported in the local newspaper, and reply to them at one of his meetings or challenge the accuracy of his facts. Very occasionally a candidate may make a personal attack on his rival, but this is normally regarded as bad form and is likely to do the attacker more harm than good.

The great majority of candidates, however, totally ignore the existence of their rivals throughout the campaign. If they are government supporters they will doggedly defend the record of the government with an occasional side swipe at the irresponsibility of the opposition, but if any names are mentioned, it will be of well-known national leaders rather than the opposition's local standard bearer. The same is broadly true, in reverse, of opposition candidates, though a former Member defending his seat is more likely to be picked out by name than a newly arrived challenger.

Although they are rarely attended by more than 200–300 people, except when a party leader is one of the speakers, and in fact the *average* audience is probably not more than 10 per cent of this size, public meetings normally constitute by far the most interesting and colourful events in the candidate's timetable.

There are certain superficial differences between meetings held by the opposing parties. At Conservative meetings the platform is invariably draped with Union Jacks, for which the Labour Party substitutes banners proclaiming party slogans. Tory meetings often conclude with the singing of 'God Save the Queen', a display of patriotism which is considered inappropriate by the other parties. A collection is invariably taken at Labour and Liberal Democrat meetings, less frequently at Conservative ones.

In other respects the pattern is fairly uniform. The speeches vary greatly in style and content, but more through differences in the background and experience of the speakers than because of political differences. The younger and less experienced they are, the more likely are they to keep pretty close to their brief – which in most cases is based on speaker's notes distributed by the various party headquarters. Local issues are likely to be stressed by town councillors and others – particularly when the opposing candidate is a stranger in the district.

The arrival of the candidate is heralded by a round of applause from his own supporters and perhaps some good-humoured banter from the other side. If the opposition is well represented in the audience a more lively and interesting meeting is likely to ensue. Hostile questions test the mettle of a candidate far more than the polite enquiries he receives from his own supporters, and at many meetings 'enemy intervention' extends to the interruption or 'heckling' of the speaker. A speaker who is quick and nimble-witted enough to score debating points against hecklers, without losing the thread of his speech, adds greatly to his stature. It is not common for heckling to get seriously out of hand but it occasionally does happen, especially in marginal constituencies where feeling is running high. In such cases it may be almost impossible for the speakers to make themselves heard and the chairman is forced to appeal for order. If he is wise he will do this in a good-humoured manner, appealing to the opponents' sportsmanship and belief in free speech and emphasising that questions will be welcomed at a later stage in the evening.

If such an appeal is ignored the chairman is placed in a tricky position. He can ask his stewards to eject people making a disturbance, but if the 'enemy' contingent is large this could prove a difficult job. He can swallow his pride and ignore the continued disorder in the hope that the speaker will eventually succeed in getting his message across. Or he can solemnly remind the audience that any person acting in a disorderly manner at a public meeting for the purpose of preventing the transaction of business is liable to a fine or imprisonment and announce that he is sending for a police constable to ensure that the law is enforced. This final course of action is virtually certain to succeed in its purpose, at any rate when the constable has arrived, but it is normally regarded as a moral defeat for the platform and is rarely resorted to.

While the candidate is making every effort to make himself known to as many voters as possible, the agent is equally busy ensuring that contact is established with every potential supporter of the party in the constituency. If the party organisation is good he will have started the campaign with a marked-up register covering the greater part of the constituency. In that case he will ask his team of canvassers to call on all the 'F' (for) voters to confirm that they are party supporters and on the 'D' or doubtful voters to see if they have moved off the fence. Those voters marked 'A' (against) are left firmly alone. Many agents find that no reasonably up-to-date canvassing records are in existence and they have to instruct their canvassers to call on every voter. In either case canvassing is regarded as much the most important single activity which has to be undertaken during elections, and every available person is pressed into service. It is normal for canvassing teams to go out on every evening of the campaign and in the daytime during weekends. Theoretically parties aim to make a 100 per cent canvas of the constituency, but most agents are more than pleased if their canvassers call on 80 per cent of the voters. It is normal to begin with the most favourable parts of the constituency and move on later to the less promising areas: so if, as often happens, a party canvasses only 50 per cent of the voters it may have called on 75 per cent of its own supporters.

In a marginal constituency it is prudent to set a target of 2000 or 3000 more favourable promises than would be necessary to win the seat. Most canvassers, particularly inexperienced ones who are much in evidence at election time, are incurably optimistic and are liable to read into a courteous reception a promise of support. It is this rather than deliberate deception which most often leads to voters being recorded in the 'F' column by canvassers representing opposing candidates. Whatever the reason, it is certain that nine candidates out of ten receive an inflated estimate of support from their canvassers.

Canvassers are asked to undertake a number of subsidiary jobs. They are liberally supplied with window bills to offer to supporters, and they are instructed to enquire about elderly or infirm voters who might require a lift to the poll or, if there is still time, to be assisted in applying for a postal vote. Canvassers are also often given leaflets to deliver 'on their rounds'. It is important for canvassers to ask to see every voter on the register at each house at which they call, and not to assume that the person who comes to the door speaks for the whole household. More families than most people imagine are divided in their voting habits, and households containing lodgers are unlikely to be politically homogeneous. A high proportion of canvassers however, despite the instructions of their agents, take the easy way out and do not bother to interview all members of a household. This is a further source of gross inaccuracies in canvassing records.

After canvassing the next biggest campaign chore has been the addressing of envelopes for the candidate's election address. In most constituencies some 50–60 thousand are required and this places a severe strain on the weaker constituency organisations. It is usual to ask each ward or local branch to be responsible for addressing the envelopes for its own area and each active member is given a quota of anything from 50 to 1000 envelopes to address, together with the appropriate portion of the election register. Elderly and housebound people who are not available for canvassing and other outdoor work are often happy to volunteer to receive a large batch of envelopes. If the election occurs in the fifth year of the Parliament some parties will already have got their envelopes addressed before the campaign begins, as they could be sure the election would be fought on the current register. Only a minority normally shows such foresight.

The election address is the traditional means by which the candidate introduces himself to the electorate. It normally contains a photograph of the candidate, and perhaps also of his wife and children, biographical details, a personal message in which he promises to devote himself to the service of the electors should he be elected and a summary of his party's programme. Often it will include a short message from the candidate's wife, addressed to women voters.

The post office is obliged at Parliamentary elections to make one free delivery to every elector on behalf of each candidate, and the great majority of candidates take advantage of this to send out their election addresses. Under the 1985 Representation of the People Act, candidates have been given the option of using an unaddressed service for the free delivery of their election communication. Most candidates have taken advantage of this, thus absolving their supporters of the chore of addressing vast numbers of envelopes.

Serious doubt is often cast on whether the trouble and expenditure

devoted by candidates to their election addresses is really worth-
while. Most candidates in fact spend between a quarter and half of
their permitted expenditure on their election address. According to
the opinion polls however, more electors are reached by means of the
election address than by any other *local* form of electioneering. In
both 1983 and 1987 the Gallup Poll reported that 49 per cent of
electors had looked at election addresses, while only 29 per cent had
been canvassed and four per cent claimed to have attended political
meetings.

An agent who has the assistance of an able and experienced
election committee to which he is willing to delegate a great deal of
responsibility, should find that, though he will work hard and for very
long hours, his campaign will run fairly smoothly. One who is unable
or unwilling to delegate is likely to find himself prey to constant
crises. Ideally each member of the election committee should be
allocated responsibility for one specific field of duties, allowing the
agent to free himself for the general oversight of the campaign. There
should be a canvassing officer, another in charge of speakers, one
responsible for the addressing of envelopes, one for dealing with the
press, one in charge of leaflet distribution, one for organising cars for
election day and one to organise the postal vote. The agent will
probably reserve for himself the planning of the candidate's timetable
and it is important that a fixed time be set aside each day for
consultation between the candidate and the agent.

Planning the schedule of meetings is especially complicated in
county constituencies where the candidate may easily be addressing
six village meetings every evening, rounding them off with a larger
meeting in one of the towns. Each meeting requires at least one or
two supporting speakers, whose main qualification must be the ability
to modify drastically the length of their speeches. It inevitably happens that on some evenings the candidate gets seriously held up at his
earlier meetings and arrives at his final meeting anything up to an
hour and a half late. A supporting speaker booked to speak for
twenty minutes has consequently to spin out his speech or fill in the
time answering questions. On another day he will find that the
candidate arrives at the meeting just as he has completed his intro-
ductory remarks and is about to embark on the main body of his
speech. In that case he must cut himself short and make way for the
candidate, with as little delay as possible.

Most agents are well conversant with electoral law and are aware
of the things which may or may not be done during an election

campaign. A much less detailed store of knowledge is normally possessed by voluntary workers, and care must be taken that through ignorance or misguided enthusiasm they do not transgress the law. If they do, they may lay themselves open, and possibly also the agent and the candidate, to heavy penalties and even to the invalidation of the election should their candidate be elected. A summary of election offences, with the penalties involved, should be prominently displayed in all committee rooms.

In practice people involved in electioneering in Britain have proved extremely law abiding and after each general election there are never more than a handful of prosecutions for election offences. The last time an election was invalidated because of an election offence was at Oxford in 1924. In Northern Ireland respect for the election laws is perhaps rather less strongly ingrained and attempts at personation (voting in the name of some other person) are not infrequent. Each party in Northern Ireland appoints special 'personation agents' who keep a close watch at each polling station to deter supporters of the other side from 'stealing' votes in this way. The disproportionately large number of postal votes cast in Northern Ireland has led to the suspicion that 'personation by post' may be widespread. The 1985 Representation of the People Act allows the Secretary of State for Northern Ireland to suspend postal voting (except for those on the permanent list of postal voters) if he is satisfied that it is necessary to do so to prevent serious abuse. The maximum fine for fraudulent postal voting practices was raised to £2000. A summary of other election offences and the penalties involved is included in Appendix 5.

Especially in marginal constituencies, agents make daily reports by telephone to their regional organisers, who are also likely to make at least one personal visit. The regional officers of both the Labour and Conservative parties do their best to organise the transfer of workers from safe and hopeless into marginal constituencies so that the maximum effort can be mounted where it will have the greatest effect. As a much higher proportion of their active members are car owners and therefore more mobile, it is clear that the Conservatives have less trouble in organising such transfers and they are in fact able to effect them on a much larger scale.

As polling day draws near the tempo of the campaign appreciably quickens. More helpers turn up every day at the committee rooms and enthusiasm and confidence mounts. Almost all voluntary election workers and most professional ones become infected with over-optimism towards the end of the campaign, unless their own party is very obviously doing badly. It is normal to over-estimate the chances both of one's candidate in the constituency and of one's party throughout the country. It would indeed be strange if it were otherwise, for so much is seen of the results of one's own campaigning and so little of the other side's that it is all but impossible to form an objective view.

A week before polling day most agents make a rapid assessment of the progress already made in canvassing and other important activities and revise their plans accordingly. Targets may be raised or lowered, or forces concentrated to recall at houses where the voters were 'out' or 'doubtful' on the first occasion that they were canvassed. All election workers are likely to be impressed at this stage by how much remains to be done and how little time is left in which to do it.

Meanwhile the agent's attention will be more and more concentrated on preparations for polling day. The transporting of elderly and disabled voters to the polls (and of many others who are unlikely themselves to summon up enough energy to get themselves there unaided) can add several hundred votes to a candidate's poll. Every effort is therefore made to secure the services of the maximum number of cars and drivers on election day and, especially, in the evening. It is illegal to hire transport for this purpose and party members who are owner drivers are strongly encouraged to volunteer their services.

Between 1948 and 1958 there was a legal restriction on the number of cars which a candidate could use for this purpose and each car had to be registered with the Returning Officer in advance. The number of cars allowed was one per candidate for every 2500 electors in boroughs and one for every 1500 in counties. The purpose of the restriction was to prevent a party which had a preponderance of wealthy supporters from turning this fact to its advantage. It was repealed by a Conservative government in 1958, on the grounds that the increasing incidence of car ownership at once reduced the party advantage involved and made the law difficult to enforce. Subsequent Labour governments made no attempt to reintroduce control in this field.

As well as compiling a roster of cars and drivers for election day, the agent will endeavour to persuade as many helpers as possible to take the day off work, so that a full-scale operation can be mounted to 'get out the vote'. Particularly in marginal constituencies, little difficulty is encountered in ensuring an adequate army of helpers on the big day.

Meanwhile the Returning Officer will be busy with his own preparations. Soon after the nominations are closed he will send out to each elector, through the post office, an official poll card. This will notify the voter of his electoral number and tell him how, where and when to vote. In the presence of the candidates, or more likely their representatives, he will also send out ballot papers to registered postal voters. In the average constituency there have been about 1000 of these (or roughly two per cent of the electorate), though the number varies widely. It is possible that the average will now increase following the wider provisions made under the 1985 and 1989 Acts. Each postal voter is sent, by post, four items:

(1) An ordinary ballot paper, duly marked or stamped.
(2) A form of declaration of identity.
(3) A small envelope for the ballot paper.
(4) A larger addressed return envelope.

The postal voter must sign the declaration of identity, and have his signature attested by one witness. He marks his X against the candidate of his choice, seals his ballot paper in the small envelope and returns it, together with the declaration of identity, in the larger envelope. The vote can be sent back to the Returning Officer at any time after it has been recorded, but it must reach him not later than 10 p.m. on polling day. On their receipt at the office of the Returning Officer the postal votes are dropped into a special ballot box.

The Returning Officer, like the agents, has to make arrangements to secure the services of a large number of assistants on polling day. Some of them will be polling clerks, whose duty will consist of presiding over polling stations. Others will have the job of counting the votes. Unlike the parties' election workers, the Returning Officer's staff will be paid for their services. The greater number of them will be local government employees, transferred for the day from other work. They will be supplemented by others engaged specially for the day. School-teachers are a favourite source of labour for polling clerks, as most schools have a holiday on election day because their premises are used as polling stations. Bank clerks, for obvious reasons, are much in demand to assist in counting the votes.

Notes

1. The most recent unopposed returns were in 1951.
2. In an earlier edition of this book the author described the above programme as 'a cracking pace'. This provoked an astonished reaction from a leading political scientist who wrote: 'American visitors are always amazed by the soft lives that British politicians lead. This, by American standards, would be an easy day'. On the other hand, the author was lightheartedly rebuked by a well-known Labour MP, later a senior Cabinet minister. 'Before your book appeared', he said, 'I had always succeeded in persuading my agent that candidates could not be expected to do any electioneering before lunchtime. Now he has me out canvassing after breakfast!'

9 The National Campaign

Seventy or eighty years ago election campaigns were conducted almost exclusively at a constituency level. Apart from organising speaking tours by the party leaders and other prominent personalities, the party headquarters played little direct part in the campaign. The newspapers were full of election news, but they were read only by a minority, and a far greater readership was claimed by regional and local papers than is the case today.

The irruption of mass readership national newspapers and, even more, the development of radio and television has changed all that. A general election was formerly a series of local contests to choose Members of Parliament, with the incidental effect of determining the political complexion of the next government. Now it is in effect a nationwide contest to choose a government and especially a prime minister. The fact that 650 individuals are in the same process elected to represent 650 different constituencies in Parliament has become a subordinate feature.

Unlike the majority of constituency parties, which are overwhelmingly dependent on voluntary labour, the party headquarters, staffed by full-time professionals, are not likely to be caught seriously unprepared by the announcement of a general election, even if it has come unexpectedly. Much of the work on which their employees have been engaged for several years past has been designed with this very moment in mind.

In some recent elections, particularly when they have come fairly late in a parliamentary term, the party machines (particularly the Conservatives') have concentrated on pre-electoral propaganda which has been launched well in advance of the date of the election. These have largely taken the form of colourful posters displayed on hoardings throughout the country, but particularly in marginal seats, and of advertisements in a large number of national and daily newspapers (political advertising on television and radio being illegal). Private business interests, allied to the Conservatives, have sometimes spent even larger sums on similar campaigns. In 1983, for the first time, there was also substantial spending by interest and pressure groups on the Labour side, such as the Greater London Council (which was facing abolition under the Tories), public sector unions and animal welfare bodies. Paradoxically the beginning of a campaign is now sometimes the cue for covering up or taking down political posters, which otherwise might be liable to be charged as election expenditure.

When the dissolution is announced the party headquarters are well prepared to produce, within a few days, speakers' handbooks outlining the party policy on a wide range of issues and documenting the failures of the opposing parties, which are quickly despatched to all Parliamentary candidates and others who are to speak on behalf of the party. These handbooks are supplemented by daily briefings on specific issues which arise during the course of the campaign. A great mass of posters, leaflets, policy statements and other propaganda material is also produced for distribution through the constituency party organisations. Some of the money subscribed to the national election funds of the parties is also disbursed to constituency parties at this stage, to ensure that even the poorest of these have some ready cash with which to finance their campaign. The Liberal and Social Democrats have been less able to extend such monetary help to their constituency branches. It is usual at the beginning of the campaign for the party leadership to depute two or three senior figures to remain in London to oversee the running of the party headquarters and to act as a campaign committee, co-ordinating the day-to-day running of the campaign and particularly to take charge of the party's television programmes and dealings with the press. It is normal to select MPs representing safe seats for this important assignment, as those with marginal constituencies could hardly be expected to leave them for the greater part of the campaign. For the same reason, in the cases of the Conservatives and the Liberals, leading peers are often included in their campaign committees.

Within a few days of the announcement of the dissolution, each party publishes its election manifesto. This is a statement of the issues which the party considers of the greatest importance and an indication, in more or less precise terms, of the party's policies to meet them. The Labour Party, which is strongly wedded to the idea that a party winning an election receives a mandate from the people to carry out definite policies, is normally more specific in its proposals. There is often a great deal of manoeuvring within the Labour Party's National Executive Committee and its 'shadow cabinet' about what items to include, which usually takes the form of a left–right struggle.

The manifestos, which run to about two to three thousand words, are given the widest possible distribution, the print orders running into millions. In addition to the large scale distribution through constituency parties, they form the basis of the policy sections in candidates' election addresses and they are widely reported in the press and on radio and television.

Despite the prominence which they are accorded, the election manifestos are seldom notable for breaking new ground. Nearly all the major proposals contained in past manifestos had already been published as official party policy and the function of the manifestos was to bring them together in a sharp and challenging manner and perhaps to add a few minor twists to give them an air of originality.

Much of the interest in the manifesto produced by the SDP–Liberal alliance in 1983 (*Working together for Britain*) was due to the fact that the two parties were offering the same programme and that it was released extremely quickly and with a minimum of friction. The Conservative manifesto (*The Challenge of our Times*) was regarded as an exceptionally bland document, but Labour's offering (*The New Hope for Britain*) was immediately seized on by its Tory opponents, who bought 3000 copies to use in support of Mrs Thatcher's contention that it was 'the most extreme manifesto that has ever yet been put before the British electorate'. In 1987 by contrast, the manifestos seemed to have far less effect on the campaign.

The manifestos will be reported and analysed in the press and media, but the only written material the vast majority of voters will receive from the parties is the election address of each candidate in their constituency. These election addresses are composed at least three weeks before election day and thus cannot reflect the issues that become especially prominent during the campaign (although it may be possible to predict what they are likely to be). They will normally tend to emphasise positive features rather than risk mention of issues where the party is seen to be on the defensive.

Table 9.1, which analyses the subjects most frequently mentioned in election addresses in 1987, gives a good idea of the range of ideas discussed and of how priorities varied between the different parties; the issues selected do not necessarily reflect the importance candidates themselves place upon them, but the anticipated reaction of the public to them and their likely impact on the election campaign.

The issues which are discussed during election campaigns obviously differ to some extent on each occasion, although certain subjects, such as the economy, public services, housing, education and defence, are almost certain to be raised at some stage at every election. Some issues may arise spontaneously during the campaign, but all parties attempt to divert attention to those issues where they

TABLE 9.1   *Subjects most mentioned in election addresses, 1987*

	Con.	Lab.	S.D.P.	Lib.
Unemployment	78	89	91	92
Inflation	64	1	47	57
Home Ownership	70	5	21	38
NHS	78	94	91	86
Education – general	59	71	93	84
Education reform	59	5	40	32
Law and Order	74	65	74	65
Defence – nuclear	80	38	74	76
Public spending/investment	14	56	55	65
Training	39	54	58	51
Pensions	47	71	84	59
'Divided Country'	3	21	58	51
'Caring'	14	27	51	35
Electoral Reform	2	0	60	54
Housing – general	20	38	65	62
Whole 'deal' for elderly	14	27	77	49
Arms control	34	11	67	65
NATO	14	15	56	57

The information in this table, which includes only the issues mentioned by 50 per cent or more of at least one party's election addresses, is drawn from a more detailed table in David Butler and Dennis Kavanagh, *The British General Election of 1987* (London: Macmillan, 1988) pp. 222–6.

perceive themselves to be strongest or their opponents most vulnerable, and these tactics will normally be planned in some detail. Nevertheless all will probably not go entirely as the parties expect; the focus of the campaign is unlikely to rest for long on questions where none of the parties find themselves actively gaining ground or their opponents discomforted. Thus in 1983, against most expectations, unemployment, despite running at a post-war record level of over three million, did not excite much interest. By contrast defence, and particularly the divergent views of leading Labour figures, emerged as a major issue. There seems to have been an increasing tendency in recent elections that a relatively small number of issues emerge, with each of the major parties trying to force their opponents onto the defensive.

The major political exchanges during elections now take place on the television screen. The 1959 election was the first of which this was really true, as in previous elections only a minority of voters had access to a television set. But the trend had become increasingly apparent ever since the first television election broadcasts, watched by less than 10 per cent of the electorate, were screened in 1951. By 1959 75 per cent of households possessed television sets and by 1987 this figure had risen to 99 per cent.

Television election broadcasts are of two kinds: those for which parties are responsible, and news and other broadcasts undertaken by the BBC and the various commercial companies. The party broadcasts – for which the broadcasting authorities make time available without financial charge – have been transmitted at each election since 1951, but those for which the broadcasting companies were responsible date from the 1959 general election.

Party political broadcasts in this form are a distinctively British phenomenon. In addition to those which take place during election campaigns, facilities are provided for their regular presentation during the periods between elections. The allocation of time for these broadcasts is made at an annual meeting between spokesmen of the three main parties and representatives of the BBC and IBA. The support secured by parties at the previous general election is taken as the general basis for determining the relative amount of broadcasting time they should have.

Representatives of the minor parties are excluded from the meetings agreeing the allocation of broadcasting time, and until 1965 neither the Scottish nor the Welsh Nationalists received any time at all. The Communist Party is particularly bitter at its exclusion and has more than once alleged that the Chief Whips of the three large parties 'have carved up the time among themselves'.

The series of party broadcasts held during an election campaign are similarly arranged at a meeting or meetings between the same participants. The criterion for the apportionment of time has normally been the number of candidates in the field at the forthcoming election rather than the number of votes achieved last time. In the 1983 general election the Social Democrat–Liberal Alliance claimed parity with the Labour and Conservative Parties, but both these parties resisted the claim. No agreement was reached, and in the end the BBC and IBA themselves decided the ratio of broadcasts, which was 5:5:4. So the Conservative and Labour Parties were awarded five broadcasts of 10 minutes each (though the Tories did not use all the time available, preferring shorter, sharper messages) and the Alliance four programmes. In addition the Scottish National Party and Plaid Cymru were allocated two and one broadcasts respectively, transmitted only in their own countries. Shorter TV broadcasts, of five minutes each, were offered to any other party putting up more than 50 candidates. Three parties qualified on this basis: the Ecology Party, the National Front and the British National Party. Radio broadcasts were allocated on a similar basis. The same ratio of 5:5:4 was also used to determine the approximate representation of the major parties in news and current affairs programmes during the election campaign. In 1987 the Alliance was given parity with the two larger parties in broadcasting time; the Green Party and, in their own countries, the Nationalists, again qualified for shorter allocations of time. (The SNP in fact went to court in an attempt to secure more air-time for themselves in Scotland, but were unsuccessful.)

The programmes are normally produced by the BBC and made available to Independent Television, though occasionally one of the independent companies is in charge of production. In the course of production the BBC watches points of broadcasting or legal policy – an appeal for monetary contributions would be disallowed, for example, as well as any libellous content. Otherwise in all political respects the content is the sole responsibility of the party concerned. The programmes were relayed simultaneously on all the television channels up to and including the 1979 election. In 1983 and 1987 they were staggered, which meant that inveterate TV-watchers could avoid them altogether by switching channels throughout the evening. Nevertheless, by the end of the campaign, no fewer than 71 per cent of the voters said that they had seen at least one Labour broadcast, 69 per cent a Conservative broadcast and 66 per cent one by the Alliance. This was a far higher figure than had been reached by any other form of party propaganda (see Table 9.2).

The use which the parties have made of their television programmes has varied considerably, and none of them has stuck to a consistent style throughout the general elections in which television broadcasts have taken place. A wide variety of techniques has been adopted – live talks delivered straight into the camera by party leaders, filmed interviews (sometimes conducted by hostile journalists, sometimes by friendly MPs), interviews with voters in the street, specially shot film sequences, newsreel material and a great many charts, graphs and animated cartoons. The parties showed great hesitancy at first in deciding whether to build their programmes round the most senior party spokesmen or to make use of their more experienced television performers, most of whom were lower down in the party hierarchy. By 1959 all parties appeared to have come round to the view that the actual party leader, whose significance to

TABLE 9.2 *Impact of campaigning (per cent of voters)*

	Yes (any)	Yes Con.	Yes Lab.	Yes All
Since the start of the campaign have you:				
Had any leaflets through the door	92	85	84	81
Seen any PEBs on TV	75	69	71	66
Been called on	49	19	20	14
Seen political posters	46	38	32	23
Received any leader's letter	17	11	9	6
Listened to an election phone-in	16	13	13	10
Heard a radio PEB	15	14	14	12
Attended a meeting	3	1	2	1

Adapted from a more detailed table in David Butler and Dennis Kavanagh, *The British General Election of 1987* (London, Macmillan, 1988) p. 215.

the electorate as an actual or potential prime minister could scarcely be exaggerated, must have the lion's share of the available time, and in all elections during the next 20 years the final broadcast of each party was reserved for a direct appeal to the voters by the leader.

In 1983, however, both the Tories and the Labour Party felt the need to dilute their leaders' impact by including other material, and Labour repeated this tactic in 1987, although the Conservatives reverted to the traditional leader's broadcast. The Alliance kept to the customary formula in both elections, but divided the time between the leaders of their two parties (David Steel and Roy Jenkins in 1983 and Steel and David Owen in 1987).

Party election broadcasts have attracted much scorn from professional broadcasters. The 1983 campaign was no exception; the distinguished American broadcaster, Walter Cronkite, described them as ranging from 'terrible to barely tolerable'. Professor Martin Harrison, who has monitored election broadcasts for the Nuffield election studies over many years, commented more judiciously:

None displayed quite the depth of unscrupulous gimmickry of some earlier campaigns, yet there was not a single moment that could be called truly moving or compelling. There were skilfully edited sequences on the winter of discontent or industrial and urban decay, but with a moment's pause for reflection (which they sought to prevent) these seemed brittle and manipulative. The justification for the broadcasts has been that they allow the parties an opportunity to speak for themselves untrammelled by editors and producers, and it is right that their freedom should extend to presentation as well as content. Yet the Conservatives felt that the best way of putting themselves across was to take only half their time and keep their leading figures out of the way as far as decently possible. Labour deployed its politicians more freely but felt the need to support them with a tireless succession of visual devices. The Alliance broadcasts were little less restless. For all the parties' complaints about being trivialised by snippety news, their own programmes were more fragmented than the most breathless news bulletin.[1]

In 1987 one Labour broadcast significantly broke with this tradition of mediocrity: a personal adulation of the party leader Neil Kinnock, thoroughly professionally produced, it was written by Colin Welland and directed by Hugh Hudson (who had collaborated on the hugely successful film *Chariots of Fire*). It immediately became one of the main talking points of the next few days, and was in many ways the outstanding incident in an otherwise rather dull election campaign. Professor Harrison called it 'a stunning invocation of the Labourism of the 1940s by the media techniques of the 1980s'. It remained, however, very much the exception.

The election programmes staged by the BBC and the commercial television companies were long hindered on the one hand by an understandable desire to do nothing which would offend any of the party authorities, and on the other by serious doubts as to the legal standing of such broadcasts. The Representation of the People Act of 1949 had laid down that any operation 'presenting the candidate or his views' should be chargeable to election expenses. Newspapers were specifically excluded from this provision, but no mention was made of radio or television. The television companies were also bound by the Television Act of 1954 which prohibited political broadcasting, other than party political broadcasts, unless it was in the form of 'properly balanced discussion or debates'.

These legal barriers partly account for the extreme timidity shown by the broadcasting authorities in the period before 1959. At no previous general election had they screened any programmes with a political content and their handling of election news items had been extremely circumspect. The Rochdale by-election in 1958, when the Granada network screened a programme in which all three candidates appeared, marked a new departure. By 1959, fortified by legal advice, both television services had resolved to take the plunge and to embark on their own election programmes.

The absence of accusations of partisanship and the high viewing figures obtained by political programmes in the 1959 election encouraged the television authorities to be much bolder in their coverage of subsequent elections. A judgment by the Electoral Court in December 1964 resulted in a further lessening of their inhibitions concerning electoral broadcasts.

The circumstances of this judgment are worth recalling. In the 1964 general election the Communist Party nominated a candidate in Kinross and West Perthshire, the constituency represented by the then Prime Minister, Sir Alec Douglas Home. Their avowed object in doing so was to claim equal broadcasting time for their nominee. The Communist claim for time was rejected, and after the election their candidate petitioned the Court to declare Sir Alec's election void, alleging that expenditure on party broadcasts by the BBC and ITA (predecessor of the IBA) was improperly incurred 'with a view to promoting the election of a candidate'. The Court held that though Sir Alec may incidentally have gained some personal electoral advantage from the broadcasts, the 'dominant motive' of the BBC and ITA was 'to give information to the public and not to promote the election of the respondents'. It therefore refused the Communists' petition.

Following this judgment, the broadcasting authorities felt free to continue to present programmes in which candidates appear as spokesmen for their parties, so long as no reference is made to the campaign in their own constituencies. But in programmes specifically concerned with constituency campaigns, including those during Parliamentary by-elections, the rule was long scrupulously adhered to that no candidate may appear unless all his opponents are included in the same programme. Subsequently it was relaxed to the extent that all candidates should be given the opportunity to appear, but it was no longer open to them to veto the appearance of their opponents by refusing to appear themselves. More recently the broadcasting authorities have been emboldened to exclude 'fringe' candidates from inclusion in programmes on individual constituencies, though taking care to mention their names and party labels.

By 1987 not only was the election given blanket coverage in all news programmes, but there was a plethora of programmes put on by the broadcasting authorities, sometimes with a phone-in facility for the general public, in which politicians of all parties took part, subject to the approximate overall ratio of time mentioned above.

The coming of regional television and of local radio meant that participation was by no means restricted to national personalities. Hundreds, perhaps thousands of candidates were assured of their minute, if not their hour of glory on the airwaves.

Most of the programmes were a great deal more entertaining, informative and hard-hitting than the Party Election Broadcasts, especially the live programmes that confronted the leading party figures with hostile voters or determined interviewers. Pride of place went to the BBC's *Election Call*, a daily morning phone-in programme broadcast simultaneously on television and radio, in which on occasions both major parties saw their representatives badly shaken by sceptical callers, but there was a host of programmes of all formats and on all channels. The emergence of breakfast television, which had been in its infancy in 1983, was a further escalation of the television coverage of the 1987 campaign, and it was here that the most publicised live television incident occurred when Labour's Denis Healey lost his temper with TV-AM interviewer Anne Diamond at the end of a long and intrusive interview about his wife's operation in a private hospital.

But it is the television news programmes which have had the greatest effect on electioneering. They have led to a major change in the way that party leaders now run their campaigns. Traditionally they set off on long tours throughout the country, taking in up to a dozen 'whistle stops' per day, and aiming to cover a high proportion of at least the medium-sized towns, as well as all the major cities during the three weeks of campaigning. Now the centre-piece of each party leader's day is a televised press conference, held at the party headquarters in London. Only after that is completed will the leader venture out into the 'provinces' for a sortie which will possibly involve only one major meeting and bring him or her back to London the same evening. Newspaper correspondents also participate in these conferences, but little attempt is made to disguise the fact that television is the main target audience.

The television viewer normally had a chance to see each party leader in action at least twice each day – once from the morning press conference, where he or she would be shown in the lunchtime and early evening news bulletins, and once, in the later news bulletins (9 p.m. on BBC 1 and 10 p.m. on ITV), when a 'live' shot would be shown from the evening meeting. BBC2 and Channel 4 may provide further, different coverage.

In 1983 Michael Foot, being an old-style campaigner, tried gamely to combine this schedule with traditional visits to a large number of constituencies, visiting 70 marginal seats during the campaign. This may have put heart into his campaign workers in the constituencies, but did not make for effective exposure on the TV screen. Mrs Thatcher preferred to conserve her energy, making only six major speeches and deliberately restricting her other visits to places where she was assured of a warm reception from her supporters or could be photographed against a newsworthy background. In 1987 all the party leaders preferred this latter approach, and future elections are likely to be fought entirely on this pattern.

Much of the remainder of the day is likely to be devoted to creating 'photo-opportunities' – incidents carefully stage-managed to provide suitable footage for the evening bulletins – and any speeches of importance will be carefully manufactured to ensure they contain moments that can be suitably excerpted to illustrate a brief news item.

At no British general election so far has there been a direct confrontation between the party leaders on the lines of the Kennedy–Nixon debates in 1960, or the more recent ones between Reagan and Carter in 1980, Reagan–Mondale in 1984 and Bush–Dukakis in 1988. Normally the Leader of the Opposition has been keen, but the Prime Minister of the day, unwilling to cede a position of equality, has shied away. The only exception was in 1979 when Prime Minister James Callaghan was willing to appear, but Margaret Thatcher (who was advised that her relative inexperience might be shown up), already virtually assured of victory, declined to take part. As Prime Minister, she was no more anxious to appear, declining to debate with Michael Foot in 1983 or with Neil Kinnock in 1987.

There is much evidence that television has enabled voters in general elections to be better informed on the issues and to be more familiar with the personalities of leading politicians than ever before. It has often been observed that television has enabled a modern political leader to speak to more people in one evening than the total number that Gladstone or Disraeli succeeded in addressing at all the meetings during their entire careers.

Television has also had its effects on other aspects of electioneering. The reporting of speeches in news bulletins enables rival political leaders to reply to each others' charges several times during the course of a day and thus the whole tempo of campaigning has been speeded up. Television has greatly increased the exposure of partisans to the propaganda of the other side and this has almost certainly led

TABLE 9.3 *Penetration of Conservative and Labour daily newspapers, 1964–83*[†]

	1964	1966	1970	1974 (Feb.)	1974 (Oct.)	1979	1983
Per cent of adult population reading . . .							
Conservative paper	60	61	54	71	31	66	75
Labour paper	49	51	52	32	32	29	24
Per cent of working-class population reading . . .							
Conservative paper	–	53	44	64	23	64	74
Labour paper	–	59	61	38	39	34	30

Note: Figures obtained by dividing Newspaper Readership Survey figures given in the Nuffield election series into the adult (15+) British population. 'Working class' is social grades C2, D and E. Some people read more than one paper. Those who read two papers supporting the same party are counted twice, inflating the figures slightly. Newspaper partisanship is defined by its preferred election outcome.
[†] Reprinted by kind permission from David Butler and Dennis Kavanagh, *The British General Election of 1983* (London: Macmillan, 1984) p. 217.

to greater sophistication in the propaganda of all parties. It has also resulted in less partisanship in the Press, as radio and television programmes are widely and justifiably regarded as impartial, and are thus used as a yardstick against which newspaper reports may be measured. Most expert observers felt, however, that there had been a marked increase in press partisanship in the 1983 campaign;[2] there was perhaps slightly greater balance in 1987.

The bulk of the press in modern elections has always been on the side of the Conservative party (see Table 9.3), although in 1987 this was less true than in the immediately preceding elections. Of the national daily newspapers, *The Guardian* and the *Daily Mirror* backed Labour, and *Today* supported the Alliance and advocated tactical voting to achieve a hung parliament, while the *Independent* remained aloof and endorsed no party. On Sundays Labour had the support of two established papers, the *Sunday Mirror* and the *People*, and the Alliance of one, the *Observer*. In addition three new Sunday newspapers were covering their first election: *Sunday Today* supported the Alliance but ceased publication halfway through the campaign, and the Labour-supporting *News on Sunday* folded shortly

TABLE 9.4   *Daily newspaper partisanship in 1987 (circulations in thousands)*

Conservative		Labour		Alliance		Neutral	
Daily Express	1697	Daily Mirror	3123	Today	307	Independent	293
Sun	3993	Guardian	494				
Daily Mail	1759						
Daily Star	1289						
Daily Telegraph	1147						
Times	442						
Financial Times	280						
Total	10607		3617		307		293

Adapted from a more detailed table in David Butler and Dennis Kavanagh, *The British General Election of 1987* (London, Macmillan, 1988) pp. 165–6.

after the election; the only commercially viable publication of the three, the *Sunday Sport*, carried a minimum of news content with no easily discernible political direction whatever.

The Conservatives, however, continued to dominate the field (see Table 9.4), with the support of three of the five quality dailies (*The Times*, the *Daily Telegraph*, and the *Financial Times*), the *Sunday Times*, the *Sunday Telegraph*, and, among the popular press, the *Daily Mail*, *Daily Express*, *Sun*, *Daily Star*, *Mail on Sunday*, *Sunday Express* and *News of the World*.

The traditional pattern may be further modified at future elections. Although the failures of several recently introduced newspapers to become established suggest there is not much room in the market for new titles, the lower costs of modern newspaper production methods seem certain to encourage further attempts and, at the very least, to maintain the increasingly competitive climate in this field; significant changes in circulation figures are possible, and editorial attitudes may well have to alter in some cases to maintain an established title's market share. Even so, the Tory predominance in the national press is unlikely to disappear in the foreseeable future.

The partisanship even of the most biased newspapers may be slightly diluted by the full page advertisements placed by the parties, which have become an increasing feature of recent campaigns – in 1987 there were over 300 pages of such advertisements, most during the final days before the election. Most of the papers will accept these from any of the political parties (although in 1987 the proprietor of

Elections in Britain Today

the *Daily Mirror*, Robert Maxwell, refused to let it carry any of the Conservatives' last week flurry of publicity, and both the *Daily Express* and the *Sun* rejected a Labour advertisement on election day which they claimed was misleading). In recent campaigns the Conservatives have been able to afford to spend considerably more on this form of publicity than the other parties, reinforcing their overall advantage in the press.

The various morning, daily and evening papers published outside London are much more uniformly pro-Conservative than is the national press. But, dependent as they are on sales to people of all political views within the area in which they are published, they tend to be less partisan in style. The majority of them give reasonably full coverage during and between elections to the activities and viewpoints of the anti-Conservative parties.

The influence that the press has on voters is difficult to measure, but it is clearly limited or the Conservative Party would win every election, as would right-wing parties in virtually every other democratic country, as in nearly all of them the press is predominantly on the side of the right. Nevertheless it is hard to believe that the Conservatives do not draw a distinct benefit from the partisanship of the press, even though it is at least partially diluted by the potent influence of television and radio which, in Britain at least, are required by law to be neutral.

The final press conferences are given on the eve of the poll and, as the campaign draws to a close, the party leaders finally set off for their own constituencies with a sense of profound relief. The extreme exertions of the preceding three weeks are over, and there is now no more that they can do to influence the result. Their absence from their constituencies during the greater part of the campaign is unlikely to have caused any undue concern, for party leaders normally represent safe seats. During the last one or two days before the votes are cast they occupy themselves in much the same way as other candidates, but with the knowledge that they will soon be set apart from them, either to taste the power and responsibility of the premiership or to assume the scarcely less onerous, but infinitely less rewarding, responsibility of leading their parties on the Opposition benches of the House of Commons.

Notes and References

1. From David Butler and Dennis Kavanagh, *The British General Election of 1983* (London: Macmillan, 1984) p. 155. Martin Harrison's chapter on Broadcasting, and Martin Harrop's on the Press, in both *The British General Election of 1983* and *The British General Election of 1987*, have been important sources for the present author in compiling this chapter.
2. See, for example, Martin Harrop's comments in Butler and Kavanagh, *op. cit.*, Chapter 9, and especially pp. 214–15.

10 Polling Day

When polling day finally arrives the limelight which has shone throughout the preceding weeks on the party leaders and the national campaigns of the parties swings decisively back to the constituencies. The morning papers carry final appeals to vote for one or other of the parties, but otherwise an uneasy quiet descends upon the national scene. The final shots have been fired on radio and television, the party headquarters have done their best or their worst, all now depends on the voter.

Polling day is a very long one for those most intimately concerned. The earliest risers are the presiding officers and poll clerks of the various polling stations. They have to be at their posts by 6.30 a.m., or thereabouts, in order to be ready to receive the first voters at 7 a.m.

Each polling station is in charge of a presiding officer, who has a number of poll clerks to help him. Most polling stations are housed in schools, but a wide variety of other premises are used in some constituencies. If no suitable building is available, a temporary prefabricated building may be erected for the occasion. Local authorities are required by law, 'as far as is reasonable and practicable to designate as polling places only places which are accessible to disabled electors'. On arrival at the polling station the presiding officer has to satisfy himself that all the necessary equipment has been installed.

Inside the polling station will be a row of voting compartments, shaped like telephone kiosks, but with a sliding curtain covering the entrance to ensure privacy. Within the compartment will be a shelf, at waist height, on which voters can mark their ballot papers. A strong indelible pencil is attached by string to the shelf. A notice giving instructions on how to vote is pinned up in each voting compartment, and is also displayed outside the polling station.

Opposite the voting compartments is a table or tables behind which the presiding officer and his assistants sit. In between, in full view of the presiding officer, stand one or more ballot boxes. The presiding officer will have been supplied with a copy of the election register for his polling district, a list of proxy and postal voters, an adequate supply of ballot papers and equipment for marking the ballot papers with the official mark. The ballot papers are printed in books, with

130

counterfoils, rather like cloakroom tickets. Serial numbers are printed on the back of each paper and each counterfoil.

The presiding officer is in sole charge of his polling station. He and his assistants have to swear a declaration of secrecy that they will not divulge, except for some purpose authorised by law, any information as to who has or has not voted or reveal to anyone before the close of the poll the nature of the official mark. A similar declaration has to be made by the candidate and his agent or representatives before they may be admitted to a polling station for any purpose except to cast their own votes.

It is the responsibility of the presiding officer to see that no unauthorised person is admitted to the polling station, that order is maintained and that the poll is conducted lawfully in every respect. At least one police constable will be on duty throughout the day at each polling station to assist the presiding officer to keep order.

Immediately before the poll opens at 7 a.m., the presiding officer must show the ballot box empty to whoever is in the polling station and then lock it and place his seal on the lock.

When the first voter arrives he will give his full name and address to the polling clerk who will tell him his number, put a tick against his name on the register, write his electoral number on the counterfoil of the ballot paper, perforate the ballot paper with the official mark and hand the ballot paper to the voter. The purpose of the official mark, the nature of which is kept secret, is to prevent the forgery of ballot papers. Poll clerks must take great care to remember to perforate each paper as it is issued, or the vote will later be invalidated through no fault of the voter.[1] It is improper to perforate ballot papers in advance, because of the risk of theft.

The voter takes his ballot paper into one of the voting compartments and marks an X against the candidate of his choice. All that the ballot papers contain are the surnames of the candidates, in alphabetical order, and their full names and addresses and descriptions, which normally refers to their party allegiance, and perhaps their occupation. A sample ballot paper is shown in Figure 10.1.

When he has marked his ballot paper the voter must fold it, and, in the view of the presiding officer, drop it into the ballot box. By this elaborate procedure the secrecy of the ballot is at once protected and the possibility of forged papers being introduced into the ballot box virtually eliminated.

If a voter spoils his ballot paper he may obtain another one on application to the presiding officer, who will mark the spoiled paper

1	**JONES** (Dorothy Jones of 418 Derby Road, Nottingham, Retired Teacher Animal Welfare candidate.)	
2	**SMITH** (James Henry Smith of 27 Roundchurch Mansions, London, S.E.22, The Labour Party Candidate.)	
3	**TAYLOR** (William Thomas Percy Taylor of 'Little- hammer', Abinger, Surrey, Conservative Party candidate.)	
4	**YOUNG** (Mary Jane Young of 14 Argyll Road, Oldham, Lancashire, SDP – Liberal Alliance candidate)	

FIGURE 10.1 *Sample ballot paper*

'cancelled' and put it on one side till the end of the day, when he has to account to the Returning Officer for all the ballot papers which he has issued.

Blind and incapacitated voters may ask the presiding officer to mark their ballot papers for them, or may bring a friend with them who will be permitted to mark their ballot papers for them.

If the election is on a Saturday, which does not normally happen in the case of Parliamentary elections though many local government elections were formerly held on that day, a Jewish voter who objects on religious grounds to voting in the prescribed manner may also request the presiding officer to mark his ballot paper for him.

By the time the first voters have cast their votes, the election agent and his helpers will already be in action. Outside each polling station will be 'tellers', each proudly sporting his party colours, who will ask voters for their electoral numbers as they leave the polling stations. There is no obligation on voters to reveal this information but the great majority of them are normally willing to do so, at least to the tellers representing their own party. Many of the tellers are school-children who are on holiday for the day and have been recruited for the job by parents who are staunch party members. Sometimes they may be paid by the party or their parents, but most of them are willing to help out for nothing. An excess of zeal may occasionally be revealed in a frosty unwillingness to cooperate with the tellers from 'the other side', but more frequently a feeling of *camaraderie* prevails and numbers are willingly swopped.

Each party will have established a sub-committee room near to the polling station which will contain a copy of the register on which will be marked all the voters who have promised to support the party's candidate. At hourly intervals, or possibly more frequently, throughout the day messengers will bring back from the tellers lists of the electoral numbers of those who have already voted so that they can be crossed off the register. An army of 'knockers up' will have been recruited to call later in the day on those who have not already voted.

Soon after breakfast the candidate, wearing an outsize rosette, will be ceremoniously introduced – probably by his agent – to the presiding officer, with whom he will exchange a few light-hearted remarks. The ostensible reason for the visit is to satisfy himself that everything is in order, though there is virtually never any question of this not being the case. During his tour the candidate will also drop into all his sub-committee rooms to give a word of encouragement to his supporters.

Throughout the day his party is likely to have one or more loud-speaker cars touring areas where its support is concentrated, urging voters to record their votes as early as possible in the day, thus reducing the pressure on the party machine during the evening. For much of the day the candidate himself is likely to be in charge of the loudspeaker, making a personal appeal to the voters to support him.

By 9 a.m. perhaps one elector in ten may have voted. Most of these would be people casting their votes on their way to work. During the daytime a steady trickle of housewives make their way to the polling stations, though many prefer to wait until the evening and to go along with their husbands.

The result is that many party workers find themselves less than fully occupied until at least 5 or 6 p.m. In the morning and afternoon sick and elderly voters are called on and offered lifts to the poll. Knockers up will be kept busy throughout the afternoon, but will find many houses empty and at others will be told to come back in the evening.

By 6 p.m. it is unusual for more than 50 per cent of the electors to have cast their votes and about that time begins an increasingly frantic effort by each party machine to get its supporters to the poll in the three hours remaining. This is especially important for the Labour Party, as working-class wives are less likely to vote earlier in the day than their middle-class counterparts. A much higher proportion of Labour votes than of Conservative ones are cast in the evening, and non-political factors such as the weather and the appeal of the evening's television programmes can have an important effect on the result in closely contested constituencies.

In the evening every available helper is mobilised to knock up voters and, wherever possible, a car is provided for every group of knockers up, so that lifts to the poll may be offered to reluctant voters. Parties with a good and well-manned organisation may well be able to knock up all their supporters who have not voted earlier, as many as six times during the course of the evening. Despite this encouragement some voters remain obdurate and refuse to turn out, others delay so long that in the end it is too late to go, a few arrive at the polling station after 10 p.m. and find it closed.

But allowing for inaccuracies in the election register, for removals and for people who are sick or away from their homes on election day, without having arranged to vote by post, the proportion of electors who actually vote in Parliamentary elections is rather high. Since 1950 it has ranged from 72 per cent to 84 per cent, which suggests that the proportion of avoidable abstentions is probably not usually much more than 10 per cent.

Promptly at 10 p.m., the presiding officer must close his polling station, even if there are electors waiting to cast their votes. He must then seal the ballot boxes, so that no more ballot papers may be inserted. He then makes out his ballot paper account. On this he must state the number of ballot papers with which he had been issued at the beginning of the day, the number of papers in the ballot box and the number of unused and spoilt papers. He must then make up packages containing the marked registers, the counterfoils and the unused ballot papers and deliver these to the Returning Officer. The police, under the direction of the Returning Officer, will collect the ballot boxes and take them straight to the place where the votes are to be counted.

The count is usually held in the town hall or other large public hall in the constituency. In nearly all borough constituencies it is held on the evening of polling day; in some counties it is postponed until the following morning. It is a crowded and lively occasion. The hall is furnished with long trestle tables at either side of which are seated the Returning Officer's assistants who are to count the votes. There is an air of expectancy as the room gradually fills up with candidates, their wives, agents and leading supporters, whose function is to act as 'counting agents' or scrutineers of the actual counting of the votes. The number of counting agents permitted to each candidate is decided by the returning officer, but the total should not be less than the number of counting assistants and each candidate must be allowed the same number. All attending the count were previously required to sign a declaration of secrecy, promising not to attempt to discover how any individual has voted or to reveal such information to any other person. Since 1986 they are no longer asked to sign, but their attention is drawn to the secrecy provisions of the Representation of the People acts and the penalties for infringing them. The press may be admitted, at the discretion of the Returning Officer, and a public gallery may also be provided.

By about 10:15 p.m. in most boroughs the first ballot boxes will arrive from the polling stations. The ballot box containing the postal votes will be among the first to arrive. Each box is emptied of its contents, which are immediately counted to make sure that they tally with the number given in the presiding officer's ballot paper account. When every box has been emptied and its contents counted the ballot papers are mixed together in one large pile, so that it is impossible to tell accurately how the voters of each polling district have recorded their votes. In the past there were often long delays in waiting for every single box to arrive before the mixing of ballot papers took place. Under the 1985 Representation of the People Act, however, it is now permissible to mix papers from several boxes at a time, providing that at least one other box is kept back to mix with the final box delivered.

The ballot papers are now sorted out into piles representing votes polled for each individual candidate. They are then counted into bundles of one hundred. All the time the counting agents, who will be standing behind the counting assistants, will be keeping an eagle eye on their activities – making sure that none of their candidate's papers have inadvertently been included amongst those of their opponents.

In a safe or hopeless constituency there is little tension, and the candidates and their supporters are much more concerned with whispered reports that may be coming in about the results in other constituencies, and the national trend to which they point. Some thoughtful Returning Officers go to the trouble of installing a television set in an anteroom and many scrutineers spend a lot of their time popping in and out to acquaint themselves with the latest position. In a marginal constituency, however, attention is firmly fixed on the counting, and as the rival piles of votes mount so do the hopes and fears of the candidates and their supporters.

In the process of sorting the votes the counting assistants come across a number of ballot papers whose validity is doubtful. They place these on one side and when all the other votes have been counted the Returning Officer adjudicates them in the presence of the candidates and their agents, giving his reasons for accepting or rejecting them in each case. There are four categories of ballot paper which must be declared void – those which do not bear the official mark, those on which votes are given for more than one candidate, those on which anything is written by which the voter can be identified and those which are unmarked.

Other papers in which the intention of the voter is unclear should be declared invalid by the Returning Officer, but where the intention is clear, but the mark has been incorrectly made he should accept their validity. Examples of incorrectly marked papers which are nevertheless valid are those where the X is placed otherwise than in the proper place, but still leaving no doubt which candidate the voter prefers; those where a tick or similar mark has been used instead of a cross and those where 'Yes' and 'No', or '1' and '2' or '1' and '0' have been written to express a preference between candidates.

When the Returning Officer has given his adjudication of the doubtful votes they should be added to their appropriate pile and the total of each candidate's votes will be recorded by the chief counting assistant who will give it to the Returning Officer. The Returning Officer will then privately inform the candidates and their agents of the result of the count. If the result is close the Returning Officer may order a recount, and any candidate may claim a recount which the Returning Officer may not reasonably refuse. If the first count shows a majority of less than 500 a demand for a recount is likely, and where the majority is less than a hundred several recounts may be held. It is also permissible for a recount to be demanded by a candidate in danger of losing his deposit where the number of his votes is close to the minimum required, even though the majority of the leading candidate may be numbered in tens of thousands.

If after several recounts there is an equality of votes between the two leading candidates, the Returning Officer draws a lot to decide which is elected. Prior to 1948 the rule was that the Returning Officer should have a casting vote. The last occasion on which this invidious situation arose in Parliamentary elections was at Ashton-under-Lyne in 1886, but there have been a number of more recent examples in local government elections.

As soon as the result of the poll has been ascertained, the Returning Officer makes a public announcement of the votes obtained by the various candidates and declares the new Member elected. It is then usual for the winning candidate to propose a vote of thanks to the Returning Officer and his staff for their conduct of the election, during which he takes the opportunity of thanking his own supporters and declaring that the result is a triumph for his party and the cause which it represents. The vote of thanks is seconded by the runner-up, who also gives his own partisan interpretation of the result, as do other candidates (if any) who are also expected to have their say. Great demonstrations of enthusiasm are made by their supporters, especially by the winning party when the seat has changed hands.

As soon as possible after the result has been declared, the Returning Officer must publish it in writing. He must also attach, to the writ which he has received from the Clerk of the Crown authorising him to conduct the election, a certificate naming the newly elected Member. The writ is then returned, post free, to the Clerk of the Crown.

The Returning Officer must also collect up all the documents concerned with the election – the ballot papers used and unused, the ballot paper accounts and rejected ballot papers, the marked copies of the election registers and lists of proxies and the counterfoils of all ballot papers – and send these to the Clerk of the Crown. All these documents will be retained for one year and then destroyed, unless an order to the contrary is made by the High Court or the House of Commons.

The validity of an election may be challenged by a petition to the High Court, which may be presented by an elector for the constituency concerned or by one of the candidates. The Court, in considering the petition, may order a scrutiny of the ballot papers and other relevant documents listed above. The High Court must report its findings to the Speaker of the House of Commons and if it has found the election invalid the House will proceed to authorise the issue of a writ for a new election.

Election petitions are rare, partly no doubt because of the great expense involved to the petitioner and partly because a Member is unlikely to be unseated if only minor irregularities are proved.[2] The most recent election petition was that against Sir Alec Douglas-Home in 1964. The Communist Party unsuccessfully attempted to unseat him on the grounds that BBC and ITA broadcasts of his by-election campaign in Kinross and West Perthshire should have given equal coverage to his Communist opponent. But the only one in the postwar period alleging irregularity in the actual constituency campaign was that brought by Sir Oswald Mosley following his defeat as a Union Movement (Fascist) candidate at North Kensington in 1959. It was unsuccessful, as was that concerning the Drake division of Plymouth in 1929, the only other petition to be made since 1924, except that concerning Mr Tony Benn, discussed on page 82, and two other petitions in the mid-1950s concerned with the election of Sinn Fein candidates who were serving prison sentences at the time of their election. In each of these three cases the issue was the qualification of the candidates not the conduct of the election. But the main reason why election petitions are seldom resorted to is the undoubted fact that major irregularities are almost unknown in modern British elections.

On election night special programmes relaying the constituency results as they become known are broadcast on radio and televised on BBC and ITV. Expert commentators, backed by computers, interpret the results and, on the basis of the trend revealed by the first contests to be counted, attempt, usually with a large measure of success, to predict what the final result will be. The computers adjust the final prediction with every constituency result that comes in.

There is lively competition to be the first constituency to declare a result. In both 1983 and 1987, the safe Tory seat of Torbay won the race, with Guildford, Basildon and Cheltenham coming close behind. In fact any constituency which consists of a highly compact urban area stands a good chance of being first, so long as its Returning Officer is prepared to spend extra money on employing more and better skilled counting agents (such as bank clerks, for example) – unless of course there is a recount.

Even before the first results are known, the commentators are furnished with the findings of 'exit' polls, in which electors are asked how they have just voted as they leave the polling booths in a representative sample of constituencies. The first time this was attempted, in October 1974, the projected result was disastrously wrong – a Labour majority of 150, when in the event the overall Labour lead was merely three seats. At the three subsequent general elections, as well as in most of the by-elections in which this technique has been employed, the predictions have been much more accurate. In 1983 the BBC exit poll, undertaken by Gallup, showed an average error in the final party vote of only 0.4 per cent. The ITN poll, conducted by the Harris Research Centre, also came very close, with an average error of 0.6 per cent. In 1987 Harris again came very close to the actual result, indicating a Conservative lead over Labour of nearly 10 per cent when the actual result put them 11 per cent ahead. The BBC did not use an exit poll in 1987; instead they asked Gallup to carry out a last minute survey, which pointed to a Conservative lead of only 5 per cent.

Normally the first result is available by 11 p.m., or soon after, and by 4 a.m., when the broadcasting programmes close down for the night, almost 600 seats will have been counted. Long before this the result of the election should be clear, unless it is extremely close. In earlier years, when only one-half to two-thirds of the seats were counted overnight, and these predominantly the more urban ones, a misleadingly large Labour lead was often built up, which would be offset on the following day when the remaining, more rural, seats were counted. Now that television coverage has induced the great majority of constituencies to declare overnight, the 'reserve' Conservative strength on the second day of counting is much smaller than it used to be.

At about 10 a.m. the following day the count is begun in the other constituencies and from 11 a.m. onwards the results are broadcast, as they come in, to about 6 p.m., by which time all but a handful of remote Scottish constituencies have declared their results. Long before this one of the party leaders will normally have conceded defeat, and it will be clear who is to govern the country for the next four or five years.

Notes

1. In Derbyshire North-East, in 1922, the Labour candidate was elected by five votes, with a larger number of unmarked ballot papers in favour of his opponent. It is clear that he owed his victory to the failure of the poll clerks to mark some of the ballot papers.
2. Butler and Rose, *The British General Election of 1959* (London: Macmillan, 1960) p. 280, quote a senior party organiser on this point: 'If we lost a seat by one vote and I could clearly prove illegal practices by the other side I wouldn't try. It would cost perhaps £5000 and they might be able to show that our man had slipped up in some way. But worse than that, it might start tit-for-tat petitions and no party could afford a lot of them. On the whole, we are both law-abiding and it's as well to leave each other alone'.

11 By-Elections, Local Elections, Euro-Elections and Referenda

Casual vacancies in the House of Commons are filled through by-elections in the constituency concerned. Such vacancies may be occasioned by the death, succession or elevation to the peerage, bankruptcy, lunacy, expulsion from the House or the acceptance of a disqualifying office by a Member of Parliament. There is no formal provision for a Member to resign his seat, but resignation is effected by applying for a disqualifying office. Two such offices – sinecures of great antiquity – are normally reserved for such a purpose – the posts of Steward of the Chiltern Hundreds and Bailiff of the Manor of Northstead.

In practice the great majority of by-elections are caused by deaths, resignations or elevation to the peerage. Between the general elections of 1945 and 1987 there were, in total, 393 by-elections. During the whole period there have been, on average, 9.4 by-elections per year, or one every five and a half weeks, yet over the 42 years, as a whole, the incidence of by-elections has halved.[1] Though the number of deaths of MPs has remained steady, the proportion who resign or are made peers has fallen sharply as governments have learned not to risk the unnecessary loss of seats by appointing their Parliamentary supporters to official posts or offering them peerages. Such preferments are now more often saved up until the end of Parliaments in order to avoid this risk, as the casualty rate in by-elections has steadily risen.

In place of the Royal Proclamation authorising a general election, the Speaker of the House of Commons issues a writ instructing the Returning Officer in the constituency concerned to make arrangements for the poll to be held. Polling day is fixed between two and three weeks after the receipt of the writ (see timetable in Appendix 4). The writ is issued following a motion approved by the House of Commons, but when the House is in recess the Speaker may issue the writ on receipt of a certificate signed by any two Members of Parliament.

By tradition the party holding the seat chooses the date on which the by-election is held, and it is the party whips who move the appropriate motion in the House, which is normally agreed without discussion. Tactical considerations clearly influence the choice of date, but if it is unduly postponed there is likely to be an adverse reaction within the constituency and the opposing parties will seek to capitalise on the unwillingness of the defending party to face a contest. Since the early 1970s there has been an informal agreement between the main parties that by-elections shall normally be held within three months of a vacancy arising. With very minor variations,[2] the legal provisions concerning a by-election are the same as in a general election. However, the limit on expenditure by candidates in a by-election is now four times that in a general election, although this was not the case before 1989.

Although a by-election campaign closely resembles that within an individual constituency at a general election, it frequently excites a great deal more interest. There is normally far stronger competition to be selected as a candidate, even for the minority party in a hopeless seat, as the publicity given to the by-election might well result in subsequent invitations from constituency parties in more attractive seats. At a general election an individual contest is merged in the national campaign and little note is taken of it outside the constituency concerned. At a by-election it holds the centre of the stage.

For this reason, too, it is more likely to attract intervention by a minor party or independent candidates, including a few who have no serious political interests and put themselves forward purely for exhibitionist reasons. For example, a total of 111 candidates contested the 16 by-elections held in Great Britain during the 1983–7 Parliament, an average of 6.9 per contest. In the general election of 1987, 2325 candidates contested 650 seats, an average of 3.6 per constituency. In 1985 the deposit required from candidates was increased from £150 to £500. This appears to have led to a slight reduction in the number of fringe candidates in by-elections, and also at general elections (the 1987 total of general election candidates was slightly down on the 1983 figure of 2579).

In fighting a by-election a constituency party can normally depend on help from outside. The party's regional organiser will probably move into the constituency for several weeks to supervise the campaign, and professional agents from other constituencies will be borrowed to undertake important specialist tasks. Other professionals from the national party headquarters may also be seconded, while voluntary workers from neighbouring constituencies can also be

expected to lend a hand. In the case of key contests in highly
marginal seats helpers may travel from all parts of the country to
support their party's nominee.

Traditionally the Prime Minister sends a personal message of
support to the government party's candidate, which is useful for
attracting press publicity, and the leaders of the opposition parties
also send similar letters to their standard-bearers. Prominent Cabinet
Ministers, and their counterparts in the other parties, descend on the
constituency to speak at election meetings and MPs are drafted in to
lead canvassing and loudspeaker drives.

The personality of the candidate in a by-election is more important
than in a general election campaign. Freed from the awesome responsibility of helping to choose a government, voters are more
prepared to cross party lines and to vote for the most attractive
candidate. Electors also appear to be more inclined to engage in
'tactical' voting at by-elections, that is to say to vote for their second
preference party if it appears to be better placed than their first
preference, in order to try to defeat the party to which they have the
greatest objection. This is perhaps the major reason why, in the
recent past, Liberal and Alliance candidates have consistently polled
better in by-elections than in general elections. Tactical voting can be
greatly stimulated by opinion polls in by-elections if, as is often the
case, they demonstrate that one of the two largest parties has no
chance of winning. This can lead to a stampede of a high proportion
of its supporters towards the Liberal Democrat candidate. Conversely
when, as in the Fulham by-election in March 1986, the polls clearly
showed the SDP–Alliance candidate to be in third place they probably
had a depressant effect on his vote.

Governments may sometimes appear to take by-elections more
seriously than their effects would warrant. It is true that it is only
rarely that a government's fate can be directly affected by the result
of a by-election, though the Labour government elected in October
1974 did eventually fall through losing too many seats in by-elections.
Its original overall majority was only three seats, and it lost seven in
all, leaving itself in a minority for the last two years of its existence.
Prime Minister James Callaghan prolonged its life through negotiat-
ing the Lib–Lab pact, but when this expired in July 1978 it became
vulnerable to the threat of all the other parties combining in a vote of
no confidence. This eventually occurred in March 1979, and the
government (which lost by a single vote) was pitched into a general
election at a time not of its own choosing and lost disastrously. The

disaster was largely self-inflicted, as Callaghan had recklessly provoked a by-election in Workington through awarding a peerage to
Fred Peart (who became Leader of the House of Lords) at a time
when the anti-Labour swing in the immediately previous by-election
was more than enough to ensure a Labour defeat at Workington,
which duly occurred.

It may seem surprising that rather more seats do not change hands
at by-elections. One reason is that relatively few of them take place in
marginal seats. Even those caused by death are disproportionately in
safe seats, as, generally speaking, it is the younger members who
represent the more marginal seats. By-elections caused by resignations or elevation to the peerage are the consequence of voluntary
decisions, and political parties are normally more cautious than to
put their marginal seats at risk, especially when they are going through a
period of unpopularity. Certainly Mrs Thatcher, whose majority was far
larger than Callaghan's, proved extremely cautious in this respect.

But it is not just the *loss* of seats which governments fear. By-
elections have long been used as a means of gauging public opinion,
and a disappointing result, even if it does not involve the loss of a
seat, can have a disastrous effect on party morale, while boosting that
of the opposition. The results of by-elections can have an influence
out of all proportion to their intrinsic importance, and this can best
be shown by discussing briefly some of the more significant results in
the post-war period.

During the Parliament of 1945–50 there was no single by-election
result which had more than a passing effect. But, cumulatively, the
by-elections contributed in no small measure to the standing of the
then Labour government. Although the Conservatives gained ground
in the great majority of the 52 contests, and won three seats from
minor parties, their failure to win a single seat from Labour was
constantly invoked as evidence that the government was still enjoying
wide support, despite other indications to the contrary.

During the course of the 1951–5 Parliament the Conservative
government actually won a seat – Sunderland South – from the
Labour opposition. This was a rare feat indeed – the great majority of
by-elections have invariably shown a swing against the government in
office, and it was almost thirty years since a government had actually
picked up a seat in a by-election. The consequence was that pressure
on the government eased perceptibly, and most observers concluded,
correctly, that the Conservatives would win the subsequent general
election.

In the period from the spring of 1962 to the summer of 1964 an almost unbroken succession of by-election disasters did immense damage to the reputation of the governments of Harold Macmillan and Sir Alec Douglas-Home, and provoked them into taking a number of ill-considered actions. The most sensational result, in March 1962, was at Orpington, hitherto regarded as an extremely safe Conservative seat. The by-election resulted in a Liberal victory; a Conservative majority of 14 760 was turned into a Liberal one of 7855. Although the Liberal revival which it appeared to foreshadow did not eventually materialise, this result largely transformed the terms in which electoral strategy was discussed. During the succeeding two years – in over 30 more by-elections – the Conservatives lost a further three seats to Labour, and suffered the further humiliation of seeing their candidate forced into third position in six Labour seats, and into fourth place in one more. The dismissal by Harold Macmillan, in July 1962, of one-third of his Cabinet, and the postponement by Sir Alec Douglas-Home of the general election until the last possible moment in 1964, were both plausibly attributed to this series of setbacks.[3]

In the 1964–6 Parliament, by-elections continued to have an important influence on the fortunes of the Labour government. The completely unexpected loss of Leyton to the Conservatives in January 1965 (when a Labour majority of 7926 was turned into a Conservative one of 205) not only led to the immediate resignation of the Foreign Secretary (Patrick Gordon Walker, who was the defeated Labour candidate), but reduced the government's precarious Parliamentary majority from five to three. It also deterred the Prime Minister from calling an early general election, which he might otherwise have been tempted to do by the favourable opinion poll findings.

A year later, in January 1966, in a keenly contested by-election at North Hull, the Labour Party increased its majority from 1181 to 5351, obtaining a swing of 4.5 per cent – the largest swing to the governing party in any by-election in a marginal seat in 32 years. This result confirmed other evidence (from opinion polls) that an early general election would produce an increased Labour Parliamentary majority, and the North Hull result certainly appears to have clinched the Prime Minister's decision to go to the country in March 1966.

The 1966–70 Labour government created a postwar record in losing 15 seats in by-elections, though as it had a large parliamentary majority these losses did not put its existence in jeopardy. Twelve of these seats were gained by the Conservative Party, but perhaps the greatest impact was made by two other by-elections, at Carmarthen and Hamilton, where Labour defeats brought Plaid Cymru and the Scottish National Party into Parliament. The Conservative government elected in 1970 had a less bumpy ride, losing five seats, four of them to the Liberals. Yet much the most striking by-election of this Parliament hardly affected the government at all. This occurred at Lincoln, where the sitting Labour MP, Dick Taverne, resigned his seat after being dropped as Labour candidate by his constituency Labour party. Running as Democratic Labour, he routed both the official Labour and Conservative candidates, winning 58.2 per cent of the poll in what has been described as 'the greatest *personal* election victory in British political history'.[4]

Taverne's victory foreshadowed the series of by-election successes in 1981–2, following the launch of the Social Democratic Party in March 1981, which enabled it to make a much greater impact than would otherwise have seemed likely. The first of these was at Warrington in July 1981, when Roy Jenkins won 42.4 per cent of the vote (against a Liberal score of nine per cent at the previous general election) and almost won a safe Labour seat. This was followed by three striking gains in Tory-held seats, by a Liberal (William Pitt) in Croydon North-West and by Social Democrats Shirley Williams, at Crosby, and Roy Jenkins, at Glasgow Hillhead. The Falklands war brought an abrupt end to the sequence, but late in the Parliament there was a further Liberal gain at Bermondsey, a former Labour stronghold where the Labour Party, seriously split over its choice of candidate, was in total disarray.

The strong Alliance showing in by-elections was repeated in the 1983–7 Parliament, when it won three seats from the Conservatives, and, in a virtual re-run of the Bermondsey episode, captured Greenwich from the Labour Party, late in the Parliament. The Parliament elected in June 1987 had very few by-elections during its first 18 months. In the first of these, the Conservatives narrowly held the marginal seat of Kensington over Labour. In the second, at Glasgow Govan, the Labour Party suffered the rare indignity for an opposition party of losing a safe seat, to the Scottish National Party, with a swing of 33 per cent. Later in this Parliament, however, the Labour Party turned in a series of strong performances, winning Conservative seats with notable swings at Vale of Glamorgan in 1989 and Mid-Staffordshire in 1990. The former Alliance parties, whose appeal was damaged by contention between the newly merged Social and Liberal

Democrats and the rump of the SDP led by Dr David Owen, failed to make any breakthroughs until Dr Owen disbanded his party in the spring of 1990. In October 1990 the Liberal Democrats captured Eastbourne from the Conservatives, in a by-election caused by the murder of the local Conservative MP, Ian Gow, by the IRA. The swing was 20.1 per cent, and the result was interpreted both as an indication that the Liberal Democrats, who had been trailing badly in the opinion polls, might be back in business, and, more certainly, that a general election was now unlikely to be held during the first half of 1991. A month later poor Tory performances in two Labour-held seats, Bootle and Bradford North, contributed to the pressures which led to the ousting of Margaret Thatcher as Tory leader and Prime Minister shortly afterwards. In March 1991, a further striking Liberal Democrat victory in the Tory-held seat of Ribble Valley hastened a government decision to abandon the unpopular Poll Tax.

Despite the influence which by-elections such as these undoubtedly had, there is a serious risk of reading too much into individual by-election results. In fact the result of any particular by-election may be wildly misleading as a reflection of the national strength of the parties. Regional and local issues which tend to cancel out in a general election may assume disproportionate importance; the turn-out, which at a general election is normally around 75 per cent, fluctuates widely (in the 1979–83 Parliament, for instance, from 33.6 to 82.4 per cent); the personal qualities of candidates have a greater effect than in a general election; and minor party and independent candidates are more likely to intervene and their influence, though marginal, is difficult to interpret.

The fallacy of drawing too many conclusions from the result of a single by-election can easily be illustrated. In November 1960 six by-elections were fought on the same day. In one of these, Carshalton, there was a swing to the Conservatives of 3.8 per cent; in another, Bolton East, there was a swing to Labour of 2.0 per cent – a difference of 5.8 per cent. In the not quite so distant past, on 28 April 1977, by-elections were held at Ashfield and Grimsby. One showed a pro-Tory swing of 20.9 per cent, the other 7.1 per cent, a difference of 13.8 per cent.

Single by-election results, then, are clearly unreliable guides to the state of public opinion, but experience has shown that groups of by-elections, held over a period of several months, do give a reasonably accurate idea of the *trend* of opinion, if their results are averaged out. They are nevertheless inherently likely to understate the actual

TABLE 11.1 *Swings in by-elections and general elections*

Government	Swings revealed in:		Improvement for party in office
	By-elections (average during Parliament)	Subsequent general election	
1945 Lab.	C 3·6	C 2·8	+ 0·8
1950 Lab.	C 4·3	C 0·9	+ 3·4
1951 Con.	C 0·2	C 2·1	+ 1·9
1955 Con.	L 4·8	C 1·1	+ 5·9
1959 Con.	L 5·5	L 3·1	+ 2·4
1964 Lab.	C 1·6	L 2·6	+ 4·2
1966 Lab.	C 16·3	C 4·7	+11·6
1970 Con.	L 5·2	L 1·4	+ 3·8
1974: Feb. Lab.	C 1·2	L 2·1	+ 3·3
Oct. Lab.	C 10·2	C 5·2	+ 5·0
1979 Con.	L 4·3*	C 4·0	+ 8·3
1983 Con.	L 7·2†	L 1·6	+ 5·6

* Based on only a minority of by-elections, excluding those where the Alliance emerged as the main challenger.
† Includes all 16 British by-elections in this Parliament. The figures conceal the fact that the Liberal–SDP Alliance were the major gainers in most of these by-elections.

level of support for the government. Year in, year out the great majority of by-elections show a swing against the government in power.

The reasons for this can only be conjectured, but it seems probable that by-elections are often used as a means of registering a 'protest vote' against particular government policies, without incurring the risk of actually overthrowing the government. The turnout at by-elections is almost invariably lower than at a general election,[5] and it may also be the case that government supporters are rather more inclined to be complacent, and to stay at home on such occasions.

In any event, Table 11.1 clearly shows that at every general election since the war the governing party has done better than the previous by-election results had indicated. In considering the significance of by-election results therefore, whilst it is usually justifiable to assume that the trend revealed by a series of by-elections over a period of time is probably correct, it would be prudent to conclude that the government's standing is a little higher than the results indicate.

LOCAL ELECTIONS

Apart from Parliamentary by-elections, the most important subsidiary elections held in Britain are those of representatives on local authorities. These are held each year in May, normally on the first Thursday of the month. Councillors are elected for a four-year term. Every four years the entire councils for the 47 non-metropolitan *counties* in England and Wales are re-elected (county council election years are 1985, 1989, 1993, and so on.). In each of the other three years in a four-year cycle, the lower-tier or *district* councils are elected (some of these may be dignified by the names of borough or city councils, but they all have the same powers). The 333 non-metropolitan district councils have an option: either the whole council can be re-elected together once every four years, or one-third of the council is re-elected in each of the non-county election years. If they choose whole council elections these are held in the mid-year of the county cycle – 1987, 1991, 1995, and so on.

Up until 1985 there were also metropolitan county councils in London and six other areas (Tyne and Wear, West Midlands, Merseyside, Greater Manchester, West Yorkshire and South Yorkshire). These were abolished by legislation passed by the Thatcher government, and the 32 *London boroughs* and 36 *metropolitan districts* now form single-tier authorities. Their members are elected *en bloc* every four years (cycle: 1986, 1990, 1994, and so on).

In Scotland there are nine *Regional* and three *Island* councils (which replaced the former counties in 1975), forming the upper tier of local government, and 53 *district* councils. All councils are elected *en bloc* every four years. The Regional and Island councils' cycle runs 1986, 1990, 1994, and so on, and the districts' 1984, 1988, 1992, and so forth.

In Northern Ireland local government is now on a single-tier basis, with 26 *district* councils elected for four-year terms on the basis of proportional representation, using the *Single Transferable Vote* (see page 220). The electoral cycle is 1985, 1989, 1993, and so on.

Except in Northern Ireland, the districts are sub-divided into a number of wards, each of which elects three councillors, one of whom retires each year if the council has decided to be elected by thirds. The counties are divided into electoral divisions returning one member each.

Voters who are qualified to vote in Parliamentary elections are also entitled to vote in local government elections for the councils in whose area they reside. In addition, peers are permitted to vote. Peers are included on the electoral register with the prefix L, indicating that they are only entitled to vote in local elections. Until 1969, occupiers of any rateable land or premises in the area of a yearly value of £10 or more (this would apply mostly to businessmen and tradesmen) were also entitled to vote and to stand as candidates. This provision was repealed by the 1969 Representation of the People Act, some 21 years after plural voting was abolished in parliamentary elections.

To be a candidate in a local election it is necessary to be 'of full age' (that is, 21 *not* 18) and a local government elector for the area of the local authority concerned, or have resided there for twelve months preceding the date of the election. There are, however, a number of disqualifications – the most important being that employees of a local authority may not seek election to it. This excludes quite a number of people, for example teachers, who would otherwise be eligible. If however a teacher is employed by a county council it would not exclude him from seeking election to a district council, even if his school were situated in its area.

As in the case of Parliamentary candidates, it is necessary to be nominated by ten electors for the ward or electoral area concerned. There is also a statutory limit to the amount of expenditure which a candidate may incur. The sum allowed is £144 for the first 500 electors and 2.9p. for each elector in excess of 500. Where there are two joint candidates the maximum expenditure for each is reduced by one-fourth, and if there are three or more joint candidates the maximum is reduced by one-third. Unlike Parliamentary candidates, few candidates in local elections spend anything near the limit laid down.

The ballot papers for local elections are similar to Parliamentary ones. The provision under the 1969 Representation of the People Act which allows candidates to include their political affiliation has almost certainly had a greater effect in local elections than in Parliamentary ones. The candidates' names are usually less well-known and less publicised, and when there were multiple vacancies it was evident that many mistakes were made, particularly when different candidates had the same or similar surnames.

In most other respects the legal provisions for the conduct of local elections are the same as for Parliamentary contests,[6] and, on a more restricted scale, the candidates run a similar type of campaign. But there are a number of important differences. At general elections between 70 and 85 per cent of the registered voters go to the polls, at local elections the figure seldom rises above 50 per cent, and the average is not more then 40 per cent. At a general election virtually all seats are contested by Labour, Conservative and Liberal Democrat candidates, while in local elections this is not the general rule, except in the main urban areas. In the past there were relatively few contests on party lines in the more rural areas, and even in towns there was a fairly large number of unopposed returns. The reorganisation of local government into larger units, which took place in 1973–4, had the effect of politicising local elections in many parts of the country where previously they had been held on non-party lines, and this has greatly reduced the incidence of unopposed returns. It is still the case, however, that regular three-party competition is far from being universal.

Nevertheless the results of local elections are closely scrutinised as guides to political trends. On rare occasions, when a particularly outstanding change in political control is registered, it can have a substantial impact on the national political scene.

More generally, the total gains and losses each year in the borough elections are taken as a barometer of the parties' standing in the country, though account has to be taken of the fact that the seats contested were last fought four years previously. With this proviso, there is much evidence that these results do give an accurate reflection of public opinion, though, as in the case of by-elections, there is a tendency to exaggerate the swing against the government party. As political barometers however, local elections have been regarded as being unsatisfactory, as they take place only once a year. In recent years this has focused attention on the previously unregarded trickle of local government by-elections which take place throughout the year. The results of these are now carefully collected and scrutinised, notably by the *New Statesman and Society*, whose political correspondent produces a rundown at monthly intervals. When taken in clusters, these have proved to be extremely sensitive indicators of movements in party support, and a useful check against opinion polls which record statements of intention rather than actual votes. In 1987 the Conservatives devoted resources to an extensive computer analysis of the local election results which played a significant role in deciding the timing of the next year's general election.

EURO-ELECTIONS

A new type of elections was introduced into Britain in June 1979, with the first direct elections to the European Parliament. Eighty-one British EuroMPs (or MEPs) were elected, at the same time as 329 other members in eight different countries, making 410 members altogether. Five years later, in June 1984, in the second direct election, 434 MEPs were elected from 10 countries, and they were later joined by a further 84 members from Spain and Portugal, who joined the European Community on 1 January 1986, making a total membership of 518. The third direct election, in which 12 countries voted simultaneously to fill the 518 seats, took place on 15–18 June 1989.

Three of the 81 British Members are elected from Northern Ireland in a three-member constituency which comprises the whole of the province. They are elected by proportional representation, under the STV system, which ensures that two Protestants and one Roman Catholic will be elected. The remaining 78 members are elected in single-member constituencies, under the first-past-the-post system, just as in elections to the House of Commons. The Euro-constituencies are much larger of course, comprising an average of eight Parliamentary constituencies joined together. Four Euro-constituencies are in Wales, eight in Scotland and 66 in England.

There is meant to be a uniform electoral system throughout the 12 member states, but so far no agreement has been reached on which system to use, mainly because the British government, and Mrs Thatcher in particular, have been unwilling to adopt a proportional system. The other 11 countries all use proportional representation in different forms, and Britain is very much the odd man out. When the legislation providing for direct elections to the European Parliament was being debated in the House of Commons, the then Labour government of James Callaghan, which depended on Liberal support, did propose a PR system, with party lists on a regional basis. It was turned down in a free vote, on 12 December 1977, by 311 votes to 224, with 90 members not voting.

The franchise for the European Parliament is the same as for the House of Commons, except that peers are able to vote, and to stand for election. The parties produce election manifestos which relate to European issues, and in some cases are drawn up jointly with like-minded parties in the other member states. But the elections have essentially been fought as part of the continuing battle of British domestic politics, with the main objective being to register support for, or opposition to, the government of the day.

So far the British public has not shown enormous interest in these elections, and the turn-out has been low (31.8 per cent in both 1978 and 1984, rising to 35.9 per cent in 1989, compared to 75.3 per cent in the 1987 general election). In Northern Ireland the turnout has been much higher (55.6 per cent in 1979, and 48.2 per cent in 1984). The absence of PR in Great Britain has meant that British representation has been much more unbalanced than that of any other member state. No Liberal or SDP member was elected in any of the three elections, despite the fact that the Alliance polled nearly one-fifth of the votes in 1984. The results of the elections are shown in Appendix 10.

One distinctive feature of the Euro-elections has been that money was made available by the European Parliament to help towards parties' election expenses. Much more money was provided in 1984 than in 1979, though it was distributed on a capricious basis. Some 69 per cent of the money was supposed to be paid out in advance, but this was only available to parties already represented in the Parliament. The remaining 31 per cent was paid out afterwards on the basis of percentage votes cast. The result was that, apart from three Northern Irish parties, only the Tories (£2.4 million), the Labour Party (£600 000) and the Scottish National Party (£100 000) received any money in advance, though the Liberals were given £150 000 by other European Liberal parties who were shocked by their exclusion. (The SDP also collected £8000 on account of a Labour MEP who had defected to them.) After the election, the Conservatives collected a further £390 000 and the Labour Party £350 000, while the Liberals got £98 000, the SDP £89 000 and the SNP a further £16 000.[7] In the subsequent Euro-election, in 1989, the parties were again heavily subsidised by the European Parliament, though the grants were distributed on a rather different basis.

REFERENDA

Apart from local polls on such issues as the Sunday opening of cinemas and public houses, referenda were unknown in Britain before the 1970s. They still form no part of the regular decision-making process, but as they have been held on three separate occasions during a period of less than six years, it would not be surprising if more were to follow in the future.

The first referendum was confined to Northern Ireland, and was boycotted by the great majority of Roman Catholic voters. Only 58.7 per cent of the electors voted on 8 March 1973, and of them 98.9 per cent wanted Northern Ireland to remain part of the United Kingdom, while 1.1 per cent supported union with the Republic of Ireland.

A much more significant development was the referendum held on 5 June 1975, in all four parts of the United Kingdom, on continued British membership of the EEC. All four countries voted in favour, the overall vote being 67.2 per cent, on a turnout of 64.5 per cent. During the course of the campaign a small amount of public money was made available to the 'umbrella' organisations which ran the 'Yes' and 'No' campaigns – £125 000 for each side. The Labour government, which had called the referendum, agreed to suspend collective responsibility so that Cabinet Ministers could campaign on both sides – 16 Members supported the pro-EEC and seven the anti-EEC cause.

The 1975 referendum was supposed to be a one-off affair, but four years later, on 1 March 1979, the people of Scotland and Wales were asked to vote on whether they wanted separate elected assemblies for the two countries. The Welsh voted decisively against, and the Scots narrowly in favour, though they failed to achieve the minimum level of 40 per cent of registered voters in favour that the House of Commons had required.

The electorate for referenda has consisted of the Parliamentary electorate plus peers. Judging by experience so far, future referenda, if any, are likely to be held on issues which cut across normal party divisions. At present, there is little evident demand for further referenda, despite the fact that opinion polls during the EEC referendum found them to be popular. There have been spasmodic demands for a referendum on capital punishment, but this has been firmly resisted by the political parties. In practice only the government of the day is in a position to initiate a referendum, and it would need to carry a bill through Parliament to enable it to be held.[8]

Notes and References

1. In the 4 years between the 1983 and 1987 general elections there were 32 by-elections, an average of eight per year, of which six produced changes, or 19 per cent. If the 16 by-elections held in Northern Ireland, because of Unionist members resigning their seats in protest against the Anglo–Irish Agreement, are excluded, there were 16 by-elections, or four per year, of which five produced changes, or 31 per cent.

2. See A. Norman Schofield, *Parliamentary Elections*, Third Edition (London: Shaw and Sons, 1959), pp. 374–76.
3. Though in the latter case the public opinion poll trends, which fully confirmed the adverse by-election results, were probably equally responsible.
4. See Chris Cook and John Ramsden, *By-elections in British Politics* (London: Macmillan, 1973), which includes accounts of many of the most significant by-elections between 1922 and 1973.
5. For instance, the turn-out in the 19 by-elections in the 1979–83 Parliament was, on average, 58.6 per cent. In the 1983 general election it was 72.5 per cent.
6. See A. Norman Schofield, *Local Elections* (London: Chas. Knight, 1962) for the detailed provisions.
7. Detailed accounts of the first two Euro-election campaigns in Britain are given in David Butler and David Marquand, *European Elections and British Politics* (London: Macmillan, 1981) and David Butler and Paul Jowett, *Party Strategies in Britain: A Study of the 1984 European Elections* (London: Macmillan, 1985). See also a special issue of *Electoral Studies*, December 1984, vol. 3, no. 3.
8. On referenda in general see David Butler and Austin Ranney (eds), *Referendums: A Comparative Study of Practice and Theory* (Washington DC: American Enterprise Institute, 1978). On the EEC referendum see David Butler and Uwe Kitzinger, *The 1975 Referendum* (London: Macmillan, 1976), Anthony King, *Britain Says Yes* (Washington DC: American Enterprise Institute, 1977) and Philip Goodhart, *Full-Hearted Consent* (London: Davis-Poynter, 1976).

12 Opinion Polls

Apart from television, the most important new factor which has influenced elections in the post-war period has been the public opinion polls. No politician worth his salt is now ignorant of the latest state of the parties, as revealed by any one of half a dozen polls; and at closely fought by-elections the predictions of the pollsters receive incomparably more attention than the pronouncements of the candidates.

This is all a comparatively recent development. On the eve of the 1945 general election the Gallup poll reported in the *News Chronicle* a Labour lead over the Conservatives of six per cent. Nobody took the slightest notice of this; least of all the *News Chronicle*. So far from predicting a runaway Labour victory, the political correspondent of that paper wrote that 'the final result may well prove very near a stalemate'. The most popular prediction in the other papers was a Conservative majority of 'around one hundred', and none of them mentioned the Gallup poll forecast. The lack of interest in the Gallup predictions in 1945 is in itself a commentary on British insularity, for nine years previously the methods of public opinion polls had been sensationally vindicated in an American presidential election.

The man who introduced opinion polling into Britain was Dr Henry Durant. In 1937 he set up the British Institute of Public Opinion, normally known as the Gallup Poll, under the sponsorship of the *News Chronicle*, which published its findings from 1938 to 1960. The British Gallup poll has close connections with its American namesake, and often co-operates with it and other Gallup affiliates in international surveys, but it has complete financial and managerial independence.

Gallup has carried out surveys of political opinion nearly every month since October 1938, has predicted the result of every general election since 1945 and of some 100 by-elections. As well as the regular questions on voting intention, a large number of further questions of a socio-political nature are included in Gallup questionnaires, which often yield valuable evidence of changing public attitudes over the years. Since the demise of the *News Chronicle* in 1960, Gallup findings have been published in *The Daily Telegraph* and the *Sunday Telegraph*.

The political polling undertaken by Gallup is only a small part of its work, though as it is so prominently publicised it acts as a standing advertisement for the commercial market research which it undertakes, and which accounts for 90 per cent of its turnover. The same applies to most of the other polling organisations which also do political polling on behalf of clients, whether they be newspapers, broadcasting organisations or political parties. Currently, five organisations in addition to Gallup are regularly active in the field. The longest standing of these is National Opinion Polls Ltd (NOP), founded in 1958 as a subsidiary company of Associated Newspapers. Its findings normally appear in the *Daily Mail* and the *Mail on Sunday*.

The Harris Research Centre, which is an offshoot of the American-based Louis Harris polling organisation, has taken over Opinion Research Centre (ORC), founded in 1965 by T. F. Thompson and Humphrey Taylor, with the Conservative Party as its first major client. Marplan, a subsidiary of McCann Erickson Advertising, started political polling in 1968, and after working for a variety of clients has produced polls mostly for *The Guardian* in recent years. The most active polling organisation is now clearly Mori (Market and Opinion Research International), run by an ebullient American pollster, Robert Worcester, whose clients include *The Times* and the *Sunday Times*, as well as the Labour Party for whom he has conducted private polling since 1970. The most recently established of the commercial polling companies is Audience Selection Ltd (ASL), a subsidiary of AGB Research, which specialises in telephone polls. It has polled for *The Sun*, and on a small scale for the Social Democratic Party. The final predictions of each of the main commercial polls, in 1987, are shown in Table 12.1. In the 1987 general election, the BBC television *Newsnight* programme established its own polling organisation, depending on social science students as interviewers, which carried out a series of polls on a panel basis (see page 213, below). Other polling organisations, notably Research Services Ltd, and the *Daily Express* Poll of Public Opinion, which was wound up in 1969, were active in earlier elections.

Between general elections, when there is less media interest, fewer polls are published, but four organisations – Gallup, Mori, NOP and Marplan – continue to conduct monthly surveys which are published in newspapers and, in more detail, in private subscription newsletters. Other polling organisations conduct once-off polls from time to time when they are commissioned to do so.

TABLE 12.1   *Record of the final polls: 1987 election*[†]

Poll by:	For:	Con.	Lab.	Alln. error	Ave.	Gap on swing	Error	F/cast on swing	Error
		(%)	(%)	(%)	(%)	(%)	(%)	(%)	(%)
Harris	TV-am	42	35	21	2.0	7	4	4.5	+2.0
Gallup	D.Tel.	41	34	23.5	1.5	7	4	4.5	+2.0
Marplan	Guard.	42	35	21	2.0	7	4	4.5	+2.0
NOP(Adj.)	Indep.	42	35	21	2.0	7	4	4.5	+2.0
ASL(Tele)	Sun	43	34	21	1.3	9	2	3.5	+1.0
MORI	Times	44	32	22	0.7	12	1	2.0	−0.5
Result of vote		43	32	23	—	11	—	2.5	—
Poll average		42	34	22	1.6	8	3	3.5	+1
Difference		−1	+2	−1	—	−3	—	−1	—

[†] Reprinted by kind permission from David Butler and Dennis Kavanagh, *The British General Election of 1987* (London: Macmillan, 1988) p. 132.

The normal national sample of each poll includes around 1000 respondents. During election campaigns, however, larger samples are by no means infrequent, particularly when the result seems likely to be close. In the past these have sometimes approached 4000, though in the 1983 and 1987 elections, when there was very little doubt that the Conservatives would win, most samples were of 2000 or less.

For the man in the street, the main interest in opinion polls is in whether they can succeed in picking the winner at a general election. In this respect the polls have a better record than they are often credited with. Apart from the old *Daily Express* poll, which few people including its proprietors took seriously, and which had the misfortune to pick the losing side twice, it has only been in 1970 (see page 159 below) that most of the polls have gone wrong. In February 1974, a hideously close contest, all the polls predicted that the Conservatives would win the most votes. They did, but owing to the vagaries of the British electoral system the Labour Party won more seats and formed the new government. The polls have never sought to translate their vote predictions into seats, which is not a calculation which can be made with precision.

The pollsters themselves do not claim that their polls should be any more accurate than plus or minus three per cent for each party's support, which means that in measuring the *gap* between two parties

TABLE 12.2   *Accuracy of 1987 polls compared to polls in previous elections*[†]

Year	Mean error gap	Average error per party	Number of polls
1964	1.8	1.3	4
1966	3.9	1.7	4
1970	6.7	2.6	5
1974 Feb.	2.5	2.2	6
1974 Oct.	4.2	1.6	4
1979	1.7	1.0	5
1983	4.8	1.7	7
1987	3.0	1.6	6
Average	3.6	1.7	5

Calculated for major parties (Conservative, Labour, and Alliance) only.
[†] Reprinted by kind permission from Richard Rose, 'Opinion Polls as Feedback Mechanisms', in Austin Ranney (ed.), *Britain at the Polls 1983* (Washington DC: American Enterprise Institute, 1985) p. 132.

the error should not be more than six per cent. Table 12.2 shows that in seven out of the last eight elections the *average* final forecast by the polls fell within this margin of error. Only in 1970 was it exceeded, and in this election four out of five polls finished up predicting the wrong winner.

The margin of error for by-elections and for individual constituencies in general elections is much larger, and there have been several examples of poll predictions being far out of line with the actual result. The most recent was the Brecon and Radnor by-election of July 1985, where the polls had shown the Labour candidate to be well in the lead, but the Liberal captured the seat.

There are good reasons why it is more difficult to get an accurate result in a single constituency than in a national sample. A scratch organisation must be set up on each occasion, and there are no previous poll results for the constituency against which to check trends. Furthermore in a national poll errors in one area tend to be cancelled out by others, in the opposite direction, elsewhere. Above all there is no way of accurately forecasting the turn-out at a by-election and of relating it to voting intention.

Things are made worse by the refusal or inability of most newspapers which sponsor local polls to provide sufficient funds for a large enough sample to be interviewed. In theory, as the electorate of the average constituency is less than 60 000, a much smaller absolute sample should yield comparable results to the minimum of 1000 which is normally regarded as essential for national surveys. In practice it does not work out like that, and there are reasons for believing that 1000 is the minimum necessary to get good results in individual constituencies. Many constituency surveys involve no more than 300–400 interviews, so it is not really surprising that some of the predictions have been hopelessly wrong. But even the best conducted local polls have shown margins of error much greater than in national forecasts.

From 1945 onwards the fame and prestige of the polls steadily increased (though in 1948, as in other countries, there was a marked setback due to the United States' polls' fiasco in picking Dewey to beat Truman in the Presidential election!).

In some respects, the 1970 British general election was a re-run of the 1948 experience in America. The Labour Party was continuously ahead in the polls from the beginning of the campaign, and the almost universal expectation was that it was going to win. The polls did not stop two weeks ahead of polling day, but all except one polling organisation (ORC) completed their interviewing at least two days before polling day ORC re-interviewed some of its respondents on election eve, and found clear evidence of last-minute switching to the Conservatives. It adjusted its figures accordingly, and forecast a Conservative win by one per cent: their actual lead over Labour was 2.4 per cent. What caused the last-minute swing is uncertain, but two events stand out. On the Sunday before the election the England football team was unexpectedly knocked out of the World Cup, a shattering blow to national morale which may well have damaged the Labour government's standing. More directly relevant was the publication the following day of misleadingly bad monthly trade figures which undermined Labour's claim to have solved the balance of payments problem.

Apart from failing to pick the winner, the other main cause for scepticism over the polls is that on occasion different polls produce strikingly different findings in surveys which are published on the same day or in the same week. To some extent, the reasons for the disparities between the polls are still a puzzle, but for the most part they can be explained by the facts that the polls are seldom strictly comparable because their fieldwork is not usually done during exactly the same period and that the polls use different sampling methods. At this point it should perhaps be stressed that the size of the sample is less important than its representative nature. A badly drawn sample of two million can be much less accurate than a well constructed one of a thousand or so, as was demonstrated in the 1936 presidential election in the United States, when the *Literary Digest* poll, with 2 376 533 respondents, predicted a landslide victory for the Republican candidate, while Gallup accurately forecast an easy win for Roosevelt.

There are two principal methods of constructing a polling sample. A *random* sample consists of taking every hundredth or thousandth name from the election register and calling on voters in their own homes. With a *quota* sample, interviewers are instructed to contact so many voters of each sex, age group, occupation and social class, worked out in proportion to the total population. Neither method provides a perfect sample, but they have different shortcomings. Under the quota method, by which people are often interviewed in the street, it is the elderly infirm who are left out. In a random sample, in which people are interviewed in their own homes, young people who tend to spend most of their time out are invariably under-represented. The random sample, which involves contacting named individuals and calling back several times if they are out, is much more expensive than the quota system. The consensus of opinion used to be that random samples were more reliable, as in theory they certainly should be. In practice however they failed to produce any better results. Because of this, and because of growing dissatisfaction with the accuracy of the election register, random sampling has now effectively been abandoned. In both the 1983 and 1987 elections all the polls used quota samples.

Occasional marked variations between the polls should not cause concern; indeed, it would be more suspicious if they were always in agreement. When there are consistent differences it is probably safer to be guided by the *average* of several polls rather than to depend exclusively on any one of them. The polls could effect improvements in their methods which should ensure a higher degree of accuracy. Such improvements (notably the employment of full-time trained interviewers in place of untrained part-timers) would be expensive, and it is unrealistic to criticise the polls for failing to implement them. The blame should rather attach to their clients, who seem to be quite happy to receive findings on the cheap.

At the time of the 1983 election, about 50 000 interviews in all were conducted by the polls, at a total cost to the newspapers and broadcasting authorities of something over £250 000. The average cost per interview worked out at £4–5.[1] In 1987, when more polls were taken than in any previous British election, the level of activity, and probably the overall cost, was half as much again. Perhaps some £400 000 was expended, but the cost per interview was unlikely to have been much higher than in 1983.

Much the greatest stimulus to the polls to improve their methods is the fact that there are several of them. Competition keeps polls on their toes: this is one field where monopoly could be very dangerous.

There has from time to time been well merited criticism about the simplistic ways that some newspapers have presented poll findings, and of the deliberately misleading partial leaking of private polls by political parties. To protect themselves from such criticism, and to force their clients to behave more responsibly, the leading polling organisations drew up a code of practice in May 1970, which was revised in January 1974. This stipulated that all published poll reports should include details of the sampling method used, the sample size and the dates of the fieldwork. It further provided that if private poll findings were leaked, full details of the poll should be made publicly available.[2] Since then there has been a noticeable improvement in the presentation of poll findings by newspapers, but there have continued to be shortcomings, particularly in the popular press. This, and evidence of more serious misuse of polls in some other countries, led the present author to argue in 1979 for the appointment of some independent authority, analogous to the Press Council, to keep a watchful eye on the activities of the polling organisations and their clients.[3]

Some critics of opinion polls have suggested that they may create a bandwagon effect in favour of the party which they report to be in the lead. Others, rather more plausibly, have hypothesised an underdog effect, arguing that some voters may be put off voting for a party which seemed to be well in the lead. Such an effect, if it exists, could have influenced the results of the two narrowly contested elections in 1974, depriving the Tories of a victory in February and reducing to a minimal level the predicted Labour majority in October. A leading pollster has privately told the present author that this was the case, but the evidence for this is inconclusive.[4]

There have been periodic attempts to ban the publication of opinion polls during election campaigns, and in 1968 the Speaker's Conference on Electoral Law recommended a 72-hour ban before polling day. The then Labour government refused to act on this recommendation, but 17 years later, in October 1985, the House of Commons rejected a Private Member's Bill to impose a ban, by the narrow margin of 128 votes to 124. A further Bill, introduced under the Ten-Minute Rule, was actually approved by 116 voters to 103 in February 1987, but made no further Parliamentary progress. Foreign experience has however shown that such bans are unworkable,[5] as well as being objectionable in principle as being designed to deprive voters of information which would in any case be available to promoters of private polls, including the political parties themselves. The former Liberal MP, Clement Freud, aptly commented on the 1985 proposal: 'the effect of the bill would be rather like banning meteorologists from forecasting the weather a week before a garden party in case anyone might be put off from going'.

Whether the polls to any great extent affect the way in which people vote, they clearly influence the morale of party activists, though even here the effect it has on their efforts cannot easily be predicted. A disappointing poll may lead to a slackening of effort or to gestures of defiance which give a sharper edge to a party's campaign – a favourable one may equally lead to complacency or renewed dedication. More importantly, polls have a very considerable influence on the behaviour of politicians. The importance of polls in informing the Prime Minister of favourable occasions for holding a general election, and even more importantly, warning him off unfavourable ones, has already been stressed in an earlier chapter.

But the whole tenor of recent election campaigns has been dominated by opinion poll findings, especially as the great majority of voters now have a reasonable idea of what the polls are saying. The 1979, 1983 and 1987 election campaigns were all fought in the knowledge that the Conservatives were a long way ahead and were virtually certain winners. In 1983 the battle for second place, in terms of votes if not in seats, between Labour and the Alliance attracted disproportionate attention solely because of the steady flow of poll findings. Indeed the Alliance parties, and before then the Liberals, have been peculiarly dependent on the polls for their credibility: the better their standing in the polls the more likely are they to attract votes. Conversely, adverse poll findings, as in the 1987 election, normally have a depressant effect on their prospects.

Although the opinion polls have established such an important role for themselves in British politics, in one respect they have played a smaller part in Britain than in the United States and some other countries. This is in the use of privately commissioned polls by the parties and by individual political leaders. Largely because of the absence of primary elections, the commissioning of polls by politi-

cians is unknown in Britain, and is likely to remain so. Even the
parties themselves were long cautious in their use of opinion polling,
and they used it mainly to test propaganda themes and for copy-
testing of posters, newspaper advertisements and other visual material.

The first campaign to be based to any significant degree on material
gleaned from the polls was that launched by the Conservatives before
the 1959 election. Labour was slower off the mark, but relied to a
similar extent on privately commissioned polls for its run-up campaign to the 1964 election. Since 1964 the Conservatives have retained the services of Opinion Research Centre, now part of the
Harris Research Centre, which originally worked almost exclusively
for them. Its former co-director, Humphrey Taylor, one of the wisest
heads in the polling world, has interpreted the polling findings to
Tory leaders during each election campaign.

The Tories have shown a highly professional attitude to polls, and
have integrated the use of their privately commissioned polls, as well
as the analysis of the mass of material available from the public polls,
into all their election planning. The Labour Party, despite having
retained the services of Mori's shrewd director, Robert Worcester,
and of his organisation, during each election from 1970 onwards,
have usually made less effective use of their private polls. This is
partly due to the suspicion with which Labour leaders such as Michael Foot (but not Harold Wilson) have regarded polls, and partly
due to the more amateur and internally divisive nature of the Labour
organisation. In 1987 there was a distinct improvement, and Labour
not only spent much more money than previously on its private polls
but made much more intelligent use of their findings.

The former Alliance parties were enthusiastic followers of the
polls, but lacked the resources to commission many private polls for
their own use. Whereas the Conservatives have been spending some
£100 000 a year on polls in recent years, and the Labour Party about
£85 000, and both parties spent an extra £120 000 during the 1987
election campaign, it is doubtful if the Alliance spent as much as
one-tenth of these amounts.[6]

Private polling has been unfavourably received in some quarters,
and allegations have been made that politicians have subordinated
their principles to the desire to win votes. Such critics appear to be
ignorant of the manner in which politicians make decisions. It is in
fact a totally unrealistic view that polls can tell a politician what
policies he ought to adopt. Any political leader who allowed them to
do so would soon develop a reputation for irresolution and lack of

consistency. The most that a poll can do for a politician or a party is to help them put over, in an effective way, the policies on which they have already decided, and to determine which policies should be stressed to particular target audiences. It is difficult to see anything improper or dishonourable in this.

Notes and References

1. See David Butler and Dennis Kavanagh, *The British General Election of 1983* (London: Macmillan, 1984) pp. 129–30.
2. See Robert M. Worcester (ed.), *Political Opinion Polling: An International Review* (London: Macmillan, 1983) pp. 109–10 for the full text of the Code of Practice.
3. 'Poll watcher wanted', *The Economist*, 13 January 1979, p. 13. Like all the articles in *The Economist*, this was unsigned.
4. See Worcester, *op. cit.*, pp. 106–7 for a discussion on the influence that polls have on voters.
5. Dick Leonard, 'Belgian Leaders should read "Areopagitica"', *Wall Street Journal (Europe)*, 18 October 1985. See also Dick Leonard, 'Opinion Polls can't be Banned', *St. Louis Post-Dispatch*, 6 December 1985.
6. Figures from Butler and Kavanagh *op. cit.*, pp. 140, 144. See Chapter 7 of this work, and also Richard Rose, 'Opinion Polls as Feedback Mechanisms' in Austin Ranney (ed.), *Britain at the Polls 1983* (Washington DC: American Enterprise Institute, 1985) pp. 108–38, for detailed assessments of the role of opinion polls in the 1983 general election.

13 How People Vote

The British voter is subjected to a heavy barrage of propaganda from all the major parties – and to occasional salvoes from minor groups and independents – during election campaigns, and to a lesser degree at other times. Earlier chapters of this book have sought to describe the various ways in which the parties seek to influence public opinion. This chapter will attempt to discern whether all this activity makes much difference to the way that people vote.

The traditional answer has been 'not much'. The general belief has been that most voters are set in their ways, and are not much influenced by what happens in election campaigns. This belief has been based on the assumption that most voters are profoundly influenced by social class factors, and in particular by the political views of their parents, which in the great majority of cases are bequeathed to their children along with their more worldly possessions. For many years this belief was largely based on conjecture, and inference from the relatively small movement in the party share of votes recorded at each successive general election. Over the past two decades however a great deal of harder evidence has been available, partly from opinion polls but more particularly from the series of election studies, based on in-depth interviewing, sponsored by the Social Science Research Council (now renamed the Economic and Social Research Council) since 1963.

This series, known as the British Election Surveys, had up to 1983 involved interviews with nearly 20 000 voters during seven general elections, and had produced three major studies,[1] as well as a substantial amount of secondary literature.[2] Much of the argument in this chapter is based on the successive findings of these surveys.[3] In part, these have confirmed traditional beliefs, though in many particulars they have challenged them. They have also suggested that the behaviour of voters has been modified over time, and that a much higher proportion of voters are now prepared to switch their votes than was the case 20 years ago.

One of the first findings of the British Election Surveys (BES) was an emphatic confirmation of the belief that most children voted the same way as their parents had done. Respondents were asked if they could remember how their parents had voted during their own childhood and were then asked their present voting intention. The

TABLE 13.1   *Present party preference by parents' Conservative or Labour preference*[†]

| Respondent's own present preference | Parents' partisanship | | |
	Both parents Conservative	Parents divided	Both parents Labour
Conservative	75%	37%	10%
Labour	14	49	81
Liberal	8	10	6
Other	—	—	—
None	3	4	3
Total	100%	100%	100%

[†] Reprinted by kind permission from David Butler and Donald Stokes, *Political Change in Britain* (London: Macmillan, 1969) p. 48.

result is shown in Table 13.1. David Butler and Donald Stokes, who were the authors of the first of the BES studies, published in 1969, constructed on the basis of their detailed findings on parental influence on voting a theory of political generations. This indicated a long-term shift from Conservative to Labour as a result of demographic changes. The reasoning behind this was that it is only since 1945 that the number of Labour voters has been approximately equal to the number of Conservatives. People who started voting before 1945 were much more likely to have Conservative-voting than Labour-voting parents. As these older voters died off, the proportion of 'hereditary' Conservatives in the electorate was bound to decline, while new generations of voters entering the electorate at the age of 18 were much more likely to be the offspring of Labour-voting parents.[4]

If this 'generational' effect was the only factor at work, it is clear that Labour would do better at every succeeding election until the 1990s, and the Conservatives worse, which has not been the case, at least since 1970. The later BES studies have concentrated more on probing what other factors have played a part, and in particular whether the traditional link between social class and voting is becoming weaker. Substantial evidence was produced to suggest that this was in fact the case, and that the simple dichotomy of middle class-Tory and working class-Labour was being attenuated.

Bo Särlvik and Ivor Crewe, who produced the second major BES study, in 1983,[5] argued not only that the working class was becoming more Tory and the middle class more Labour, but that long-term partisan commitments were getting weaker for a large number of voters. Table 13.2 shows how support among Labour identifiers for Labour principles had declined over a ten-year-period, while Table 13.3 revealed a strikingly high level of support for professed Tory objectives among Labour voters. Figure 13.1 shows that the strength of partisan commitment among both Tory and Labour identifiers was weakening during this period. Later studies by the same authors showed this trend continuing up until 1983.

Särlvik and Crewe described this process as one of dealignment, and suggested that it was a reason behind the much larger swings in by-elections which have occurred in the period since 1966. The authors of the third BES study,[6] Anthony Heath, Roger Jowell and John Curtice, however challenge the thesis that class divisions are

TABLE 13.2 *Falling support for Labour principles*

	All Labour identifiers			'Core' Labour identifiers		
	1964 %	Feb 1974 %	Change 1964– Feb '74 %	1964 %	Feb 1974 %	Change 1964– Feb '74 %
In favour of nationalising more industries	57	50	–7	64	50	–14
In favour of spending more on social services	89	61	–28	92	57	–35
In favour of retaining close ties between trade unions and the Labour party	38	29	–9	50	34	–16
Whose sympathies are generally for strikers	37	23	–14	33	25	–8
Who do not believe that the trade unions have 'too much power'	59	44	–15	74	52	–22
Perceiving 'a great deal' of difference between the parties	49	33	–16	62	41	–21
Average (mean)	55	40	–15	63	43	–20

SOURCE *The Economist*, 11 March 1978

TABLE 13.3 *Labour voters on Tory aims*

| | Should the next government attempt to achieve these objectives? | | |
	Should %	Should not %	Don't know %
Reduce violent crime and vandalism	95	3	2
Reduce Supplementary Benefit for strikers, on assumption that they are getting strike pay from their unions	63	30	7
End secondary picketing by strikers	78	14	8
Reduce income tax, especially for the higher paid	52	45	3
Give council house tenants the right to buy their homes, with discounts for people who have lived in them for three years or more	75	20	5
Reduce the number of civil servants	70	22	8
Sell off parts of some state owned companies	40	49	11

SOURCE   The *Observer*, 22 April 1979

becoming less important as a factor in voting. They argue that what has happened is not so much a decline in class influence as a change in the relative size of the different classes. Once account is taken of this, the class connection with voting is as strong as ever, they assert.[7] Table 13.4 shows the substantial changes in class sizes that occurred between 1964 and 1983, with the salariat increasing by half, and the working class declining from nearly half the electorate to barely a third. Table 13.5 shows how people in these five different class categories voted in 1983. The Conservative Party held a large lead in the four higher groupings (particularly the petty bourgeoisie, defined as 'farmers, small proprietors and own-account manual workers' or 'independents'), while Labour remained well ahead in the residual working class. (The Alliance support was more evenly distributed.)

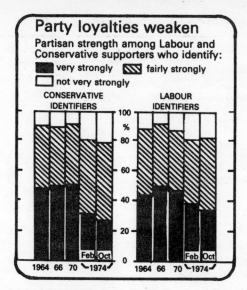

FIGURE 13.1   *Party loyalties weaken*

SOURCE   *The Economist*, 11 March 1978

TABLE 13.4   *Class composition of the electorate: 1964 and 1983*[†]

	1964	1983
	%	%
Salariat	18	27
Routine nonmanual	18	24
Petty bourgeoisie	7	8
Foremen and technicians	10	7
Working class	47	34
Total	100	100
N =	1475	3790

[†] Reprinted by kind permission from Anthony Heath, Roger Jowell and John Curtice, *How Britain Votes* (Oxford: Pergamon Press, 1985) p. 36.

It should be noted that the class categorisation adopted by Heath *et al.* is different from that used in the great majority of voting studies, which is based on standard market research designations. These divide the population into six occupational categories, as follows:

TABLE 13.5 *Head of household's class and vote*[†]

Head of household's class	Conservative	Labour	Alliance	Others	
Salariat	54	14	31	1	100% (N = 923)
Routine nonmanual	49	24	25	2	100% (N = 495)
Petty bourgeoisie	69	13	17	1	100% (N = 291)
Foremen and technicians	45	28	26	1	100% (N = 266)
Working class	30	48	21	1	100% (N = 1089)

[†] Reprinted by kind permission from Anthony Heath, Roger Jowell and John Curtice, op. cit., p. 27.

A Higher managerial or professional
B Lower managerial or administrative
C1 Skilled or supervisory non-manual, lower non-manual
C2 Skilled manual
D Unskilled manual
E Residual, on pension or other state benefit

Table 13.6 shows how the 1983 vote divided, accordingly to this classification. All studies agree that occupational differences are more significant politically than differences in income, as such, though there is a considerable overlap, the more prestigious occupations being normally, but not invariably, better paid. Heath *et al.* hypothesised also that the actual working situation was of importance, in particular whether a voter was in a position of authority over others and whether he was directly exposed to market forces in earning his or her livelihood. In both cases this proved likely to sharply increase the probability of voting Conservative. Hence the 'petty bourgeoisie' class in their findings, which is drawn effectively

TABLE 13.6 *Social grade and vote*[†]

Social grade	Conservative	Labour	Alliance	Others	
Grade A	69	7	23	1	100% (N = 160)
Grade B	55	13	31	1	100% (N = 764)
Grade C1	54	20	24	2	100% (N = 595)
Grade C2	38	39	22	1	100% (N = 930)
Grade D	30	47	22	1	100% (N = 609)

[†] Reprinted by kind permission from Anthony Heath, Roger Jowell and John Curtice, *op. cit.*, p. 26.

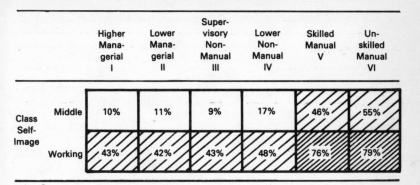

		Higher Mana-gerial I	Lower Mana-gerial II	Super-visory Non-Manual III	Lower Non-Manual IV	Skilled Manual V	Un-skilled Manual VI
Class Self-Image	Middle	10%	11%	9%	17%	46%	55%
	Working	43%	42%	43%	48%	76%	79%

FIGURE 13.2   *Proportion Labour among major party supporters by occupational level and class self-image, 1963* [†]

[†]Reprinted by kind permission from David Butler and Donald Stokes, *Political Change in Britain* (London: Macmillan, 1969) p. 78.

from among the B, C1 and C2 categories, but contains a much higher incidence of Conservative voters than any of these three groupings.

One striking finding has been that subjective class feelings are a clearer indication of political partisanship than a voter's objective position in the social system. That is to say that people with middle class occupations who regard themselves as working class have been much more likely to vote Labour, while the reverse is the case with voters in working class occupations who regard themselves as middle class. This is illustrated by Figure 13.2, drawn from the Butler-Stokes survey.

Another important factor is trade union membership, with members being much more likely to vote Labour than non-members, irrespective of their occupational level (Table 13.7).

Another significant influence on voting, according to many studies, is housing, with owner occupiers being more likely to vote Tory and council tenants Labour, irrespective of class differences. Table 13.8 demonstrates this clearly in relation to the 1983 election.

Where they live seems to be a factor in influencing how people vote. As everybody knows, there are profound regional differences in voting patterns, with the Conservatives and the Alliance being much stronger in the South of England, and Labour in Scotland, Wales and the North. Figures for 1983 from the Heath study illustrate this point (Table 13.9). To a large extent, these figures can be explained by social class differences between the regions, but this is far from being

TABLE 13.7　*Support for labour among union and non-union families by occupational grade, 1964[†]*

	Super-visory non-manual III	Lower non-manual IV	Skilled manual V	Non-skilled manual VI
Proportion voting Labour				
Among union families	42%	56%	72%	78%
Among non-union families	18%	20%	53%	62%
Difference	24%	36%	19%	16%
	(n = 220)	(n = 121)	(n = 519)	(n = 314)

[†] Reprinted by kind permission from David Butler and Donald Stokes, *Political Change in Britain*, op. cit., p. 156.

TABLE 13.8　*Housing, class and vote[†]*

	Conservative	Labour	Alliance	Others	
Salariat:					
Owner-occupiers	56	12	31	1	100% (N = 744)
Private tenants	54	5	34	7	100% (N = 39)
Council tenants	33	36	28	3	100% (N = 71)
Intermediate classes:					
Owner-occupiers	59	14	26	1	100% (N = 844)
Private tenants	54	23	18	5	100% (N = 112)
Council tenants	25	50	23	2	100% (N = 252)
Working class:					
Owner-occupiers	39	37	23	1	100% (N = 463)
Private tenants	28	47	22	3	100% (N = 83)
Council tenants	20	62	17	1	100% (N = 441)

[†] Reprinted by kind permission from Anthony Heath, Roger Jowell and John Curtice, op. cit., p. 46.

the whole story. There is, apparently, a 'neighbourhood effect', which means that even working class voters in the South are more inclined to vote Conservative, and middle class voters in the north and in Scotland and Wales to vote Labour. Similarly there is a marked urban–rural division, with urban voters, irrespective of class, being more likely to vote Labour, and rural voters more inclined to vote Conservative. People living in predominantly middle class

TABLE 13.9   *Region and vote*[†]

	Conservative	Labour	Alliance	Others	
Scotland	22	45	23	10	100% (N = 280)
Wales	34	40	23	3	100% (N = 167)
North	39	37	24	0	100% (N = 812)
Midlands	52	27	22	0	101% (N = 573)
South	53	19	28	0	100% (N = 1217)

[†]Reprinted by kind permission from Anthony Heath, Roger Jowell and John Curtice, op. cit., p. 75.

TABLE 13.10   *Class, neighbourhood, region and vote*[†]

	Percentage voting Conservative	
	North	South
Salaried individuals		
in salaried wards	54 (78)	54 (269)
in mixed wards	51 (40)	60 (140)
in working-class wards	40 (81)	— (14)
All salaried individuals	48 (199)	57 (423)
Intermediate-class individuals		
in salaried wards	56 (87)	63 (251)
in mixed wards	60 (79)	53 (236)
in working-class wards	39 (142)	40 (28)
All intermediate-class individuals	49 (308)	57 (515)
Working-class individuals		
in salaried wards	46 (22)	49 (106)
in mixed wards	31 (57)	40 (145)
in working-class wards	20 (235)	19 (40)
All working class individuals	24 (314)	40 (291)
Figures in brackets give cell sizes		

[†]Reprinted by kind permission from Anthony Heath, Roger Jowell and John Curtice, op. cit., p. 83.

neighbourhoods are more likely to be Tory voters, whatever their own class background, and those in working class areas Labour. The separate effects of region and neighbourhood are indicated in Table 13.10.

TABLE 13.11   *Class, education and vote*[†]

	Conservative	Labour	Alliance	Others		
Salariat						
degree	42	16	41	1	100%	(N = 131)
'O' level or above	54	12	33	1	100%	(N = 501)
below 'O' level	60	17	22	2	101%	(N = 231)
Intermediate classes						
degree	—	—	—	—	—	(N = 21)
'O' level or above	57	17	25	1	100%	(N = 441)
below 'O' level	49	25	24	2	100%	(N = 748)
Working class						
degree	—	—	—	—	—	(N = 4)
'O' level or above	40	36	22	2	100%	(N = 169)
below 'O' level	28	52	20	1	101%	(N = 815)

[†]Reprinted by kind permission from Anthony Heath, Roger Jowell and John Curtice, op. cit., p. 67.

Education is a more complicated factor, as its effect seems to vary according to social class. Among the working class the better somebody is educated the more likely they are to vote Conservative. In the middle class, the better educated, and particularly those who have benefited from higher education, are less likely to vote Conservative (see Table 13.11). Heath *et al.* surmise that this may be because higher education exposes people to 'liberal values' (on such issues as the death penalty, free speech, defence expenditure, the common market and stiff jail sentences) which are more likely to lead to people voting Labour or Alliance rather than Conservative.

For many years polls and electoral studies showed women to be more Conservative than men, but this may be entirely explicable by the fact that there happened to be many more women among other groups (mainly pre-1945 voters) which were predisposed to vote Conservative. Most of the pre-1945 voters are now dead, and by 1983 there was no evidence of any significant gender-related differences in voting (the Heath *et al.* survey figures for 1983 showed 46 per cent of men and 44 per cent of women voting Tory).

One fact that stands out concerning all the factors discussed so far is that the correlation between any one of them and voting intention is in every case a lot less than 100 per cent. Although each factor may predispose an individual to vote in a certain way, large numbers of them do not in fact do so. Should they therefore be regarded as 'deviants', or is there another important countervailing factor at work which in large measure cancels out these particular influences? Heath *et al.* have no doubt that there is, and that this factor is ideology, or the settled opinions of voters.

In other words, voters are thinking animals, who are not the mere creatures of economic determinism. If their own values or beliefs or perceptions conflict with their economic circumstances they are fully capable of giving them priority. If no conflict arises, their beliefs naturally reinforce the economic influences, and people to whom this applies form the bedrock support for the Conservative and Labour Parties. Where there is a conflict, however, one is likely to encounter less extreme partisanship, a willingness to consider the claims of the other side, perhaps to vary one's vote from one election to the next, and a greater propensity to support alternatives, such as the Alliance, or the SNP in Scotland. No researcher has been able to demonstrate mathematically the relative strength of economic and ideological factors, but Anthony Heath asserts categorically that 'values and perceptions explain much more of the variance in vote than does social class, but then they always have done'.[8]

All the factors discussed so far, insofar as they influence consciously or unconsciously the actions of voters, are permanent or long-term and are therefore likely to affect the orientation or identification of voters over a long period. Other factors, such as the impact of individual candidates or party leaders, the effect of campaign techniques, the success or failure of governments in dealing with transient issues, may well affect actual decisions on how to vote in particular elections. These factors may confirm or challenge the long-term identification of voters. Moreover a voter who consistently votes contrary to his long-term identification because of short-term factors may well end up by changing his identification as well.

The greater volatility of voters – in other democracies as well as in Britain – suggests that long-term identification may be becoming weaker, a thesis strongly supported by the Särlvik–Crewe study, which showed a declining number of voters who identified with one or other party, and a diminishing sense of commitment even among identifiers.[9] This weakening sense of identification has provided an opportunity for the Liberal–Social Democratic Alliance, without however guaranteeing its success.

It has been suggested that rising living standards and improved educational opportunities have resulted in fewer voters being influenced by class considerations. According to this theory a new generation of 'postmaterialist voters' has arrived, 'people who have been brought up in an economically secure environment . . . who will grow up to place greater emphasis on higher needs such as freedom of speech and a humane society'. Heath *et al.* credit the American writers R. Inglehart and A. Maslow with this concept:

> Maslow postulates that man has a hierarchy of needs: needs for food and shelter come at the bottom of the hierarchy and tend to receive highest priority until they are satisfied. Once they are satisfied people move on to higher needs culminating in ones such as 'self-actualisation'. Inglehart claims to follow this account and argues that people who experienced 'formative affluence' will grow up to place more emphasis on values such as democracy and freedom of speech.[10]

Heath *et al.* see the development of 'postmaterialist values' as a countervailing factor to the advantage that the Conservative Party might otherwise expect to gain from the numerical decline of the working class.

Another theory, derived from the writings of another American author, Anthony Downs, [11] sees the parties as competitors in a market place, modifying their offerings in response to the preferences of the customers (voters). This theory is also explored by Heath *et al.*, in particular the evidence that the Labour Party had wilfully refused to modify its policies in the direction indicated by voter preferences. [12] What is probable is that a growing number of voters are becoming more susceptible to short-term influences.

A perceptive analysis of the electorate was made by Dr Mark Abrams as long ago as 1964. Referring to the Labour and Conservative parties, he then wrote:

> 'each party can rely upon the unwavering support of approximately one-third of the electorate. Their devotion is unaffected by any shortcomings in party leadership, party programme, constituency, candidate or party organisation. . . . The remaining uncommitted one-third of the electorate do not form a homogeneous group. Its members are drawn from both sexes, all social statuses, and all age groups . . . no more than half of them will usually vote.'[13]

This final third of the electorate (sometimes referred to as the floating vote) was made up of a number of overlapping sub-groups. These were Liberal voters, abstainers, lukewarm supporters of either party and genuine floaters. Liberal voters were a much more heterogeneous collection than their Labour or Conservative counterparts. A large proportion of both Labour and Conservative voters were regular supporters of their party. It is doubtful if more than a third of the electors who voted for Liberal candidates regarded themselves as Liberals. The remainder were mostly disgruntled supporters of the larger parties or those who voted Liberal at a particular election because of the personal qualities of the candidate.

Now, over 25 years later, Abrams's analysis is probably still essentially valid, except that the number of unwavering supporters of both the largest parties has undoubtedly declined, so that it is perhaps only about one-half, rather than two-thirds of the electorate, which is permanently committed. The Liberal Democrat vote remains distinctly 'softer' than that of its two larger rivals.

Abstainers are, again, a very mixed group. Some are persistent abstainers, and some only temporary. There are, first, what might be termed 'involuntary' abstainers – those who have been accidentally left off the register, or who have moved and inadvertently failed to claim a postal vote, or who are ill or who for some other pressing reason genuinely find it difficult to get along to the polling station on election day. At a rough estimate, these might add up to about 12 per cent of the electorate, which leaves an equal number of 'voluntary' abstainers – people who could easily cast their votes but who choose not to do so.

Probably a small proportion of these are discriminating electors who choose not to vote because they do not approve of the candidates or parties which are running in their constituencies. For example, it seems likely that in Scotland in 1979 one-seventh of would-be Liberal voters in constituencies without Liberal candidates stayed at home rather than give their votes to non-Liberals.[14] But the majority of abstainers are among the least discriminating of electors – those who have the least interest in and the smallest knowledge of current political issues. They tend to be concentrated amongst the poorest and least educated sections of the population, the very old, the very young and more among women than among men. Successive polls have shown that among non-voters a higher proportion are sympathetic to Labour than to the Conservatives, and it is generally considered that a high turn-out favours Labour, while a low one is to the advantage of the Tories. Recent evidence suggests that the

TABLE 13.12   *Flow of the vote from 1979 to 1983 (percent of voters)*[†]

Voted in 1983	Conservative	Labour	Alliance	Did not vote	Too young
			Voted in 1979		
Conservative	77	7	14	22	28
Labour	4	63	9	12	17
Alliance	13	22	72	14	20
Other	*	1	*	*	2
Did not vote	6	7	5	52	32
N =	1521	1252	382	357	396

[†] Reprinted by kind permission from Ivor Crewe, 'How to Win a Landslide without Really Trying', in Austin Ranney (ed.), *Britain at the Polls 1983* (Washington DC: American Enterprise Institute, 1985) p. 166.

Liberal Democrats, and the former Alliance parties, also benefit from a high turnout. [15]

Finally, and most elusive, are the people who actually switch their votes from one major party to the other. According to a Gallup Poll survey conducted for the BBC in 1983, which asked people how they had previously voted in 1979, some seven per cent of Labour voters switched over to the Tories, while four per cent of Tories switched to Labour (see Table 13.12). This survey suggested that only some 67 per cent (2129 voters out of 3155) of those who had voted for the Labour, Conservative or Liberal Parties maintained their support unchanged from one election to the next.

But despite the increasing interest which sociologists have, since 1945, shown in elections and in voting habits, relatively little is known about what actually causes people to change their voting allegiances. The same Gallup survey (Table 13.13) suggests that television broadcasts and discussions within the family are the two most important influences at work. There is evidence[16] that many more people switch over between elections rather than during election campaigns. This led the parties to begin their campaigning at a much earlier stage than in the past. The elections of 1959 and 1964 were marked by very heavy expenditure, particularly on the Conservative side, on advertising campaigns launched well before the date that the elections were announced. Such massive expenditure on advertising has however not been maintained in subsequent elections, partly because of the great expenditure involved but also because of accumulating evidence that it is only through television,

TABLE 13.13   *Campaign's effect on vote choice (percent of votes)*[†]

Reason for vote choice	All voters	Late deciders	Loyalists	Switchers
Because of a				
Conservative broadcast on TV	6	14	5	8
Labour broadcast on TV	5	12	5	7
Alliance broadcast on TV	9	26	6	22
Because of a				
Conservative newspaper advert/ poster I saw	1	4	1	2
Labour newspaper advert/ poster I saw	2	5	2	1
Alliance newspaper advert/ poster I saw	1	5	1	4
Because I was persuaded by . . .				
my wife/husband	2	2	2	3
my parents/children	3	4	3	1
somebody at work	1	2	1	1
a party worker	1	5	1	2

[†] Reprinted by kind permission from Ivor Crewe, 'How to Win a Landslide without Really Trying', op. cit., p. 164.
SOURCE   BBC TV/Gallup survey, 8–9 June 1983 ($N = 4, 141$).
NOTE   Question was worded, "When you finally decided which way to vote was it for one or more reasons on this card?"

where political advertising is banned, that a measurable effect could be made on voters.[17]

But the majority of voters seem to be immune to direct influence by the political parties. The different items in a party's programme and the promises which it makes seem to make little difference to people's voting intentions. A glance at the charts produced by the Gallup Poll showing the fluctuations in the level of support of the different parties in the period since 1945 shows less correlation than one might expect with major political events and with the triumphs and disasters of ministers and opposition leaders. A closer examination reveals a high correlation with the general level of economic activity in the country. It was long thought that the unemployment level was much the most sensitive political indicator. Yet the experience in the years following 1979, when a Conservative government presided over a massive increase in unemployment with little apparent adverse effect on its fortunes, cast severe doubt on this belief. It seems rather that a cluster of factors which together add up to a general sense of wellbeing, or its converse, are responsible for shifts in support for governments and opposition parties. Apart from unemployment, these include inflation, mortgage and other interest rates, the balance of payments and the level of the exchange rate. For each of these factors, whether the current trend is up or down is probably more important than its actual level.

Much more than the actual policies on which political parties fight elections, voters may also be influenced by such factors as the personalities of the party leaders, the perceived degree of unity or disunity within a party, its general air of competence or its absence, and the extent to which its approach fits in with the voters' sense of fairness.[18] The voters are also aware of general images, whose roots may go back far into the past. Thus the Labour Party will be seen by its supporters as the party which is opposed to privilege, which is for the welfare state, which cares for ordinary people, and by its opponents as the party of nationalisation and controls, of extravagant financial policies and as the party which is *only* for the workers. The Conservative Party is seen by its supporters as the party for people who want to get on, for business efficiency and for making Britain's voice heard in the world. Its opponents see it as the party of the rich, the privileged and the old-fashioned. The Liberal Democrats are seen as being fresh, open-minded, uncommitted to sectional interests and untainted by governmental failures in the recent past. Their opponents see them as inexperienced, opportunist and unwilling to take sides. Nevertheless a large proportion of voters, though they remain committed to one party or the other, are willing to admit that their opponents have many virtues. Extreme partisanship is rare.[19]

Support for the parties seems sometimes to be governed more by the activities of their natural allies than by what they do themselves. If businessmen are seen to be behaving in an abnormally rapacious manner, or a takeover battle is fought with obvious disregard to the public interest, it is the Conservative Party which suffers. Similarly if trade unions appear to be behaving irresponsibly and, especially if strikes occur which inconvenience the public without at the same time strongly convincing them of the justice of the strikers' case, the Labour Party takes a hard knock. This is rough justice, perhaps, but each party gains considerably in financial and other ways from its alliances so they hardly complain too loudly at the compensating disadvantages.

If the national campaigns of the parties appear to have had only a limited effect on people's voting, what of the campaigns in the constituencies? In the period before the First World War many voters were probably directly influenced by these campaigns. But, as we have seen, the growth of the mass media has shifted attention overwhelmingly away from the individual candidates towards the party leaders. The result has been that neither the personality of the candidate nor the quality of his campaign has much effect on the average voter.

Nearly all authorities agree that virtually no candidate, however outstanding, is worth more than 500 extra votes to his party from one election to the next, and the great majority of candidates are clearly worth much less. This is not true of by-elections, where voters are relieved of the responsibility of helping to choose a government and more of them feel freer to give weight to personality factors. It is also less true of Liberal Democrat and Nationalist candidates than of those representing the two larger parties. But it remains true that in the great majority of constituencies, the most distinguished of statesmen can hope to win very few extra votes than would the most mediocre of the party hacks. If there are constituencies where the personality of the candidate and, even more important, the trouble which he is prepared to take to serve his constituents are still significant factors, they are those in the most remote parts of Scotland and Wales. But there are probably less than a dozen of these remaining. Recent evidence does suggest, however, that the *cumulative* effect of a sitting Member of Parliament, measured over several successive elections, may be rather greater than had been imagined. A good constituency Member may build up personal support over the years, which means that he will poll markedly better than the normal support for his party. Conversely an unpopular Member may do substantially worse, especially if he is elderly and has outstayed his welcome.[20]

Nor does the efficiency of the party machine in the constituencies appear to have much influence on the result. Every party worker is vividly aware of specific voters who were got to the poll *only* because of his powers of persuasion or because he gave them a lift to the poll at the last possible hour. But the sum total of these achievements does not amount to a great deal. The number of people voting in constituencies in which each party has a high level of organisation is only fractionally higher than the turn-out in those constituencies where party organisation is most rudimentary.

One field in which organisation does make a measurable contribution is postal voting. There is no doubt that the Conservatives have been much more successful in registering postal voters than their opponents. As around 2–3 per cent of votes cast in recent general elections have been postal votes, it is clear that in closely contested constituencies postal voters can spell the difference between victory and defeat. It seems highly probable that the Conservatives have gained between five and 15 extra seats at each election since 1950 because of their greater success in this sphere. This may be a small number, but in closely contested elections, such as 1950, 1964 and October 1974, this factor may well have made the difference between a precarious and a reasonably comfortable overall majority for the Labour party.

It is probably inevitable that the Conservatives should gain some advantage from the postal vote. Middle-class voters generally are more aware of their civic rights and more ready to claim them than are manual workers and their families. But the decisive edge which the Conservatives have achieved, which ensures them more than 75 per cent of the postal votes in most constituencies, is a direct result of their more professional organisation. It is here that their ability to employ many more agents than the Labour Party, and to provide them more often with clerical assistance, has paid dividends. Although Labour certainly now shows more awareness of the importance of the postal vote than it did in 1950, it has only very partially succeeded in closing the gap. It is probably true that a big majority of Labour voters who move house or are taken seriously ill in the months preceding a general election do not record their votes. The number of lost Conservative votes is substantially less. The extension of postal voting to holidaymakers, from 1987 onwards, is likely further to increase the Conservative advantage.

Notes and References

1. David Butler and Donald Stokes, *Political Change in Britain* (London: Macmillan, 1974, 2nd edition); Bo Särlvik and Ivor Crewe, *Decade of Dealignment* (Cambridge University Press, 1983); Anthony Heath, Roger Jowell and John Curtice, *How Britain Votes* (Oxford: Pergamon Press, 1985).
2. See the detailed bibliography in Heath, Jowell and Curtice, op cit., pp. 239–46.

3. For a description of the methodology of these surveys see Heath, Jowell and Curtice, op. cit., Appendix 11, pp. 230–4.
4. A strikingly similar 'generational effect' among American voters, which may largely have accounted for a long-term swing from Republican to Democrat, had earlier been detected by Angus Campbell, Philip Converse, Warren Miller and Donald Stokes, *The American Voter* (New York: Wiley, 1960) especially pp. 45–6.
5. Bo Särlvik and Ivor Crewe, op. cit. See also Ivor Crewe, Bo Särlvik and James Alt, 'Partisan Dealignment in Britain 1964–74' in *British Journal of Political Science*, vol. 7, pp. 129–90.
6. Heath, Jowell and Curtice, op. cit.
7. *Ibid.*, pp. 35–9.
8. Anthony Heath, 'Comment on Dennis Kavanagh's "How We Vote Now"', in *Electoral Studies*, vol. 5, no. 1, April 1986, p. 30.
9. See Crewe, Särlvik and Alt, op. cit.
10. Heath, Jowell and Curtice, op. cit., p. 62.
11. Anthony Downs, *An Economic Theory of Democracy*(New York: Harper, 1957), and see, more recently, David Robertson, *Class and the British Electorate* (Oxford: Blackwell, 1984).
12. See, in particular, Chapter 7 of Heath, Jowell and Curtice, op. cit.
13. See 'Opinion Polls and Party Propaganda', *Public Opinion Quarterly*, vol. 28, Spring 1964, pp. 13–19.
14. See John Curtice and Michael Steed, 'An Analysis of the Voting', in David Butler and Dennis Kavanagh, *The British General Election of 1979* (London: Macmillan, 1980) p. 422.
15. See Ian McAllister and Anthony Mughan, 'Differential Turnout and Party Advantage in British General Elections, 1964–83' in *Electoral Studies*, vol. 5, no. 2, August 1986, pp. 143–52.
16. See Joseph Trenaman and Denis McQuail, *Television and the Political Image* (London: Methuen, 1961).
17. See Michael Pinto-Duschinsky, *British Political Finance 1830–1980*, (Washington DC: American Enterprise Institute, 1981) pp. 274–6.
18. See Heath, Jowell and Curtice, op cit., Chapter 11, pp. 157–69.
19. See Mark Abrams, *Public Opinion Quarterly*, vol. 28, Spring 1964.
20. P. M. Williams, 'Two Notes on the British Electoral System', in *Parliamentary Affairs*, Winter 1966–7, pp. 13–30.

14 How Much Does it Cost?

The cost of elections is less in the United Kingdom than in some other democratic countries and, in particular, substantially less than in the United States. But total election expenses do amount to a considerable sum, both those chargeable to the Exchequer and to local authorities and those for which the candidates and the political parties are responsible. (This chapter deals solely with the cost of general elections; statistics are not readily available of expenses incurred in local elections, though the sums involved are undoubtedly lower. Expenditure on Parliamentary by-elections is similar to that in individual constituencies at a general election. Reference is made to the cost of Euro-elections in Chapter 11.

There are three categories of expenditure chargeable to public funds – the cost of printing and compiling the register, the Returning Officers' expenses and the cost of the public facilities made available free of charge to candidates and political parties. These consist of the free postal delivery of electoral communications, the free hire of meeting halls and the provision of free broadcasting time for party election broadcasts on television and radio.

Under the 1948 Representation of the People Act provision was made for the compilation of two election registers each year. In 1949, as an economy cut, the number was reduced to one, thereby effecting a saving of about £650 000 per year. At present prices it would probably cost about £2 million to reintroduce a second register and thus ensure that it was kept more up-to-date.

The cost of the election register is borne equally by the Treasury and the local authorities. It is of course an annual charge and the cost in 1986–7 was £28.9 million. As the register is used annually for local government elections, and every five years for elections to the European Parliament, it would be unrealistic to count the whole cost of maintaining the register as part of the expense of a general election.

Other costs charged to the public, through the Treasury's Consolidated Fund, are the Returning Officers' expenses. The total expense reported in 1987 was around £2 million, an average of £3100 per constituency. This included the cost of publishing the notice of the election, receiving and publicising the nominations, and of sending out poll cards to all electors. The actual cost to the local authorities is however much greater than this sum suggests, as no account is taken of the cost of the temporary diversion of local government staff from other work during elections, nor of the cost of employing polling-station clerks on election day and of people to count the votes after the poll has closed.

The Treasury derives one small but regular source of income from elections – the forfeiture of deposits. This has brought in the following sums in post-war general elections:

TABLE 14.1   *Lost deposits*

Year	Number of lost deposits	Total sum
1945	163	£ 24 450
1950	461	£ 69 150
1951	96	£ 14 400
1955	100	£ 15 000
1959	116	£ 17 400
1964	186	£ 28 050
1966	237	£ 35 550
1970	408	£ 61 200
1974: Feb.	321	£ 48 150
Oct.	442	£ 66 300
1979	1001	£150 150
1983	739	£110 850
1987	290	£145 000

The Post Office is reimbursed by the Treasury for the cost of the free postal delivery, but no precise figures are available for the cost to local authorities of making halls available free to candidates, or to the broadcasting authorities of the provision of free air time. Various estimates have been made of what the commercial charges would be for such services, the most precise by Michael Pinto-Duschinsky.[1] He calculated that the Labour and Conservative parties were each subsidised to the extent of £3 073 000 during the 1979 general election (£311 000 each for free postage, £62 000 for the free hire of halls and £2.7 million for party political broadcasts). His total estimate for the Liberal party was £1 800 000, but he made no calculations for smaller parties and independents. His overall figure for the three main parties in 1979 was just under £8 million. On this basis, and allowing for inflation, the cost for the 1983 election would have been in the region of £12.5 million, and that for the 1987 election around £17 million. The probable cost for an election in 1991 or 1992 would be somewhat over £22 million.

When every allowance is made for indirect expenses, it seems improbable that the 1987 general election cost the public purse more than about £45 million plus a proportion of the *annual* cost of maintaining the election register.

The cost to candidates and their parties of fighting elections is, of course, additional to this. The amount of money which may be spent on behalf of a candidate during the actual election campaign is strictly limited by law. The campaign is usually regarded as dating from the announcement of a dissolution in the case of a general election or the date that the vacancy occurs in the case of a by-election, though the law is woolly on this point. It may be that only the shorter period following the actual dissolution (or issue of a writ) is in fact covered by the law. On the other hand the campaign might be held to date from the announcement of a candidature, and this is why all parties are careful to describe their standard bearers as *prospective* candidates until the announcement of the dissolution. The point has never been contested in the courts and, in practice, all candidates play safe and return their expenses for the longer period.

Until 1918 the whole of the Returning Officers' expenses in each constituency was chargeable to the candidates, and this constituted a considerable extra burden, especially for poorer candidates and parties. Since 1883 there has been a restriction on the amount which can be spent on behalf of each candidate, and though the electorate greatly increased and the value of money depreciated, the level of permitted expenditure was lowered both in 1918 and in 1948. The effect of this was that the actual money expended was lower in the 1966 general election (£1 130 882) than in 1906 (£1 166 858). Since then the rate of inflation has been so high that the actual amount expended grew by over seven times between 1966 and 1987, when the total expenditure was £8 039 174. Yet in real terms the expenditure level is far lower than in the early years of this century.

The level of permitted expenditure was formally laid down by Act of Parliament, which meant that a new Act needed to be passed whenever an increase was considered desirable because of the erosion in the value of money. Since 1978 however, the Home Secretary has been permitted to enact new limits by an order in council, subject to an affirmative vote by both Houses of Parliament. In 1989 the maximum expenditure permitted for each candidate was raised to

£3648 plus 4.1p. per elector in county constituencies: and £3 648 plus 3.1p. per elector in borough constituencies. Following a change in the law in 1989, these limits apply only to general elections; in a by-election the permitted expenditure is exactly four times as great.

Candidates' personal expenses are excluded from the limitation. Its effect is that in the average constituency the maximum expenditure permitted is about £5800 per candidate. The average maximum for county constituencies is about £6100 and that for boroughs around £5500, but as the former often contain widely scattered areas of population difficult to organise, the differential can easily be justified.

Within 35 days after the declaration of the result the agent of each candidate has to submit to the Returning Officer a complete statement of expenses incurred, together with the relevant bills and receipts. Within the following 10 days the Returning Officer is required to publish in at least two local newspapers a summary (under seven heads) of the expenses of all candidates concerned. Within a year of the election a summary of all the accounts, together with other relevant information, is published as a Parliamentary Paper, under the title, *Return of Election Expenses*. The amounts expended by all candidates and by those of the three main parties in general elections since 1945 were as follows:

TABLE 14.2 *Expenditure by parliamentary candidates*

Year	Candidates	Total expenditure	Average per candidate	Con.	Lab.	Lib./All.
		£	£	£	£	£
1945	1468	1 073 216	645	780	593	532
1950	1868	1 170 114	628	777	694	459
1951	1376	946 013	688	773	658	488
1955	1409	904 677	642	735	611	423
1959	1536	1 051 217	684	761	705	532
1964	1757	1 229 203	699	790	751	579
1966	1707	1 136 882	667	766	726	501
1970	1786	1 392 796	761	949	828	525
1974: Feb.	2135	1 780 542	951	1197	1127	745
Oct.	2252	2 168 514	963	1275	1163	725
1979	2576	3 557 441	1381	2190	1897	1013
1983	2579	6 145 264	2383	3320	2927	2520
1987	2325	8 039 174	3457	4400	3900	3400

In 1987 Conservative candidates spent on average 78 per cent of the permitted maximum, Labour candidates 69 per cent and Liberal–SDP candidates 61 per cent. Minor party and independent candidates spent a great deal less. The average for all candidates was 59.6 per cent.

Table 14.3 shows the returns made by the four candidates in a borough constituency, Oxford West and Abingdon, where the maximum permitted expenditure was £6028.59p.

TABLE 14.3   *Election expenses in Oxford West and Abingdon, 1987*

Nature of expenditure	John Patten (Con.)	Christopher Huhne (SDP/All.)	John Power (Lab.)	Donald Smith (Green)
	£	£	£	£
Agents	603.00	0.00	40.00	0.00
Clerks, etc.	578.45	0.00	0.00	0.00
Printing, stationery, etc.	2 803.70	4 647.10	5024.35	781.90
Public meetings	54.07	129.40	7.00	0.00
Committee rooms	243.05	301.00	0.00	0.00
Miscellaneous matters	1 644.50	688.71	743.73	5.36
Net total *	5 926.77	5 766.21	5814.08	787.26
Personal expenses	120.00	85.00	600.00	5.30
Grand total	6 046.77	5 851.21	6414.08	792.56
Votes polled	25 171	20 293	8108	695

* The maximum permitted expenditure, not including personal expenses, for this constituency was £6028.59.

All parties consistently spend more money in respect of their successful candidates than on behalf of their unsuccessful nominees, but it is in the highly marginal seats that candidates of all parties tend to spend very near the maximum permitted. Evasion of the law had apparently been fairly widespread in marginal constituencies, according to David Butler who wrote after the 1959 election:

Agents quite often admitted to subterfuges, some plainly legal, some more dubious, by which they kept their official expenses down. Sympathetic printers could undercharge, knowing that no objection would be raised to a compensating overcharge outside election time. Equipment needed solely for the campaign could be bought in advance and then hired to the agent at a very low notional figure. Although the likelihood of either side scrutinising its rivals' accounts or launching a petition is very small, it is unfortunate that the law should be so much circumvented.[2]

With more realistic spending limits, it is possible that the incidence of evasion has declined since 1959, except in key by-elections where it has been evident that over-spending has occurred. It was for this reason that the limit for by-elections was quadrupled in 1989, and it is to be hoped that it will be adhered to in future.

Restriction of expenditure is highly desirable if money is not to talk at election time. A far more serious problem, however, is the lack of any limitation on amounts which can be spent nationally and in the period between elections. These amounts have now begun to dwarf the total sums spent on behalf of all candidates. In the 1983 general election the central expenditure of the Conservative party was £3.6 million (including £2.8 million on advertising), while the Labour Party spend £1.9 million, the Liberals £250 000 and the SDP £600 000.[3]

The inequality between the parties' expenditure, and concern that both the Conservative and Labour parties were dependent on sectional interests (business and trade unions, respectively) for the great bulk of their funds, has led to a demand – which the author of this book was the first to articulate[4] – for the election expenses of British political parties to be partially reimbursed from public funds. This now happens in a majority of democratic countries in Europe, as well as in Australia, Canada and the United States (presidential elections only, so far). An independent committee of inquiry was set up in 1975, under Lord Houghton, to look into this problem. It reported in 1976, and a majority of its members were in favour of introducing such a system in Britain. Its main recommendations were:

We recommend the introduction of a system of state financial aid for political parties in the United Kingdom.

Such aid should take the form of:

(i) annual grants to be paid from Exchequer funds to the central organisations of the parties for their general purposes, the amounts being determined according to the extent of each party's electoral support;

(ii) at local level, a limited reimbursement of the election expenses of Parliamentary and local government candidates. In order to qualify for a grant a party must at the previous general election have either:

(a) saved the deposits of its candidates in at least six constituencies; or

(b) had at least two of its candidates returned as Members; or

(c) had one of its candidates returned as a Member, and received as a party a total of not less than 150 000 votes.

The amount of the annual grant payable to each of the qualifying parties shall be calculated on the basis of 5p for each vote cast for candidates at the previous general election.

The scheme for the limited reimbursement of candidates' election expenses should apply to all Parliamentary elections, and to all elections for county and district councils in England and Wales, regional, island and district councils in Scotland, and the Greater London Council and London borough councils.

Reimbursement should be restricted to those candidates who poll at least one-eighth of the votes cast, and the amount to be reimbursed should be the candidate's actual election expenses up to a limit of half his legally permitted maximum expenditure. Payment shall be made directly to the candidate.[5]

The Houghton report was not acted on, despite the fact that the Labour Party, then in power, was broadly in favour of its proposals. The Leader of the House of Commons, Michael Foot, to whom the report was presented, was however unenthusiastic and made no effort to implement it. The Thatcher government, elected in 1979, was openly hostile, but the Labour Party and both Alliance parties have subsequently endorsed the principle of public funding, and legislation may be expected to be introduced by the next non-Conservative government.[6] In the meantime the only public money available to parties is the relatively small sum paid each year since 1975 to meet the specifically Parliamentary expenses of opposition parties, who lack the Civil Service assistance available to the government. In the 1988–89 Parliamentary session, just over £1 150 000 was paid out, of which the Labour Party received £839 700, the Liberal Democrats £187 190, the SDP £56 120, the SNP £18 270, Plaid Cymru £10 800 and the Northern Irish parties shared £51 410.

Notes and References

1. Michael Pinto-Duschinsky, *British Political Finance 1830–1980* (Washington DC: American Enterprise Institute, 1981) p. 267.
2. David Butler and Richard Rose, *The British General Election of 1959* (London: Macmillan, 1960) pp. 144–5.
3. See David Butler and Dennis Kavanagh, *The British General Election of 1983* (London: Macmillan, 1984) p. 267.
4. Dick Leonard, *Paying for Party Politics* (London: Political and Economic Planning, 1975). See also my chapter 'Contrasts in selected Western Democracies: Germany, Sweden, Britain' in Herbert E. Alexander (ed.), *Political Finance* (Beverly Hills and London: Sage Publications, 1979) pp. 41–73.
5. *Report of the Committee on Financial Aid to Political Parties*, Cmnd 6601 (London: HMSO, 1976).
6. For a thorough discussion of the issue, by an opponent of public funding, see Michael Pinto-Duschinsky, op. cit. A less ambitious proposal for public funding was put forward by a committee set up by the Hansard Society, under the chairmanship of Edmund Dell, see *Paying for Politics* (London: Hansard Society for Parliamentary Government, 1981).

15 An Evolving System

In 1254 the Sheriff of each county was ordered to send two knights, chosen by the county, 'to consider what aid they would give the King in his great necessity'; 11 years later the Parliament summoned by Simon de Montfort contained not only two knights from each county, but also two citizens from each city and two burgesses from each borough. The Parliaments of the thirteenth century were very different from those of today, and no doubt there were even greater differences in the manner of their election. Nevertheless a statute approved by the Parliament of Edward I, in 1275, stipulating that the elections should be 'free' is still in force today, and the gradual evolution of the present system can be traced back through hundreds of Acts of Parliament spanning the centuries in between.

This evolution is a continuing process. In 1985 alone for instance, three important changes were made – postal voting was extended to holiday-makers, British citizens who had been living abroad for five years or less became eligible to vote, and the deposit for candidates was increased from £150 to £500, while the qualifying limit for its return was reduced from one-eighth to one-twentieth of the votes cast. In 1989 two further significant changes were made: the right to vote was extended to citizens who had been living abroad for up to 20 years, while the maximum permitted expenditure by candidates in by-elections was increased to four times the level permitted in by-elections. In fact, the two most distinctive features of the British electoral system are its antiquity and its capacity to absorb changes. While some parts of the electoral law remain intact for centuries, others are liable to be amended at virtually any time. The great majority of amendments are of a minor character.

The period of most significant change was, of course, the hundred or so years following the passage of the Great Reform Bill of 1832 when, as described briefly in Chapter 3 above, the struggle for universal suffrage was fought and won. Almost as important as the extension of the franchise, was such legislation as the Ballot Act of 1872, which secured the secrecy of the ballot, and the Corrupt Practices Act of 1883, which effectively eliminated bribery from British elections.

The advances won in the nineteenth and early twentieth centuries were consolidated in the Representation of the People Acts of 1948 and 1949, and subsequently again in the 1983 Act, which forms the basis of the present system. Changes in the law since 1949 have been mostly in a minor key, seeking to improve the detailed working of an established system rather than to effect any radical alteration. A typical example was the Elections (Welsh Forms) Act of 1964, which provided that Welsh translations of election forms could be used in Wales and Monmouthshire. Less typical, because its motivation was partisan advantage, was the Representation of the People (Amendment) Act of 1958 which, as described in Chapter 8 above, removed the restriction on the use of motor-cars prescribed by the 1948 Act.

Fairly frequent attempts are made by MPs to introduce changes through Private Members' Bills. The great majority of these attempts are unsuccessful. Nevertheless, an average of one Act of Parliament per year – nearly all of them government bills – have been enacted in recent years. Between 1969 and 1989, 19 Acts were passed, not including those concerned with local government elections or with referenda. The list was as follows:

Representation of the People Act 1969
Representation of the People Act 1974
Representation of the People (No. 2) Act 1974
Recess Elections Act 1975
House of Commons Disqualification Act 1975
Representation of the People (Armed Forces) Act 1976
Representation of the People Act 1977
Returning Officers (Scotland) Act 1977
European Assembly Elections Act 1978
Representation of the People Act 1978
House of Commons (Redistribution of Seats) Act 1979
Representation of the People Act 1979
Representation of the People Act 1980
European Assembly Elections Act 1981
Representation of the People Act 1981
Representation of the People Act 1983
Representation of the People Act 1985
Parliamentary Constituencies Act 1986
Representation of the People Act 1989

The 1948 and 1949 Acts, although they introduced a number of important innovations, are basically nineteenth century in form, and the legal provisions relating to elections are in many respects similar to those in force one hundred years ago. What has transformed election campaigns out of all recognition in the past century has primarily been not the change in the law but the technological and sociological developments which have taken place. It would be pointless to elaborate on them in a work of this kind, but it may be useful just to list the four changes which appear to have had the greatest effect upon British elections.

First there has been the revolution in transportation, which has enabled politicians to travel rapidly round the country – the growth of railways in the mid-nineteenth century and, even more important, the spread of the motor-car, which has also greatly affected local campaigning. In a densely populated but geographically small country, however, the aeroplane and the helicopter have so far made little impact upon electioneering, their use being effectively limited to the party leaders.

Second has been the development of mass media of communication – newspapers with national circulation, telegraphs, radio and, later, television. More humbly, the telephone has also made an incalculable contribution. Third has been the spread of education, which has tended to lag behind some other developed countries, especially in so far as higher education is concerned, and, finally, the development of highly centralised party machines.

In a number of respects electoral law has tended to lag behind these developments, and for many years failed, for example, to take account of the consequences of broadcasting for electoral campaigning. A fairly recent tradition has been established that an attempt at all-party agreement should precede any important changes in electoral law, and inter-party conferences under the chairmanship of the Speaker of the House of Commons preceded the Representation of the People Acts of 1918, 1948 and 1969 (though in each case the Act did not exactly follow the recommendations of the Speaker's Conference). Other Speaker's Conferences sat in 1929–30, 1972–4 and 1977–8. These conferences, which are made up entirely of Members of Parliament, meet in private under the Speaker's chairmanship. They hear evidence from interested parties and from expert witnesses before considering their recommendations. The initiative for convening them is taken by the government, which consults the opposition about the terms of reference before the members are appointed.

The 1965–8 Conference is a good example of the procedure. Shortly after the 1964 general election the new Prime Minister,

Harold Wilson, invited the Speaker to preside over a conference on electoral law, and on 12 May 1965 the Speaker informed the House of Commons that he had agreed to do so. Apart from the Speaker, 29 Members of Parliament, whose names were suggested by the party whips, made up the conference. The MPs were appointed in approximate proportion to party membership of the House of Commons; 15 were Labour, 13 Conservative and one Liberal. The terms of reference of the Conference were as follows:

To examine and, if possible, to submit agreed resolutions on the following matters relating to Parliamentary elections:
  (a) Reform of the franchise, with particular reference to the minimum age for voting and registration procedure generally;
  (b) Methods of election, with particular reference to preferential voting;
  (c) Conduct of elections, with particular reference to:
     (i) the problem of absent voting generally;
     (ii) use of the official mark on ballot papers and of electoral numbers on counterfoils;
     (iii) polling hours;
     (iv) appointment of polling day as a public holiday;
     (v) provisions relating to undue influence; and
     (vi) returning officers for county constituencies;
  (d) Election expenses generally;
  (e) Use of broadcasting; and
  (f) Cost of election petitions and application for relief.

The Conference allowed a period of time for interested organisations or individuals to submit representations, and in November 1965 began its considerations. In view of the narrow Parliamentary majority an early general election was anticipated and the Conference agreed to submit interim reports on a number of urgent matters on which early legislation might be practicable.

Three such reports were produced between 28 December 1965 and 7 March 1966, but the dissolution of Parliament on 10 March prevented any action before the 1966 general election. The Conference was reappointed, with a partially different membership, after the 1966 general election, and produced a further series of reports. Amongst other proposals, it advocated an increase in the permitted level of election expenditure, the exemption of broadcasting from the provisions relating to election expenses and the lowering of the voting age from 21 to 18. Most of its other proposals were negative: no change to proportional representation or the Alternative Vote, no party labels on ballot papers, no postal votes for the over-70s or for holiday-makers, no provision for meeting candidates' election expenses out of public funds, no requirement that employees should be given time off work in order to vote, and rejection of the proposals that polling day should be a public holiday and that political expenditure should be restricted outside the actual campaign period.

One highly controversial proposal was endorsed by a majority of the Conference. By nine votes to five, it agreed that 'There should be no broadcast, or publication in a newspaper or other periodical, of the result of a public opinion poll or of betting odds on the likely result of a parliamentary election during the period of seventy-two hours before the close of the poll. This proposal, which was greeted with incredulity by the pollsters themselves and by most political commentators, presumably reflected belief by MPs in the bandwagon theory, discussed on page 161 above.

The government introduced the 1969 Representation of the People Act after receiving the final report from the Conference. Several of its recommendations – including votes at 18 and the exemption of broadcasting as an election expense – were reflected in its provisions, but others were not. The Act did provide for party labels to be included on ballot papers (by allowing up to six descriptive words to be added), but it included no provision to restrict the publication of opinion polls. It also extended the time that polling stations remain open in Parliamentary elections, from 9 pm to 10 pm, which had not been recommended by the Conference.

There will probably be further Conferences from time to time, and governments will continue to pick and choose from their recommendations, or allow a free vote in the House of Commons as has occurred quite frequently in the past. But any substantial change in the system – such as the introduction of proportional representation, or even the payment or partial payment of election expenses out of public funds – will be an essentially political decision, and is unlikely to result from such a Conference. Short of such a radical change, the system is likely to continue to evolve in an unspectacular way, with one or two minor changes being introduced each year.

Appendix 1: General Election Results, 1945–1987

Year	Parties	Candidates	MPs elected	Unopposed returns	Lost deposits	Total vote	Percentage vote
1945	Conservative	624	213	2	6	9 988 306	39.8
	Labour	604	393	1	2	11 995 152	47.8
	Liberal	306	12	–	64	2 248 226	9.0
	Others	148	22	–	91	854 294	2.8
Turnout: 72.7%		1 682	640	3	163	25 085 978	100.0
Swing (to Lab.)* 11.3%							
1950	Conservative	620	298	2	5	12 502 567	43.5
	Labour	617	315	–	–	13 266 592	46.1
	Liberal	475	9	–	319	2 621 548	9.1
	Others	156	3	–	137	381 964	1.3
Turnout: 84.0%		1 868	625	2	461	28 772 671	100.0
Swing (to Con.)* 2.8%							
1951	Conservative	617	321	4	3	13 717 538	48.0
	Labour	617	295	–	1	13 948 605	48.8
	Liberal	109	6	–	66	730 556	2.5
	Others	23	3	–	26	198 969	0.7
Turnout: 82.5%		1 376	625	4	96	28 595 668	100.0
Swing (to Con.)* 0.9%							

continued on page 198

Appendix 1: *continued*

Year	Parties	Candidates	MPs elected	Unopposed returns	Lost deposits	Total vote	Percentage vote
1955	**Conservative**	623	344	–	3	13 286 569	49.7
	Labour	620	277	–	1	12 404 970	46.4
	Liberal	110	6	–	60	722 405	2.7
	Others	56	3	–	36	346 554	1.2
		1 409	630	–	100	26 760 493	100.0
Turnout: 76.7% Swing (to Con.)* 2.1%							
1959	**Conservative**	625	365	–	2	13 749 830	49.4
	Labour	621	258	–	1	12 215 538	43.8
	Liberal	216	6	–	55	1 638 571	5.9
	Others	74	1	–	58	255 302	0.9
		1 536	630	–	116	27 859 241	100.0
Turnout: 78.8% Swing (to Con.)* 1.1%							
1964	Conservative	629	303	–	5	12 001 396	43.4
	Labour	628	317	–	8	12 205 814	44.1
	Liberal	365	9	–	53	3 092 878	11.2
	Others	135	1	–	121	348 914	1.3
		1 757	630	–	187	27 649 002	100.0
Turnout: 77.0% Swing (to Lab.)* 3.1%							

1966						
Conservative	629	253	–	9	11 418 413	41.9
Labour	621	363	–	3	13 056 659	47.9
Liberal	311	12	–	104	2 327 470	8.5
Others	146	2	–	121	456 909	1.7
	1 707	630	–	237	27 259 743	100.0
Turnout: 75.8%						
Swing (to Lab.)* 2.6%						
1970						
Conservative	628	330	–	10	13 145 123	46.4
Labour	624	287	–	6	12 179 341	43.0
Liberal	332	6	–	184	2 117 035	7.5
Others	253	7	–	208	903 299	3.1
	1 837	630	–	408	28 344 798	100.0
Turnout: 72.0%						
Swing (to Con.)* 4.7%						
Feb. 1974						
Conservative	623	297	–	8	11 868 906	37.9
Labour	623	301	–	25	11 639 243	37.1
Liberal	517	14	–	23	6 063 470	19.3
Others	372	23	–	265	1 762 047	5.7
	2 135	635	–	321	31 333 226	100.0
Turnout: 78.7%						
Swing (to Lab.)* 1.3%						
Oct. 1974						
Conservative	623	277	–	28	10 464 817	35.8
Labour	623	319	–	13	11 457 079	39.2
Liberal	619	13	–	125	5 346 754	18.3
Others	387	26	–	276	1 920 528	6.7
	2 252	635	–	442	29 189 178	100.0
Turnout: 72.8%						
Swing (to Lab.)* 2.1%						

continued on page 200

Appendix 1: *continued*

Year	Parties	Candidates	MPs elected	Unopposed returns	Lost deposits	Total vote	Percentage vote
1979	**Conservative**	622	339	–	3	13 697 923	43.9
	Labour	622	268	–	22	11 506 661	36.9
	Liberal	576	11	–	303	4 305 197	13.8
	Others	756	17	–	673	1 711 581	5.4
		2 576	635	–	1 001	31 221 362	100.0
Turnout: 76.0% Swing (to Con.)* 5.2%							
1983	**Conservative**	633	397	–	5	13 012 316	42.4
	Labour	633	209	–	119	8 456 934	27.6
	Liberal-SDP	633	23	–	10	7 780 949	25.4
	Others	680	21	–	605	1 420 938	4.6
		2 579	650	–	739	30 671 137	100.0
Turnout: 72.7% Swing (to Con.)* 3.9%							
1987	**Conservative**	633	376	–	0	13 763 066	42.3
	Labour	633	229	–	0	10 029 778	30.8
	Liberal-SDP	633	22	–	1	7 341 290	22.6
	Others	426	23	–	289	1 402 003	4.3
		2 325	650	–	290	32 536 137	100.0
Turnout: 75.3% Swing (to Lab.)* 1.6%							

* The swing (between the Conservative and Labour Parties) shown here is calculated on the total national vote, *not* on the average of the swings in all constituencies contested.

Appendix 2: Election Statistics, 1987

Electors	43 665 986
Postal voters	947 748
Polling districts	35 042
Polling stations	46 566
Members	650
Candidates	2 325
Candidates' expenses:	£
Personal expenses	266 547
Agents	326 927
Clerks	107 974
Printing	6 612 952
Public meetings	88 652
Committee rooms	260 756
Miscellaneous	641 913
Total (excluding personal expenses)	8 039 174
Votes polled	32 529 578

SOURCE   *Return of the Expenses of each Candidate at the General Election of June 1987*, House of Commons Paper 426, April 1988.

Appendix 3: Proxy and Postal Voters

The following categories of registered voters may claim the right to appoint *proxies* to vote on their behalf:

An elector who is likely to be at sea, or abroad, on account of his employment or on account of his service in the auxiliary or reserve forces at the time. (**RPF 7**)

All service voters. (**F/VOTE/33**)

Wives of servicemen abroad. (**F/VOTE/34**)

Voters employed in the service of the Crown in a post outside the United Kingdom. (**E 79**)

Wives of Crown servants residing outside the United Kingdom with their husbands. (**E 80**)

Holiday-makers (**RPF 9**)

Overseas Electors (**Overseas Elector's Declaration**)

Applications to appoint a proxy must be made, on an appropriate form, at least 13 days before polling day (excluding Saturdays, Sundays and public holidays). The names of the forms required are given in brackets after each category. RPF forms are obtainable from the constituency returning officer (that is, at the local town hall); service forms from commanding officers, and forms for Crown servants and their wives from their own government departments. Overseas Elector's Declarations are obtainable from British consulates or embassies abroad. Two proxies are named on the form, the second of whom would be entitled to vote on behalf of the elector only if the first proxy indicates within five days of being approached by the Returning Officer that he is unable to act on behalf of the absent voter. A proxy records the vote at the same polling station at which the absent voter would otherwise be entitled to vote.

Postal votes may be claimed for an *indefinite* period by those unable, or unlikely to be able, to go to vote in person, because of:

(1) The general nature of their employment, service or occupation (for example, long-distance lorry drivers and merchant seamen). (**RPF 7**)

(2) Blindness or other physical incapacity (the signature of a doctor or other qualified person is needed on the application form except in the case of registered blind persons and people in receipt of a mobility allowance). (**RPF 7B**)

(3) No longer residing at the qualifying address (if they cannot reasonably be expected to vote in person at the polling station for their old address.) (**RPF 9**)

(4) Having to make a journey by sea or air in order to be able to vote in

person. (This applies mostly to Scottish electors who live on islands away from a polling station.) (**RPF 7A**)

In addition, a postal vote may be claimed for a *particular election only*, by reason of:

(1) Service as a member of the reserve or auxiliary forces. (**RPF 9**)
(2) Employment on date of poll as a constable, or by the Returning Officer. (**RPF 9**)
(3) At a general election being a candidate or a candidate's spouse in some other constituency. (**RPF 9**)
(4) At a general election being a Returning Officer, deputy Returning Officer or acting returning officer, or being employed by a Returning Officer, in some other constituency. (**RPF 9**)
(5) Absence from home on polling day, for example on holiday. (**RPF 9**)
(6) Illness (a doctor's signature is needed on the application form). (**RPF 9**)

A service voter serving in the UK, even though he has appointed a proxy, may vote at his polling station personally if a ballot paper has not already been issued to his proxy.

Any proxy voter who himself falls into one of the above categories may apply to vote by post.

Appendix 4: Election Timetable

The following chart lists the important days to remember during a general election campaign. It is important to remember to exclude Saturdays, Sundays and bank holidays (and the weekdays immediately before and after a bank holiday) in the count of seventeen days between the Proclamation and polling day.

TABLE A4.1

General election	Example		
Day	*Chart days*	*Calendar dates*	
0. Proclamation			
1. Receipt of writ	0	F	5 Proclamation
2.	–	S	6
3. Notice of election	–	Su	7
4. First day for Nomination and last day for normal claims for postal or proxy votes	1	M	8 Receipt of Writ
	2	T	9 Notice of Election
	3	W	10
	4	T	11
5.	5	F	12 First day for Nomination
6. Last day for Nomination	–	S	13 Last normal day to claim proxy or postal votes
7.	–	Su	14
8.	6	M	15 Last day for Nomination
9.	7	T	16
10.	8	W	17
11. Last day for ill voters to claim postal or proxy votes	9	T	18
	10	F	19
	–	S	20
12.	–	Su	21
13.	11	M	22
14.	12	T	23
15.	13	W	24
16.	14	T	25
17. Polling day	15	F	26
	–	S	27
	–	Su	28
	16	M	29
	17	T	30 Polling day

In a by-election, some discretion is allowed in the choice of polling day, as the following table shows.

TABLE A4.2 *By-election*

	Day
Receipt of Writ	1
	2
Notice of Election	3
	4
	5
Earliest final Nom.	6
	7
Latest final Nom.	8
	9
	10
	11
	12
	13
	14
	15
	16
Earliest Poll	17
	18
Latest Poll	19

Appendix 5: Corrupt and Illegal Practices

Offences

BRIBERY. No gift, loan, or promise of money or money's worth must be made to a voter to induce him either to vote or abstain from voting.

The offer or promise of a situation or employment to a voter or anyone connected with him, if made with the same object, is also bribery.

The consequences are the same whether bribery is committed before, during, or after an election.

Giving or paying money for the purpose of bribery is equivalent to the offence itself.

A gift or promise to a third person to procure a vote is bribery. Payment for loss of time, wages, or travelling expenses is equal to bribery.

Any person who receives a bribe, or bargains for employment or reward in consideration of his vote, is guilty of bribery.

TREATING. No meat, drinks, entertainment or provisions can be paid for or provided for any person at any time, in order to induce him, or any other person, to vote or abstain from voting. The gift of tickets to be exchanged for refreshment is regarded as treating.

Treating the wives or relatives of voters is also forbidden.

The receiver of any meat, drink, etc., is equally guilty, and liable to the same consequences.*

UNDUE INFLUENCE. No force, threat, restraint, or fraud may be used to compel an elector to vote or abstain.

Using or threatening any spiritual or temporal injury is undue influence.

The withdrawal of custom, or a threat to do so, comes under this prohibition. A threat to evict a tenant will also be undue influence.

UNAUTHORISED EXPENDITURE. Incurring expenditure on account of holding public meetings or issuing advertisements, circulars or publications, by any person, other than the election agent, for the purpose of promoting or procuring the election of any candidate at a Parliamentary election, unless authorised in writing by such election agent and returned as an expense by the person incurring it.

PERSONATION. Applying for a ballot paper in the name of another person, whether alive or dead.

Aiding or abetting the commission of the offence of personation.

206

ELECTION OFFENCES
PRACTICES

Penalties

On indictment, 12 months imprisonment or an unlimited fine, or both. On summary conviction, six months' imprisonment, a fine not exceeding £2000, or both.

Deprivation of the right of voting for five years.

Removal from, and disqualification for, any public office.

Payment of costs of an election inquiry in certain cases.

If committed by the candidate he also loses his seat, if elected, and is disqualified for ten years from representing the constituency and is disqualified for five years from sitting for any other constituency.

If committed by any agent the election is void, and the candidate is disqualified for seven years.

NOTE   Any recognised active worker may be held to be 'an agent'.

On indictment, two years' imprisonment, an unlimited fine, or both.

Five years' incapacity to vote, or hold any public office.

If committed by any agent, the candidate loses his seat.

Appendix 5: *continued*

ILLEGAL

Offences

CONVEYANCE. Paying or receiving money for conveyance of voters to or
from the poll.
    (Private conveyances lent gratuitously can alone be employed; hackney
carriages are prohibited except when hired by voters for their own exclus-
ive use.)
ADVERTISING. Paying money to an elector for exhibiting bills, etc.
The receiver is also guilty.
VOTING when prohibited, or inducing a prohibited elector to vote.
VOTING twice in the same constituency in the same election.
FALSE STATEMENT. Publishing a false statement of the withdrawal of
any candidate or as to his character.
ILLEGAL PROXY VOTING. Voting or attempting to vote in person after
having appointed a proxy, and while such appointment is uncancelled.
    Voting or attempting to vote as proxy on behalf of more than two absent
voters at an election in any constituency, unless voting as the husband or
wife, or the parent, brother or sister of the absent voter.
    Voting or attempting to vote at any election under the authority of a
proxy paper when the person knows or has reasonable grounds for sup-
posing that the proxy paper has been cancelled, or that the elector on
whose behalf it has been issued is dead or not entitled to vote at that
election.
POLL CARDS. Issuing at a Parliamentary election any poll card or document resembling an official poll card.

PUBLISHING BILLS, placards or posters, without the printer's name and
address. (The election agent alone, or sub-agents in counties, may issue
any printed matter at the election.) Any process for multiplying copies of a
document other than by copying it by hand is deemed to be printing.

ILLEGAL PAYMENT, EMPLOY-
LENDING OR USING, for the conveyance of voters, horses or vehicles
usually kept for hire.
EMPLOYMENT of any person as a canvasser.
USING A COMMITTEE ROOM in any public elementary school.
A fine not exceeding £2000.

FORGERY
FORGERY or counterfeiting a ballot paper is not a corrupt or illegal
practice as such, but under the Forgery and Counterfeiting Act of 1981 is
subject to a maximum penalty of 10 years' imprisonment or an unlimited
fine, or both. On summary conviction, the maximum penalty is six months'
imprisonment or a maximum fine of £2000, or both.

*NOTE REFRESHMENT FOR WORKERS: Whilst it is much better,
and more prudent, to leave all workers, whether paid or unpaid, to find their
own refreshments, the view has been expressed by some judges that 'the

PRACTICES

Penalties

A fine not exceeding £2000.
Incapacity to vote for five years.
If committed by a candidate or an agent, the election may be rendered void.

If the offender be the candidate or his agent, the full penalty attaching to an illegal practice as above.
If any other person, a fine not exceeding £2000.

MENT, AND HIRING

A fine not exceeding £2000.

giving of refreshments to persons employed at the election, if *bona fide* and honestly done, *is not treating*, even though the workers be voters, if care be taken to confine it to persons actually engaged on the election'.

Appendix 6: Occupations of Candidates and MPs, 1987[†]

Occupation	Conservative		Labour		Liberal		SDP	
	elected	defeated	elected	defeated	elected	defeated	elected	defeated
Professions:								
Barrister	43	33	9	4	4	11	1	15
Solicitor	21	19	9	13	1	19	–	17
Doctor/dentist	3	4	2	4	1	5	1	11
Architect/surveyor	7	2	–	–	–	3	–	1
Civil/chartered engineer	6	7	–	4	–	5	–	6
Chartered sec./accountant	17	12	2	6	–	9	–	4
Civil Servant/local govt.	13	3	8	28	1	15	1	9
Armed services	15	7	–	–	1	1	–	2
Teachers:								
University	6	3	11	15	2	13	–	15
Adult	2	8	15	47	–	24	–	20
School	17	18	29	82	2	34	–	39
Other consultants	3	3	2	5	–	11	–	10
Scientific research	3	1	6	2	–	3	–	4
Total	156 (42%)	120 (50%)	93 (40%)	210 (52%)	10 (59%)	153 (50%)	3 (60%)	153 (51%)
Business:								
Company director	39	21	2	1	–	14	–	12
Company executive	75	39	12	6	–	39	–	41
Commerce/insurance	18	13	9	9	–	10	–	12

Management/clerical	4	7	16	18	2	12	–	7
General business	3	8	2	2	–	8	–	3
Total	139 (37%)	88 (34%)	41 (10%)	36 (9%)	2 (12%)	83 (27%)	0 (0%)	75 (25%)
Miscellaneous:								
Miscellaneous white collar	8	5	18	54	1	21	1	17
Politician/pol. organiser	21	14	12	21	1	17	–	8
Publisher/journalist	26	12	14	9	2	13	1	16
Farmer	16	6	2	1	1	2	–	7
Housewife	7	–	–	4	–	6	–	5
Student	–	2	–	1	–	2	–	3
Local administration	–	2	4	7	–	9	–	2
Total	78 (20%)	41 (14%)	50 (21%)	97 (24%)	5 (30%)	70 (22%)	2 (40%)	58 (19%)
Manual workers:								
Miner	1	1	16	1	–	–	–	2
Skilled worker	2	7	44	41	–	4	–	13
Semi/unskilled worker	–	–	6	14	–	–	–	–
Total	3 (1%)	8 (3%)	66 (29%)	56 (14%)	0 (0%)	4 (1%)	0 (0%)	15 (5%)
Grand Total	376	257	229	404	17	310	5	301

† Reprinted by kind permission from Byron Criddle, 'Candidates' in David Butler and Dennis Kavanagh, *The British General Election of 1987* (London: Macmillan, 1988) pp. 204–5.

Appendix 7: Opinion Poll Surveys, 1987

Polls on voting intention, May–June 1987[†]

Dates	Fieldwork sampling	Company (Publication)	C. (%)	Lab. (%)	Aln (%)	Other (%)	Total (%)	C.-L. (%)	C./Lab. swing (%)
6–11.5	1 735(180)	NOP (Standard)	46	28	25	1	100	+18	−1
7–11.5	1 085(110)	GALLUP (Telegraph)	39	28	30	3	100	+11	+2.5
8–12.5	1 445(103)	MARPLAN (Guardian)	43	29	25	3	100	+14	+1
8–12.5	1 934(178)	MORI (Sunday Times)	44	31	23	2	100	+13	+1.5
11–13.5	1 424(73)	MORI (Times) (Adj)	43	32	23	2	100	+11	+2.5
11–14.5	1 521(65)	MORI (S/T) (Pnl)	44	30	25	1	100	+14	+1
13.5	1 020(50)	MARPLAN (D. Express)	41	30	26	3	100	+11	+2.5
13–15.5	1 040(97)	HARRIS (Observer)	42	33	23	2	100	+9	+3.5
13–15.5	3 164(100)	HARRIS (W/W) (Adj)	40	34	25	1	100	+6	+5
14–17.5	2 410(60)	NEWSNIGHT (Adj)	40	34	24	2	100	+6	+5
16–17.5	1 058(97)	HARRIS (TV-am)	42	32	24	2	100	+10	+3
18.5	1 072(54)	MARPLAN (Today)	41	33	24	2	100	+8	+4
19.5	1 976(52)	NOP (I'dent) (Adj)	42	34	23	1	100	+8	+4
19–20.5	2 640(197)	GALLUP (Telegraph)	42	33	23	2	100	+9	+3.5
18–21.5	1 079(98)	HARRIS (TV-am)	43	36	20	1	100	+7	+4.5
20–21.5	1 328(65)	MORI (S/T) (Pnl)	44	31	24	1	100	+13	+1.5
20–21.5	1 066(97)	HARRIS (Observer)	41	34	22	3	100	+7	+4.5
21.5	1 517(103)	MARPLAN (Guardian)	41	33	21	5	100	+8	+4
20–22.5	1 432(140)	GALLUP (S'graph) (Pnl)	42	33	23	2	100	+9	+3.5
20–22.5	1 386(66)	HARRIS (W/W) (Adj) (Pnl)	42	35	22	1	100	+7	+4.5

22–25.5	HARRIS (TV-am)	1 075(98)	42	37	21	0	100	+5	+5.5
26.5	MARPLAN (Today)	1 035(69)	42	35	20	3	100	+7	+4.5
26.5	NOP (I'dent) (Adj)	978(52)	42	35	21	2	100	+7	+4.5
26–27.5	GALLUP (Telegraph)	2 506(194)	44.5	36	18	1.5	100	+8.5	+3.8
27–28.5	MORI (S/T) (Pnl)	1 188(65)	44	32	23	1	100	+12	+2
27–28.5	HARRIS (Observer)	1 072(98)	41	37	21	1	100	+4	+6
27–28.5	HARRIS (W/W) (Adj) (Pnl)	1 296(66)	41	37	21	1	100	+4	+6
26–29.5	HARRIS (TV-am)	1 067(97)	45	32	22	1	100	+13	+1.5
28.5	MARPLAN (G'dian)	1 553(103)	44	32	21	3	100	+12	+2
27–29.5	GALLUP (S'graph) (Adj)	1 271(140)	41.5	34	22.5	2	100	+7.5	+4.3
29.5	MARPLAN (S.E'ss) (Adj)	1 302(50)	45	31	23	1	100	+14	+1
29–30.5	MORI (Times) (Adj)	1 420(73)	44	32	22	2	100	+12	+2
30.5–1.6	NEWSNIGHT (Adj) (Pnl)	2 116(60)	40	36	22	2	100	+4	+6
30.5–2.6	HARRIS (TV-am)	1 573(100)	42	36	20	2	100	+6	+5
1.6	MARPLAN (Today)	1 063(69)	44	33	21	2	100	+11	+2.5
2.6	NOP (I'dent) (Adj)	989(52)	43	34	20	3	100	+9	+3.5
2–3.6	GALLUP (Telegraph)	2 553(200)	40.5	36.5	21.5	1.5	100	+4	+6
3–4.6	MORI (S/T) (Adj) (Pnl)	1 305(65)	43	32	24	1	100	+11	+2.5
3–4.6	HARRIS (Observer)	1 087(98)	44	33	21	2	100	+11	+2.5
4.6	MARPLAN (Guardian)	1 576(103)	44	34	20	2	100	+10	+3
3–5.6	HARRIS (W/W) (Adj)	1 100(60)	40	35	24	1	100	+5	+5.5
3–5.6	GALLUP (S'graph) (Pnl)	1 275(145)	41.5	34.5	22.5	1.5	100	+7	+4.5
3–6.6	HARRIS (TV-am)	2 102(98)	43	33	22	2	100	+10	+3
5.6	MARPLAN (S.E'ss) (Adj)	1 300(23)	47	30	21	2	100	+17	-0.5
5.6	MARPLAN (Today)	1 065(69)	43	35	21	1	100	+8	+4
5–6.6	MORI (Times) (Adj)	1 443(73)	43	34	21	2	100	+9	+3.5
7–8.6	NEWSNIGHT (Adj) (Pnl)	2 023(60)	39	36	24	1	100	+3	+6.5
8.6	MARPLAN (Guardian)	1 575(103)	45	32	21	2	100	+13	+1.5

continued on page 214

Appendix 7: *continued*

Dates	Fieldwork sampling	Company (Publication)	C. (%)	Lab. (%)	Aln (%)	Other (%)	Total (%)	C.-L. (%)	C./Lab. swing (%)
8–9.6	2 122(99)	HARRIS (TV-am)	42	35	21	2	100	+7	+4.5
8–9.6	2 005(195)	GALLUP (Telegraph)	41	34	23.5	1.5	100	+7	+4.5
9.6	1 086(69)	MARPLAN (Today)	43	35	21	1	100	+8	+4
9.6	1 702*	ASL (The Sun)	43	34	21	2	100	+9	+3.5
9–10.6	1 668(165)	MORI (Times)	44	32	22	2	100	+12	+2
10.6	1 633(103)	MARPLAN (Guardian)	42	35	21	2	100	+7	+4.5
10.6	1 668(52)	NOP (I'dent) (Adj)	42	35	21	2	100	+7	+4.5
11 June	Final Result		43	32	23	2	100	+11	+2.5

ABBREVIATIONS: 'Adj' indicates a marginals poll adjusted to reflect the whole country; 'Pnl' indicates a panel survey; W/W – Weekend World; I'dent – The Independent; S/T – Sunday Times; S'graph – Sunday Telegraph; S.Ex'ss – Sunday Express; ASL – Audience Selection Ltd.; * – Telephone poll.

† Reprinted by kind permission from David Butler and Dennis Kavanagh, *The British General Election of 1987* (London: Macmillan, 1988) p. 125.

Appendix 8: Other Electoral Systems[†]

There are three broad categories of electoral systems: plurality, majoritarian and proportional representation (PR).

The Plurality System

This system awards seat(s) to the candidate(s) who get the most votes even if this is less than an absolute majority. This is often known, particularly in the United Kingdom, where it is used for Parliamentary and all other elections except non-Parliamentary ones in Northern Ireland, as the 'first past the post' system.

Most frequently it is used in single-Member constituencies, but it may equally be applied to multi-Member constituencies where the voter normally has as many votes as there are seats to be filled (for example, in some local government elections in the UK). A unique example of the use of multi-Member constituencies, where the elector has only one vote, is in Japan, whose electoral system is known as the *single non-transferable vote*.

Plurality systems are very widely used for Parliamentary elections, though they are nowadays mostly restricted to countries (including the USA) which were once under British rule. For presidential elections however, where by definition only one person is to be elected, the plurality system is more widely employed. Of the 13 democratic countries directly electing their president, six use plurality voting.

The Majoritarian System

This means that only candidates winning more than 50 per cent of the votes cast may be elected. The system has two sub-categories: the *two-ballot* system and the *alternative vote*.

In the two-ballot system, which is normally restricted to single-member constituencies, a second round of voting is held if no candidate gains more than 50 per cent of the votes cast in the first ballot. The second ballot is often legally limited to the two leading candidates in the first round. Historically it has been the system used most frequently in France in Parliamentary elections, but it was temporarily replaced by a proportional system in 1986. It is widely used, however, in presidential elections. Seven of the countries directly electing their presidents, including France, use the two-ballot system.

[†] This appendix is largely based, by kind permission of The Economist Publishing Company, on the introduction I wrote to Dick Leonard and Richard Natkiel, *World Atlas of Elections* (London: Economist Publishing Co., 1986).

The alternative vote is used for the election of the Australian House of Representatives. Voters number the candidates in the order of their choice, and if no candidate wins more than 50 per cent of the votes cast the bottom candidate is eliminated and his votes are redistributed to their second choices. Further candidates may be eliminated until one candidate achieves an absolute majority. The alternative vote is also used in the Republic of Ireland in the event of Parliamentary by-elections and for the election of the president.

Proportional Representation

This is the final broad category of election systems. As its name implies, it attempts to relate the allocation of seats as closely as possible to the distribution of votes. By definition, this requires more than one vacancy, so multiMember constituencies are necessary.

This system is divided between two main sub-categories and a number of sub-sub-categories. The sub-categories are: *largest remainder* and *highest average*. These refer to the mathematical formulae by which the seats are allocated, as there is no way of ensuring 100 per cent proportionality.

The largest remainder method is the simplest means of allocation. It involves setting a quota of votes which party lists of candidates must achieve in order to be guaranteed a seat. The most common quota is the *Hare quota*, named after Thomas Hare, a Victorian lawyer and associate of John Stuart Mill. This is derived by dividing the number of votes cast by the number of seats to fill. For example, in a four-member constituency where 20 000 votes have been cast the quota will be 5000.

TABLE A8.1   *Four-member constituency. 20,000 votes cast. Hare quota: 5,000*

Party	Votes	Quota	Seats	Remainder	Seats	Total seats
A	8 200	5000	1	3200	1	2
B	6 100	5000	1	1100	0	1
C	3 000	–	0	3000	1	1
D	2 700	–	0	2700	0	0
Total	20 000		2		2	4

In the example shown in Table A8.1 only two of the four parties achieve an electoral quota. So only two of the four seats can be directly allocated: one each to parties A and B. But under the *largest remainder* system the third seat also goes to party A and the fourth seat to party C. The *largest remainder* system is regarded as being favourable to smaller parties, and it is noteworthy in the above example that party C gets as many seats as party B while getting less than half the number of votes.

The *highest average* system was devised by another nineteenth-century lawyer, the Belgian Victor D'Hondt, after whom it is named. Its central idea is to divide each party's votes by successive divisors, and then allocate the

TABLE A8.2 *Four-member constituency. 20,000 votes cast. Division by D'Hondt divisors*

Party	Votes	Divisor: 1	Divisor: 2	Divisor: 3	Total seats
A	8 200	8200 (1)	4100 (3)	2733	2
B	6 100	6100 (1)	3050 (4)	2033	2
C	3 000	3000	1500	1000	0
D	2 700	2700	1350	900	0
Total	20 000				4

seats to the parties in descending order of quotients. Table A8.2 shows the same results in votes as Table A8.1, but under the D'Hondt system the allocation of seats is different.

In the example in Table A8.2 the first seat will go to party A, the second to party B, the third to party A and the fourth to party B whose second quotient is 50 more than the first quotient of party C. Party C is left without a seat, which suggests that the D'Hondt system is less favourable to smaller parties than the Hare quota.

It is possible to combine both methods by first applying the Hare quota and then allocating the remaining seats by D'Hondt divisors. Different quotas and divisors have also been devised, with the objective of giving greater or lesser advantages to large, small or medium-sized parties.

Two different quotas, whose practical effect is to allocate more seats by quota, leaving fewer to the remainders, are the *Hagenbach-Bischoff quota* and the *Imperiali quota*. The Hagenbach-Bischoff quota involves dividing the total votes cast by the number of seats plus one, and the Imperiali quota by the number of seats plus two.

Alternative divisors to those used in the D'Hondt system are the *Sainte-Laguë* and the *Sainte-Laguë modified divisors*. The first of these involves dividing each party's votes by 1, 3, 5, 7, and so on, instead of by 1, 2, 3, 4, and so on. The second, which has been adopted in several Scandinavian countries, involves setting the first divisor at 1.4 instead of 1 (1.4, 3, 5, 7, and so on). This has the effect of strengthening medium-sized parties in a multi-party system.

Several countries practise a double allocation of seats, in so far as remainders are transferred to a regional or national pool before the remaining seats are allocated. The effect is usually to make the overall result more proportional.

Many countries apply a threshold, in any event, before parties can qualify for seats, either at a constituency or at national level. The size of the threshold varies from country to country, but the most common figure is five per cent. Other things being equal, the larger the number of seats in each constituency the more proportional a system will be. The extreme examples are Israel and the Netherlands, in each of which the entire country forms one constituency.

A particular form of proportional representation is the *single transferable vote* (STV), which is used for Parliamentary elections in the Republic of Ireland. Under this system the voter may list all the candidates on a ballot paper in his order of preference. The total number of votes cast is divided by the number of seats plus one, and one is added to the quotient. This is known as the *Droop* quota. Candidates achieving the Droop quota are allocated seats, and any excess votes are transferred to their second preferences. The process is repeated until all the seats have been filled, if necessary eliminating the bottom candidates and transferring their votes in the same way. The counting of votes under STV is a complicated procedure, often requiring a long series of separate counts. An example from the Irish general election of February 1982 is shown in Appendix 9.

The STV system, as used in the Republic of Ireland, is less proportional than most party list systems, mainly because the constituencies are relatively small (three to five Members), but it gives a much larger choice of individual candidates to the voter.

TABLE A8.3   *Quotas and divisors: the formulae*

---

1. Hare quota $= \dfrac{\text{Votes}}{\text{Seats}}$

2. Hagenbach-Bischoff quota $= \dfrac{\text{Votes}}{\text{Seats} + 1}$

3. Imperiali quota $= \dfrac{\text{Votes}}{\text{Seats} + 2}$

4. Droop quota $= \dfrac{\text{Votes}}{\text{Seats} + 1} + 1$

5. D'Hondt divisors: 1, 2, 3, 4, 5, etc
6. Sainte-Laguë divisors: 1, 3, 5, 7, 9, etc
7. Sainte-Laguë modified divisors: 1. 4, 3, 5, 7, 9, etc

One other device, which also produces this effect, is *panachage*, as practised in Switzerland and Luxembourg. These countries employ party list systems, but the voter has as many votes as there are seats to be filled and may, if he chooses, distribute his choices between candidates on several different lists.

West Germany employs a hybrid system, in that one half of the Parliamentary seats are filled by plurality, using single-Member constituencies, while the other half are filled by party lists, using the D'Hondt system. The objective is to achieve overall proportionality, while preserving the advantages of single-member constituencies. If a party is over-represented by constituency Members, it will be allocated relatively fewer, or none at all, of the list seats, while parties which are under-represented are compensated through the allocation of the list Seats.

This system has become known in Britain as the *Additional Member System* (AMS), and a variant of it was recommended by a Commission appointed by the Hansard Society which reported in 1976.* Apart from STV, which is the preferred alternative of the Liberal Democratic Party, AMS is the only PR system to have attracted any significant support in the UK.

WHO USES WHAT?

There are some 39 well established democracies in the world (those with a population of more than 200 000). The following lists indicate the electoral systems used by each country for their Parliamentary lower chamber elections.

Plurality (first-past-the post)	Majoritarian	PR
Bahamas	Australia (Alternative Vote)	Austria
Barbados	France (two ballots)	Belgium
Botswana		Colombia
Canada		Costa Rica
Fiji		Cyprus
India		Denmark
Jamaica		Dominican Republic
Japan (SNTV)*		Ecuador
New Zealand		Finland
Papua New Guinea		West Germany (AMS)
Solomon Islands		Greece
Trinidad and Tobago		Iceland
United Kingdom		Ireland (STV)
United States of America		Israel
		Italy
		Luxembourg
		Netherlands
		Norway
		Portugal
		Spain
		Sweden
		Switzerland
		Venezuela

* Single Non-transferable Vote.

*Report of the Hansard Society Commission on Electoral Reform (London, 1976).

Appendix 9: The Single Transferable Vote

The Single Transferable Vote is a very simple system of voting, the voter merely numbering the candidates 1, 2, 3 and so on in the order of his preference. The counting of the votes is more complicated, as the following not untypical result from Galway West, in the Republic of Ireland's general election of February 1982, illustrates. It took seven counts before the five seats were filled, only one candidate securing enough first preference votes to secure election on the first count.

TABLE A9.1 Galway West result, general election February 1982 †

Galway West (5 seats)
Total valid poll 48,572   Quota 8.096
Turnout 67.5%

Candidate and party	Count 1 [a]	Count 2 [b]	Count 3 [c]	Count 4 [d]	Count 5 [e]	Count 6 [f]	Count 7 [g]
*Molloy (FF)	9,545*	−1,449					
*Donnellan (FG)	6,105	+38 6,143	+51 6,194	+30 6,224	+2,181 8,405*		
*Higgins (Lab)	5,718	+129 5,847	+715 6,562	+214 6,776	+554 7,330	+2,970 10,300*	−2,204
Fahey (FF)	6,019	+352 6,371	+99 6,470	+294 6,764	+97 6,861	+379 7,240	+431 7,671*
*Geoghegan-Quinn (FF)	4,139	+475 4,614	+47 4,661	+1,716 6,377	+87 6,464	+221 6,685	+196 6,881
*Killilea (FF)	5,624	+198 5,822	+35 5,857	+242 6,099	+29 6,128	+212 6,340	+145 6,485
McCormack (FG)	3,952	+24 3,976	+38 4,014	+41 4,055	+1,014 5,069**		
Coogan (FG)	3,746	+47 3,793	+145 3,938	+105 4,043**			
O'Connor (FF)	2,513	+171 2,684	+33 2,717**				
Brick (SFWP)	1,211	+15 1,226**					
Spoilt/non-trans.	391	0	63	75	81	1,287	1,432

TABLE A9.2   *First preference votes and seats won*[†]

Party	N votes	% votes	Seats won
FF	27 840	57.3	3
FG	13 803	28.4	1
Lab	5 718	11.8	1
SFWP	1 211	2.5	0

[†] Adopted with kind permission from Paul McKee, 'The Republic of Ireland', in Vernon Bogdanor and David Butler (eds), *Democracy and Elections: Electoral Systems and their Political Consequences* (Cambridge University Press, 1983) pp. 170–1

GENERAL NOTES

(i) The quota = $\dfrac{48\ 572}{5 + 1}$ + 1 = 8096 (ignoring any fractions).

(ii) The party abbreviations following each candidate's name are:

FF   Fianna Fail. (Literally translated this party name is 'soldiers of destiny'.)

FG   Fine Gael. (Literally translated the party name is 'family group of the Gaels'.)

Lab   Labour.

SFWP Sinn Fein the Workers' Party.

(iii) An asterisk preceding a candidate's name, for example, *Molloy, indicates a Member of the previous Dail, that is, a sitting Member.

A single asterisk following a number of votes indicates that the votes of that candidate have exceeded the quota and hence the candidate has been elected on that count.

A double asterisk following a number of votes indicates that the candidate has been eliminated as a result of that particular count and the votes are to be transferred in the following count.

(iv) The candidates are listed in descending order of the final vote obtained by the candidate. This vote will be obtained in the count which results in the candidate being elected or eliminated. An alternative presentation which could be used is to list the candidates in alphabetical order, as they are on the ballot paper.

a Count 1: first preference votes counted, Molloy (FF) elected.

b Count 2: distribution of surplus votes of Molloy (FF), Brick (SFWP) eliminated.

c Count 3 transfer of votes of Brick (SFWP), O'Connor (FF) eliminated.

d Count 4: transfer of votes of O'Connor (FF), Coogan (FG) eliminated.

e Count 5: transfer of votes of Coogan (FG), Donnellan (FG) elected, McCormack (FG) eliminated.

f Count 6: transfer of votes of McCormack (FG), Higgins (Lab.) elected.

g Count 7: distribution of surplus votes of Higgins (Lab.) Fahey (FF) and Geoghegan-Quinn (FF) elected without reaching quota.

Appendix 10: Results of Euro-elections, 1979, 1984 and 1989

1979:

Great Britain (7.8 seats)   Turnout: 31.8%

Party	Votes	%	Seats
Conservative Party	6 508 492	50.6	60
Labour Party	4 253 247	33.0	17
Liberal Party	1 690 638	13.1	0
Scottish National Party	247 836	1.9	1
Plaid Cymru	83 399	0.6	0
Others	90 318	0.8	0
Total	12 873 930	100.0	78

Northern Ireland (3 seats)   S.T.V. system of P.R.   Turnout: 55.6%

Party	First Preference Votes	%	Seats
Democratic Unionist Party	170 688	29.8	1
Social Democratic Labour Party	140 622	24.6	1
Official Unionist Party	125 169	21.9	1
Others	135 760	23.7	0
Total	572 239	100.0	3

1984:

Great Britain (78 seats)   Turnout 31.8%

Party	Votes	%	Seats
Conservative Party	5 426 866	40.8	45
Labour Party	4 865 224	36.5	32
Liberal/SDP Alliance	2 591 659	19.5	0
Scottish National Party	230 594	1.7	1
Plaid Cymru	103 031	0.8	0
Others	95 524	0.7	0
Total	13 312 898	100.0	78

Northern Ireland (3 seats)   S.T.V. system of P.R.   Turnout: 64.4%

Party	First Preference Votes	%	Seats
Democratic Unionist Party	230 251	33.6	1
Social Democratic and Labour Party	151 399	22.1	1
Official Unionist Party	147 169	21.5	1
Provisional Sinn Fein	91 476	13.3	0
Alliance Party of Northern Ireland	34 046	5.0	0
Others	30 976	4.6	0
Total	685 317	100.0	3

1989:

Great Britain (78 seats)   Turnout: 35.9%

Party	Votes	%	Seats
Conservative Party	5 224 037	34.1	32
Labour	6 153 604	40.2	45
SLD	986 292	6.4	0
SDP	75 886	0.5	0
Scottish National Party	406 686	2.6	1
Plaid Cymru	115 062	0.7	0
Green Party	2 292 705	15.0	0
Others	39 971	0.3	0
Total	15 353 154	100.0	78

Northern Ireland (3 seats)   S.T.V. system of P.R.   Turnout: 48.8%

Party	First Preference Votes	%	Seats
Democratic Unionist Party	160 110	29.6	1
Social Democratic and Labour Party	136 335	25.2	1
Official Unionist	118 785	22.0	1
Provisional Sinn Fein	48 914	9.1	0
APNI	27 905	5.2	0
Others	42 762	7.9	0
Totals	534 811	100.0	3

Bibliography

ELECTION RESULTS

Full results of general elections, together with biographical details of Members and of defeated candidates are published shortly after each election in *The Times Guide to the House of Commons* (London: Times Books). The series goes back to 1929, and also appeared after the elections of January 1910, December 1910 and 1918.

Less detailed results are given also in *Dod's Parliamentary Companion*, published annually, *Vacher's Parliamentary Guide*, quarterly and *Whitaker's Almanack*, annually.

Tabulated results for all constituencies from 1885 to 1983 inclusive are included in four volumes compiled by F. W. S. Craig: *British Parliamentary Election Results 1885–1918* (Chichester: Parliamentary Research Services, 1969); *British Parliamentary Election Results 1918–49* (Chichester: Parliamentary Research Services, 1969); *British Parliamentary Election Results 1950–70* (Chichester: Parliamentary Research Services, 1971) and *Britain Votes 3* (Chichester: Parliamentary Research Services, 1984). Summaries are included in *British Political Facts 1900–1990* by David Butler and Gareth Butler (London: Macmillan, 1991).

Results of elections to the European Parliament are given in *The Times Guide to the European Parliament*, (Times Books, 1979, 1984 and 1989) and in *Europe Votes 2: European Parliamentary Election Results 1979–84*, Thomas T. Mackie and F. W. S. Craig (eds) (Chichester: Parliamentary Research Services, 1985).

GENERAL ELECTIONS

A general overview of all the elections from 1945 to 1987 is given in *British General Elections Since 1945* by David Butler (Oxford: Basil Blackwell, 1989). More detailed accounts of individual elections are provided in a series of books sponsored by Nuffield College, Oxford: *The British General Election of 1945* by R. B. McCallum and Alison Readman (London: Macmillan, 1947); *The British General Election of 1950* by H. G. Nicholas (London: Macmillan, 1951); *The British General Election of 1951* by D. E. Butler (London: Macmillan, 1952); *The British General Election of 1955* by D. E. Butler (London: Macmillan, 1955); *The British General Election of 1959* by D. E. Butler and Richard Rose (London: Macmillan, 1960); *The British General Election of 1964* by D. E. Butler and Anthony King (London: Macmillan, 1965); *The British General Election of 1966* by D. E. Butler and Anthony King (London: Macmillan, 1966); *The British General Election of 1970* by David Butler and Michael Pinto-Duschinsky (London: Macmillan,

1971); *The British General Election of February 1974* by David Butler and Dennis Kavanagh (London: Macmillan, 1974); *The British General Election of October 1974* by David Butler and Dennis Kavanagh (London: Macmillan, 1975); *The British General Election of 1979* by David Butler and Dennis Kavanagh (London: Macmillan, 1980); *The British General Election of 1983* by David Butler and Dennis Kavanagh (London: Macmillan, 1984) and *The British General Election of 1987* by David Butler and Dennis Kavanagh (London: Macmillan, 1988).

A rival series, published by the American Enterprise Institute in Washington DC, has appeared since 1974. The titles have been *Britain at the Polls: The Parliamentary Elections of 1974*, edited by Howard R. Penniman; *Britain at the Polls 1979*, edited by Howard R. Penniman and *Britain at the Polls 1983*, edited by Austin Ranney.

The 1983 general election produced a record crop of more detailed studies of various aspects of the campaign. These included *The General Election Campaign of 1983*, edited by Ivor Crewe and Martin Harrop (Cambridge University Press, 1986), *British Democracy at the Crossroads* by Patrick Dunleavy and C. T. Husbands (London: Allen & Unwin, 1985), *The Geography of English Politics: the 1983 General Election* by R. J. Johnston (London: Croom Helm, 1983) and *The Nationwide Competition for Votes: The 1983 British Election* by Ian McAllister and Richard Rose (London: Frances Pinter, 1984).

Books on the 1987 election include *Political Communications: The General Election Campaign of 1987*, edited by Ivor Crewe and Martin Harrop (Cambridge, University Press, 1989) and *How Voters Change* by William Miller, Harold Clarke, Martin Harrop, Lawrence Leduc and Paul Whiteley (Oxford: Clarendon Press, 1990).

Similar volumes on Euro-election campaigns are *European Elections and British Politics* by David Butler and David Marquand (London: Macmillan, 1981) and *Party Strategies in Britain: A Study of the 1984 European Elections* by David Butler and Paul Jowett (London: Macmillan, 1985).

Three studies appeared on the 1975 Referendum campaign: *The 1975 Referendum* by David Butler and Uwe Kitzinger (London: Macmillan, 1976); *Britain says Yes* by Anthony King (Washington DC: American Enterprise Institute, 1977) and *Full-hearted Consent* by Philip Goodhart (London: Davis-Poynter, 1976). On the 1979 Scottish referendum, see *The Referendum Experience, Scotland 1979*, edited by Jean Bochel, David Denver and Alan MacCartney (Aberdeen University Press, 1981).

CONSTITUENCIES

A large amount of demographical and statistical data on the current Parliamentary constituencies is contained in *British Parliamentary Constituencies: A Statistical Compendium* by Ivor Crewe and Anthony Fox (London: Faber, 1984). Their relationship to the previous constituencies before the redistribution which took effect in 1983 is precisely defined in *The BBC/ITN Guide to the New Parliamentary Constituencies* (Chichester: Parliamentary Research Services, 1983). A more political analysis is contained in two books by Robert Waller, *The Almanac of British Politics* (London: Croom Helm, 1983) and *The Atlas of British Politics* (London: Croom Helm, 1984).

THE ELECTORAL SYSTEM

The fullest account of its development is *The Electoral System in Britain since 1918* by D. E. Butler (Oxford University Press, 1963, second edition). Critical assessments are made in *Political Representation and Elections in Britain* by P. J. Pulzer (London: Allen and Unwin, 1968) and *British Elections* by Geoffrey Alderman (London: Batsford, 1978).

Information on other electoral systems and on elections in other democratic countries is contained in *Democracy and Elections: Electoral Systems and their Political Consequences*, Vernon Bogdanor and David Butler (eds) (Cambridge University Press, 1983), *Democracy at the Polls: A Comparative Study of Competitive National Elections*, David Butler, Howard R. Penniman and Austin Ranney (eds) (Washington DC: American Enterprise Institute, 1981), *How Democracies Vote* by Enid Lakeman (London: Faber, 1974, 4th edition), *World Atlas of Elections: Voting Patterns in 39 Democracies* by Dick Leonard and Richard Natkiel (London: Economist Publishing Company, 1986) and *The International Almanac of Electoral History* by Thomas T. Mackie and Richard Rose (London: Macmillan, 1982, second edition).

VOTING STUDIES

The major works are the three successive volumes reporting the findings of the British Election Surveys between 1963 and 1983. These were *Political Change in Britain* by David Butler and Donald Stokes (London: Macmillan, 1974, second edition), *Decade of Dealignment* by Bo Särlvik and Ivor Crewe (Cambridge University Press, 1983) and *How Britain Votes* by Anthony Heath, Roger Jowell and John Curtice (Oxford: Pergamon Press, 1985). A separate volume on Scotland is *The End of British Politics?* by W. L. Miller (Oxford: Clarendon Press, 1981). An offshoot of this series is *Class and the British Electorate* by David Robertson (Oxford: Basil Blackwell, 1984). See also *How Voters Decide* by Hilde T. Himmelweit, Patrick Humphreys and Marianne Jaeger (Milton Keynes: Open University Press, 1985, second edition).

CANDIDATES

Three books, none of them recent, which cover the field comprehensively are *Pathways to Parliament* by Austin Ranney (Madison: University of Wisconsin Press, and London: Macmillan, 1965); *The Selectorate* by Peter Paterson (London: MacGibbon and Kee, 1967) and *The Selection of Parliamentary Candidates* by Michael Rush (London: Nelson, 1969). On Members of Parliament see *The Commons in Perspective* by Philip Norton (Oxford:

Martin Robertson, 1981) and *The Backbenchers* by P. G. Richards (London: Faber, 1972).

POLITICAL PARTIES

The standard work, *British Political Parties* by R. T. McKenzie (London: Heinemann, 1963, second edition) is now seriously out of date. A rather more recent study is *The Problem of Party Government* by Richard Rose (Harmondsworth: Penguin Books, 1976). Two more up-to-date studies are *The British Party System* by S. Ingle (Oxford: Basil Blackwell, 1989, second edition) and *UK Political Parties Since 1945*, Anthony Seldon (ed.) (New York: Philip Allan, 1990). There are many books on individual parties, such as *The Conservative Party from Heath to Thatcher* by Robert Behrens (London: Saxon House, 1980); *The Politics of the Labour Party*, Dennis Kavanagh (ed.) (London: Allen & Unwin, 1982), *Liberal Party Politics*, Vernon Bogdanor (ed.) (Oxford University Press, 1983) and *Breaking the Mould? The Birth and Prospects of the Social Democratic Party* by Ian Bradley (Oxford: Martin Robertson, 1981).

OPINION POLLS

An excellent summary of the history and methods of opinion polls in Britain is contained in *Political Opinion Polling: An International Review*, Robert M. Worcester (ed.) (London: Macmillan, 1983). See also *Polls, Politics and Populism* by John Clemens (Aldershot: Gower Publishing, 1983) and *Political Opinion Polls* by Frank Teer and James D. Spence (London: Hutchinson, 1973).

PARTY FINANCE

A comprehensive historical account is contained in *British Political Finance 1830–1980* by Michael Pinto-Duschinsky (Washington DC: American Enterprise Institute, 1981). On the case for public subsidies see the Houghton Report, *Report of the Committee on Financial Aid to Political Parties* (London: HMSO, Cmnd. 6601, 1976) and *Paying for Party Politics: The Case for Public Subsidies* by Dick Leonard (London: Political and Economic Planning, 1975).

GENERAL POLITICAL BACKGROUND

Two excellent surveys, both recently revised, are *The Government and Politics of Britain* by John P. Mackintosh, revised by P. G. Richards (London; Hutchinson, 1984, 6th edition) and *Politics in England* by Richard Rose (London, Faber: 1985).

ELECTION LAW

The standard reference book is *Schofield's Election Law* by A. J. Little (London: Shaw and Sons, 1984). See also *Erskine May's Treatise on the Law, Privileges, Proceedings and Usage of Parliament* (London: Butterworth, 1983, 20th edition) and *Law and the Electoral Process* by H. F. Rawlings (London: Sweet and Maxwell, 1988).

Index

This is a lively and authoritative account by a leading political journalist and former MP of how the British electoral system works. It is addressed primarily to intelligent voters, but also to students of political science, government and British Constitution at universities, colleges and schools. It answers central questions such as: When are elections held? Who can vote? What happens on polling day? And how does one become an MP? It explains clearly how and why constituency boundaries have to be altered, how the parties are organized, how campaigns are conducted, the role of the media, how reliable opinion polls are and what happens at by-elections. It deals also with local elections, referenda and elections to the European Parliament and describes clearly the main features of other electoral systems, including the main variations of proportional representation. The annexes contain a mass of electoral statistics and a thorough bibliography.

For a note on the author, please see the back flap

Dick Leonard, a leading political journalist, is currently European Community Correspondent for the *Observer*. He was previously an assistant editor of *The Economist*, and his syndicated articles appear in newspapers throughout the world. He also teaches a university course in journalism. A former Labour MP for Romford, and Parliamentary Private Secretary to Anthony Crosland, his previous books include *Guide to the General Election*, *The Backbencher and Parliament* (co-editor with Valentine Herman), *Paying for Party Politics*, *World Atlas of Elections* (with Richard Natkiel) and *Pocket Guide to the European Community*.